SPEAKING CLEARLY

SPEAKING CLEARLY
Improving Voice and Diction

Jeffrey C. Hahner

Martin A. Sokoloff

Sandra Salisch

Geoffrey D. Needler

Pace University

Random House   New York

This book is dedicated to our
patient and understanding families,
especially Vivienne and Beth Sokoloff
and Bette and Tim Hahner.

First Edition
987654321
Copyright © 1983 by Random House, Inc.

Library of Congress Cataloging in Publication Data
Main entry under title:
Speaking clearly.
Includes bibliographies and index.
1. Speech therapy. 2. Voice. 3. Diction.
I. Hahner, Jeffrey C.
RC423.S634 1983   428.3   82–16502
ISBN 0–394–32806–X

Manufactured in the United States of America

Cover and text design by Karin Gerdes Kincheloe

PERMISSIONS ACKNOWLEDGMENTS

PERMISSIONS ACKNOWLEDGMENTS

Preface

Taking (and teaching) a college course in voice and diction can often be a real challenge. Many students who enroll with high hopes for dramatic changes in speech don't achieve those changes or find that they are, at most, very temporary. One of the main reasons is lack of time. The students usually have been speaking for at least seventeen years and would like to successfully change their way of speaking in just one short semester or one even shorter summer session. Furthermore, they aren't going to attempt this in a one-to-one setting with an instructor, but on a time-sharing basis in the classroom. Also, it's probably not the only course the students are taking at the time, and all the other pressures of life also make themselves felt and compete for the students' attention. In addition, the students frequently feel uncomfortable about carrying over what they're learning in class to everyday communication situations. So if taking (and teaching) a course in voice and diction is a challenge, it's because conditions are far from ideal.

Our purpose in writing this book is to eliminate some of the obstacles to success in voice and diction courses, and to increase the chances for the significant, lasting changes in voice and diction that most students seek.

This book is the result of twenty years of teaching voice and diction courses to thousands of students. During that time we've been able to identify many of the factors that spell success in speech improvement. We've pooled our knowledge, our experience, and the materials that we've developed over the years to provide a book that capitalizes on the success factors. This book brings you the things we do that *work*: specific materials and approaches we use that have proven themselves in the classroom.

One such approach is the use of voice and diction drills that are presented in increasing order of difficulty. Our drills distinguish between the less and more difficult productions of a given sound and prevent students from trying to progress too rapidly or start at levels inappropriate for beginners. These drills give the students early rewards and help them to develop a healthy, positive attitude. Along this line, we've tried to avoid the use of tongue-twisters. The sentences in the drills are designed to present the target sounds at a frequency close to that of normal conversation. Words are familiar, and they can be phased into the students' everyday conversations.

We have also kept in mind the fact that students of voice and diction sometimes find it awkward or embarrassing to drill aloud on materials that, while providing ample practice on target sounds, may not make sense as far as content is concerned. We've made every effort to create materials that students can feel comfortable practicing, either alone or as part of a classroom group. We've found that students tend to resist using practice materials that sound "silly."

As voice and diction instructors and speech pathologists, we've found it extremely helpful to use ear-training techniques to help our students develop accurate auditory "pictures" of the correct production of target sounds. In this way, students can learn to monitor and self-correct their own productions of the sounds as well as learn to produce the sounds more easily. We have provided, in Appendix A, an outline of the step-by-step ear-training process that can be applied in the classroom by the instructor or individually by the students as an out-of-class assignment. It is also possible to use the ear-training steps as a means to assess each student's ability to discriminate between standard and nonstandard productions of target sounds.

In many cases, students who have particularly hard-to-correct problems need additional help. We've provided Appendix B as a special section that covers, in a step-by-step way, such problems as lingual and lateral lisps. We've tried to give the students some self-help measures and provide carry-over materials for students who are concurrently engaged in speech therapy. In addition, we've tried to offer guidance to instructors who may feel unsure of themselves in these more specialized areas. Students who use Appendix B can be assigned practice on their own, thus allowing more class time for activities involving larger numbers of students.

This book also addresses two other major concerns. One is our belief that students in beginning courses in voice and diction ought to gain a certain sense of perspective as to where their own vocal and articulatory styles fit into their overall communication styles. For example, we consider paralinguistic elements such as loudness, rate, intonation and voice quality, to be essential aspects of a person's nonverbal communication. Accordingly, Chapters 4 and 5 are devoted to voice production and vocal expressiveness. But there are other nonverbal elements, such as kinesics and proxemics, that also are an important part of a person's total communication package. Chapter 6 completes the perspective on aspects of nonverbal communication.

Finally, in our experience we have found that significant numbers of beginning students in voice and diction have a high degree of apprehension about the course in general, and they suffer varying degrees of stagefright when asked to read or speak aloud in the classroom. We have included Chapter 2 to give students information about the nature and causes of stagefright and to provide them with concrete ways to manage stagefright successfully.

We wrote this book because we wanted to share what we do in teaching voice and diction. We feel that what we're doing works well for us; we're confident that it will work well for others, too.

The manuscript was reviewed by several of our colleagues, whom we would like to thank here for their helpful critiques. They were: Randall Capps, Western Kentucky University; June Kable, Midwestern State University; Alphonse Keasley, Jr., University of Colorado—Boulder; Barbara H. Moran, Johnson C. Smith University; Charles Parker, North Carolina State University; Carol Ashburn Roach, University of Alabama—Huntsville; Carla Waal, University of Missouri—Columbia; and Lynn Wells, Saddleback Community College.

We would also like to express our heartfelt thanks to all those who were kind enough to give of themselves to help bring this project to completion, particularly: Roth Wilkofsky, Kathleen Domenig, Deborah Connor-Coker, and John Sturman at Random House; Pat Sgarro, Jerry Goldberg, Dawn Knipe, Dr. Alfred Dumais, Nancy Kaplan, Charley Sayers, and all our students at Pace; and for giving us the initial shove, Howard Lockwood, the "dean" of publishers' representatives.

Finally, we must state that this book would not have been possible without the enthusiastic encouragement of the late Dr. Joseph J. Miranne, Jr., first chairman and founder of the Department of Speech and Drama at Pace University.

J.C.H.
M.A.S.
S.S.
G.D.N.

Contents

part one

Introduction to Speech Communication

Why do you communicate? *How* do you do it? Why do some people communicate more effectively than others? How can I gain more self-confidence? How can I become a more effective speaker?

These are typical of the questions asked by people like you who are about to start working on voice and diction. Part I of this book will answer these and other questions you may have and start you on the way to *speaking clearly*.

1

Overview

Recently a series of employment interviews were held on our campus. Several seniors who were considered to be likely candidates for jobs with highly rated accounting firms appeared for their interviews. They were all shined and polished, and they had boned up on all they should know to make favorable impressions on the interviewers. Their academic credentials were highly suitable; they were all set. What happened? You guessed it! They failed the interviews.

Why? The interviewers told the Director of our Career Planning Center that the speech patterns of those students were more appropriate for manual laborers than professional accountants, and that these particular students would not be considered for employment.

Consider this case: one of our students in a voice and diction class, a rather petite young woman, made her first tape recording. This woman was also a student teacher, and during the conference that followed the recording session, she complained that she was having trouble maintaining discipline in her student teaching assignment. She said that she was assigned to teach several high school English classes and that most of the students towered over her physically. They paid little attention to her instructions, and she was feeling increasingly frustrated. She had never heard herself on tape before, and when she did, she realized that her voice was quite high-pitched and weak. She said, "I sound just like a little girl." After some voice retraining she returned to class. She found that with her "new" voice she was able to get her students' attention and really get down to the business of teaching.

These incidents, and many others like them, are familiar to anyone who is trained to observe the way people speak. As you think over some of your own communication history, you can probably remember several times when you made snap judgments about people solely on the basis of how they presented themselves through speaking. In other words, *how* a person says something, rather than *what* that person says, forms a lasting impression. You form these impressions because you've come to believe that a person's personality is reflected in the way he or she speaks. What if your first impression is wrong? If your relationship with that individual continues, it will take a long time for you to change your opinion.

A person's communication patterns are usually very informative as to what kind of person he or she is. We can tell a good deal about someone by the way he pronounces words; from the loudness, quality, and inflection of his voice; the way he uses gestures; the way he stands; what he does with his eyes and face. We make judgments mostly without being aware of the basis on which we are making them; but we make them just the same.

For most of us, the truth is we have not one but several styles of communicating. For example, we usually talk quite differently when we're speaking with our friends than we do when we're being interviewed for a job. Chances are in any of these situations we're trying to make a good impression and get the other person to respond to us in a favorable way.

INTRODUCTION TO SPEECH COMMUNICATION

"But," you may say, "I've been talking all my life, and I haven't had any trouble. Why should I study speech? What will it do for me?" The answers to these questions—the reasons for studying speech—will, of course, vary from student to student. For one student the reason might be a desire to communicate effectively. You may have no difficulty communicating in the specific geographic and social environment called home, but in a different environment, your present speech patterns might be so different from those around you that people pay more attention to the *way* you speak than to *what* you have to say. For another student the reason might be a wish to make a good impression. It may be that your present speech patterns could, at one time or another, prevent you from getting that job you're after, that promotion you deserve, that date with that person who is so special to you.

Perhaps it is the way you pronounce certain words or how loudly you speak or the quality of your voice or some other aspect of your speech that, in some way, prevents your communication from being as effective as you would like. The result is you may not be successful in getting the desired response from those with whom you are communicating.

Once they've thought about these reasons, most of our students say, "Okay, you've convinced me. But I *can't* change the way I speak; I'm too old! I'd just be wasting my time." We don't agree! First, you don't have to learn to speak all over again. You only have to add another speaking style to those you already possess, to be used when it's appropriate for the particular speaker, listener, or occasion. Second, the ability to learn new speech patterns doesn't depend on your age but on your motivation. It's simply a matter of learning new muscle habits and developing dormant listening skills. If you *want* to do it, you *can!* How long it takes you to improve your speech depends on how badly you want to do it and the amount of time you're willing to spend on practice.

THE COMMUNICATION PROCESS

Now is a good time to talk about communication: what it is, how it operates, and what influence your speech has on your communication and its effectiveness.

Communication is the process whereby an idea, thought, or feeling that arises in the mind of one person is conveyed to the mind of someone else. For example, say there's someone that you enjoyed meeting. You might want to convey to him or her this message: "I like you, and I would like a chance to get to know you better."

The first step in the process would be for your brain to reach back into its file of experiences and dig out the words that would best express the idea. To come up with the appropriate words, your brain would probably review a number of different ways to express the same idea and, based on your attitudes, values, and past experiences, select those words you think would result in the most effective, least risky, way of conveying your message.

The next step would be for your brain to regulate the various structures and muscles your body uses to produce speech so that you could transmit the words of your message. These words, when spoken, exist in the form of sounds or vibrations of the air molecules surrounding you. When these vibrations reach the ear of another person (hopefully the person you intended should hear them), the vibrations change into nerve impulses that travel to the brain where they are translated into ideas.

So at this point, you have directed a message toward a person you'd like to get to know better, and you hope that person shares your feeling. But then you get a response far from the one you were hoping for. Why might this have happened? Chances are you were a victim of communication noise.

Noise

In an ideal situation, the message created in the brain of the other person would be exactly the same as the one that originated in yours. Most of the time this doesn't happen, though, because of a number of factors that operate in almost all communication situations. These factors are frequently called barriers to communication or simply noise. Noise exists in human speech communication because, at this time, we have no way to link the speaker's brain directly to the listener's. In a way, we could compare you and your listener to a television station and a TV set; they're miles apart, but an attempt is made to have a picture appear on the TV set that is the same as the one in the studio. When the picture is different, it's because of noise. The noise could be generated at the source ("Please stand by . . .") by something between your set and the studio (an electrical storm), or by something wrong inside your TV set (crossed wires). Similarly, speech communication noises exist: environmental, listener-generated, and speaker-generated.

Environmental Noise

Just as a TV signal can be distorted while it's traveling between the studio and your set at home, so can your communication be subjected to distortion from noise between you and your listener.

The noise may be *acoustic,* that is, other sounds (not generated by speaker or listener) that block out speech or make hearing difficult. It is hard to understand conversations at a loud party, for example. For the same reason, people who live near busy airports learn to lip-read and use it to make themselves understood every time a jet takes off. The effect of acoustic noise on speech is that if you hear the words at all, you still can't be sure you heard them correctly.

There are *visual* noises, too. Have you ever sat in a classroom trying to pay attention to a lecture or discussion while your eyes and mind kept straying through the window to something happening outside? That something outside the window is a visual noise. (We also use, however, the visual sense to help us understand speech; there's less chance of error when you can see the speaker's lips.)

These are just a few illustrations of how environmental factors can disrupt communication or at least make it more difficult.

Listener-generated Noise

The receiver of the communication, though, can also be at fault. Think, for a moment, about all the factors you bring to each communication situation and how they might affect the way you listen to, understand, and integrate what someone is saying to you. How do you feel about the speaker, for instance? Do you like, respect, or admire that person? If so, you are much more likely to be open and receptive to what that person has to say. If you dislike, fear, or distrust the speaker, chances are you won't accept or agree with very much of what he or she says. How do you feel about the way the other person talks? Does that particular accent or way of pronouncing words turn you off?

Another factor to consider is how you feel about the subject you are talking about. Do you have a lot of fixed ideas, attitudes, or values about the subject? Is it something that you feel very strongly about? It's likely that if your answers to the last two questions are yes, your mind will be fairly closed to ideas or attitudes that differ from yours.

Do you react emotionally to certain words or phrases that have strong associations to you? How would you feel, for instance, if someone called you or your ideas dumb, communistic, "reactionary!" How willing would you be to listen objectively to that person?

These are all examples of factors existing within the listener that may increase or diminish the likelihood of effective communication taking place.

Speaker-generated Noise

Speakers can create noise that interferes with accurate message transmission through a number of different types of behaviors. Disturbing *linguistic behaviors* can constitute "noise" experienced as faulty grammar or *syntax,* incorrect word choices, or faulty production of any of the sounds that make up the words. *Paralinguistic behaviors* might include such interferences as uneven loudness, rate, or rhythm; inappropriate pitch or stress patterns; and unusual or abnormal voice qualities. *Extraverbal behaviors* can also cause problems;

your gestures or facial expressions might not be appropriate for your message. All these behaviors can take the attention of your listener away from *what* is being said and focus it on *how* it is being said.

In this text, we deal primarily with the behaviors that constitute speaker-generated noise: those parts of your speech pattern that may call attention to themselves or in some way make your message hard to understand or cause your listener to misinterpret your message. We'll present both theory and practical exercises to help you eliminate such noise and to help you make your spoken communication more effective.

HOW TO USE THIS BOOK

This book contains a wide variety of materials related to voice and diction. First, browse through the entire book. See how it's laid out, what's covered in each appendix, how the index is organized. Once you're familiar with the book, you can use it more effectively.

Chapters

Each chapter is a complete unit in itself and can be used separately. This means your instructor can assign chapter readings in whatever order he or she prefers.

Chapter 2

We strongly recommend that you read Chapter 2 next. It deals with reducing stagefright and anxiety. Read the chapter and try the practice activities according to your own needs, or as your instructor assigns.

Chapter 3

Chapter 3 deals entirely with the theory of speech—the anatomy and physiology—and requires no drill materials.

Chapters 4 and 5

In Chapters 4 and 5, guided activities for voice analysis and improvement are alternated with theory about effective voice characteristics. We've divided in-

INTRODUCTION TO SPEECH COMMUNICATION

structions for carrying out vocal exercises and activities according to the level of difficulty for self-directed student practice.

Chapter 6

The subject of Chapter 6 is nonverbal communication, and it will help you become aware of some of the barriers to communication that may be generated by poor nonverbal or extraverbal behaviors on the part of the speaker. Here, again, we have alternated explanatory materials on theory with specific suggestions for exercises you can do, either in class or outside class, to reinforce and clarify the theory.

Chapter 7

Chapter 7 presents the theory as well as practical applications of the International Phonetic Alphabet (I.P.A.) for the purpose of teaching you the component sounds of American English. The drill materials in Chapter 7 will help you master the dual skills of transcribing in I.P.A. and reading orally from I.P.A. symbols.

Chapters 8 and 9

The drill materials in Chapter 7 become the framework for each of the sounds presented in Chapters 8 and 9. Wherever possible, we've arranged the drills into two or three levels of difficulty. This allows you to practice with less or more difficult materials, depending on your level of skill at producing the particular sound.

We've tried to design our practice sentences so that they are as close as possible to what people might say in normal conversation. We have made every effort to avoid "loading" each sentence with a lot of words containing the sound being practiced. Our clinical experience has shown us that loaded sentences (tongue twisters) are not particularly useful in helping you correct misarticulated sounds.

Appendixes

Appendix A

We think you'll find Appendix A especially helpful. It has the strange title of "Ear Training," and what it covers is not listening but auditory discrimination. Read this section thoroughly and make sure to do the exercises. You'll find them effective in teaching you the differences between the standard and nonstandard sounds of our language.

Appendix B

Appendix B covers special explanations and drills for some hard-to-correct speech problems. Your instructor may suggest that you use this section, or you may want to use it on your own if you're having trouble with the sounds this section covers.

Appendix C

Appendix C will help you check and correct your pronunciation of a number of words that are frequently mispronounced.

Appendix D

Appendix D is a glossary of terms we use with which you may not be familiar. We've tried to minimize the use of technical terms, but there are several we felt we couldn't do without.

Appendix E

Appendix E provides a number of tear-out Speech Evaluation Checklists. You can use them to evaluate your own speech as well as the speech of others.

FEEDBACK

We've tried to bring you the best book we could that would help you learn the principles of voice and diction and to put those principles into practice as effectively as possible. If you have any suggestions as to how we can improve the book, give us some feedback. Write to us at Pace University, Pace Plaza, New York, NY 10038. We'd like to hear from you.

INTRODUCTION TO SPEECH COMMUNICATION

2

Dealing with Nervousness

When you first started reading this book, you probably thought about the future: presenting yourself as a public speaker. You may have pictured yourself in front of the class, giving a speech. You also may have thought back to a time you made a presentation in another class or appeared in a school play. As you thought about those occasions, chances are strange things began to happen to you: your mouth began to feel dry, your stomach became a little bit shaky, your hands became slightly sweaty and cold. What was happening? You were feeling some of the symptoms of stagefright.

Stagefright is the biggest problem students face in speech classes. Each student usually believes that he or she is the only one with stagefright and is, therefore, abnormal. Most people believe that stagefright indicates some kind of flaw in a person's personality. This kind of thinking can create a devastating cycle: people become *afraid of their stagefright*. Each time they must speak in front of an audience, they get nervous; their nervousness causes them to make the mistakes they were afraid of making, which causes them to be at least as nervous the next time they must speak to an audience. Every year in our freshman speech courses we get graduating seniors who have delayed taking the course for four whole years simply because of their fear.

One of the reasons stagefright is such a problem is people don't usually talk about it; no one wants to admit that he or she has stagefright. We've learned a lot about stagefright over the years, and we'd like to share some of what we've learned with you. Let's start by clearing up some misconceptions about stagefright.

BELIEF: Stagefright is abnormal.

FACT: Stagefright is normal; almost everyone has it.

Other than those related to health and safety, what's the #1 fear in the nation? That's right; stagefright! Numerous surveys of inexperienced speakers show that, on the average, 75% admit to having stagefright and more than 35% think it's a serious problem. Surprisingly, stagefright is also considered to be a problem by about 76% of experienced speakers—lecturers, politicians, and business people. Those who perform for a living also have stagefright. In a recent *TV Guide* article, Olivia Newton-John told how her stagefright leaves her shaking and crying before a performance. And Jane Fonda has admitted to having "tremendous fear," a sentiment echoed by Sir Laurence Olivier, and many others.

The point we're trying to make is that *stagefright is perfectly normal!* It's so normal, in fact, many speech experts feel that the person who does *not* have stagefright should be considered *abnormal*.

BELIEF: Stagefright is always harmful.

FACT: Stagefright can be helpful.

You may be surprised to learn that stagefright can actually help you become a better speaker. It's true! When you're feeling the symptoms of stagefright, you become alert and alive, and you're better able to listen and adjust to the situation. You are also more "up" and appear more eager and involved in getting your message across to your listeners. If you don't have stagefright, you run the risk of putting your audience to sleep.

BELIEF: Stagefright should be eliminated.

FACT: You should understand, expect, accept, control, and use stagefright to make yourself a more effective speaker.

Let's see just what stagefright is, what causes it, and how it works.

Stagefright is a *normal* state of anxiety. It occurs when you're faced with a speaking situation that has an unpredictable outcome. Public speaking is not the only situation in which you may experience stagefright. It's quite common in job interviews, telephone calls, business meetings, classroom reports, club announcements, even meeting your prospective in-laws.

What Causes Stagefright?

Stagefright is a speaker's response to a "fight or flight" situation. Here's an example of such a situation. You're taking a walk in the woods on a pleasant autumn afternoon. Strolling around the base of a huge tree, you get the shock of your life! Suddenly, unexpectedly, you come face to face with a giant, hungry, growling, grizzly bear! What are you going to do? Whatever you do, you probably won't stop to think about it because at this point your body goes on "automatic pilot." It reacts automatically to prepare itself to either fight the bear or run away as far as is humanly possible. A number of things happen very quickly: your muscles tense; your heartbeat and breathing speed up; glands in your body begin to secrete essential fluids.

Bodily functions that are usually controlled voluntarily are now running on pure emotion. You act now, think later. And you may not become aware of your actions until *after* they have occurred. The mother of one of the authors surprised a burglar in her home in the middle of the night. She bodily threw him out of the house and then sat trembling by the phone for two hours before she could control herself enough to call the police.

The same kind of situation can occur in speech. You may face an audience and experience fear for any number of reasons. Your body interprets the feelings of fear to mean you are facing a real physical threat, such as the bear in the forest or the burglar in the house. As a result, your "automatic pilot" prepares your body to either fight the audience or run away from it, and your mind no longer controls what your body does.

The Physical Symptoms of Stagefright

The symptoms of stagefright are easily explained, now that you understand what causes it. They all relate to the fact that your body is ready to run or fight.

Butterflies in the Stomach

This is one of the first symptoms. Energy in your body needs to be pumped to those parts that are going to get it out of danger. Since the process of digestion requires a lot of energy, that process halts and energy is diverted to the arms and legs. The food you've eaten just sits in your stomach, undigested, until the danger is past.

Dry Mouth

The process of digestion begins in the mouth with the secretion of saliva. Since saliva production has been halted, too, your mouth becomes very dry. And it does not matter how much water you drink; it stays dry.

Rapid Breathing

Increased energy demands mean an increased need for oxygen, so your breathing speeds up accordingly.

Rapid Heart Rate

The heart must circulate the blood through the body more quickly in order to distribute oxygen to the skeletal muscles you'll use in running or fighting.

INTRODUCTION TO SPEECH COMMUNICATION

Trembling Hands, Weak Knees, Unsteady Voice

Almost all your skeletal muscles are under tension. As a result, they begin to tremble. Voice production is controlled by skeletal muscles, too, and you can hear the results of the excess tension.

Perspiration

Even though your mouth becomes dry, your body becomes increasingly wet with perspiration. This is simply an attempt to control body temperature. Because there is more blood circulating near the surface of the body, there is more body heat. Your body sends perspiration to the surface, and as the perspiration evaporates, it cools your body.

These symptoms are the ones most commonly experienced in stagefright. We're sure you can add some of your own to the list.

What Can You Do About Stagefright?

For most people, the symptoms of stagefright can be quite unnerving. Think back to the first time you can remember experiencing stagefright. What frightened you more, the speaking itself or the fact that your body was doing strange, terrible things to you?

The point is this: if you don't understand what's happening to you, more fear can develop. In other words, *stagefright can be fear of fear!*

Let's repeat what we said earlier: you shouldn't try to eliminate stagefright. Instead, you should *understand it, expect it, accept it, control it,* and *use it* to make you a more effective speaker. Don't expect that your fear is going to magically vanish once you learn its secrets. If you think you can be *totally* free from stagefright, you're probably setting yourself up for failure.

Dealing with stagefright involves three treatment stages: long-term, short-term, and what we call "first aid."

Long-term Treatments

Understand Your Stagefright

By learning about the causes and symptoms of stagefright, you take away the fear of the unknown. When you realize that stagefright is perfectly normal, you remove a lot of unnecessary doubt about your sanity.

Talk About Stagefright

Think about times you've had stagefright. Discuss those times with someone who is close to you. You'll find that talking it over clears up some of the mystery about it. You'll also find that the person with whom you're talking will want to share similar experiences with you.

Be Realistic About the Situation

Remember that your audience is nothing like the imaginary bear you faced in the woods. The audience can't cause you any physical harm. In fact, most audiences and listeners are genuinely interested in what you have to say, and they want you to do well. That's especially true in speech classes, where your fellow students would rather listen to you than think about their own cases of stagefright.

Put Things in Perspective

One way to put things in perspective is to play the game we call, "What's the worst that can happen?" Here's what we mean; imagine that when you get up to read in front of the class today, you're going to make a mistake. The professor is going to flunk you, your grade average will drop below 2.00, and you'll be dismissed from college. You probably won't be able to get a job without a college degree and you won't be eligible to collect unemployment. Your parents will throw you out of the house, and then you'll be forced to beg for food in the streets. All because of this one speech assignment.

When playing this game, let your imagination run wild. The result will make your fears seem kind of silly. Once you are able to poke fun at your fears, they will no longer seem more important than they really are.

Gain as Much Experience as Possible

Try to speak before an audience as much as you can, in as many different situations as you can. Each time you speak, you'll feel a little more confident. Experience really is the best teacher.

Short-term Treatments

Be Prepared

Know what you're doing, and you'll feel much more confident and more at ease. Don't worry about how you look or sound; you'll find that your memory seems better and that ideas and words flow more smoothly.

Practice, Practice, Practice!

By "practice" we don't mean a silent reading; we mean saying the words out loud! If you don't practice out loud, you won't have much confidence in yourself. How many times should you practice? There's no magic number; just practice as much as you feel you need. Try to practice in front of another person to get the feeling of saying the words to someone other than yourself. Pick someone who can be objective. We don't recommend brothers or sisters for this because they usually delight in making you feel even worse (if that's possible). If no one is available, use a mirror. And don't forget your trusty tape recorder; it doesn't lie.

Don't practice on the day of your presentation. Chances are you'll be more nervous than usual that day. Nervousness causes errors that cause more nervousness, causing even more errors, causing even more nervousness, causing . . . and so on, reducing you to a mass of quivering jelly. We recommend that your last practice session be on the night before you're due to talk. Last minute preparations really don't help at all.

Talk About What's Happening Now

Explain to yourself, or to others, what's happening to your body. For example, when you feel the first symptoms of stagefright, you might say, "Oh-oh, my mouth is starting to feel dry, and my tongue is like a big ball of cotton. I guess that means my digestion is starting to slow down. Yup, I must be right; I can feel some butterflies starting to fly. I wish I hadn't eaten that pepperoni pizza for lunch. Now my hands are beginning to sweat, and I can feel a slight trembling in my knees. I guess I'm caught in an approach–avoidance conflict. Let's see, what's going to come next? I should start to feel my heart pounding . . ." When you talk about what's happening to you in such an objective way, the physical feelings seem less frightening and almost become welcome signs of normality. You have removed some of the mystery, and you feel more in control.

Check Out the Room

Look over the room before you speak; it won't feel so strange later on. Make sure everything is set up and works. Do you need a desk or lectern, does the mike work, is the tape recorder plugged in, and so on? By looking over the room before your presentation, things become a little less uncertain.

Burn Up Excess Energy

Remember, your body begins to go on automatic pilot quite a while before you actually have to speak, and tension builds up in your muscles. There are some things you can do that will help you feel more relaxed: jog around the building, but don't overdo it; get off the bus or subway a few stops early and walk the rest of the way; take the stairs instead of the elevator, and so forth. Engaging in mild forms of exercise will help you get rid of excess energy. Just make sure you don't exhaust yourself.

Relaxation exercises will also help. Try slow, easy breathing. Think pleasant thoughts. Part by part, mentally dispel the tension in your body. Roll your head around to relax your neck. (For specific instructions for these and other relaxation procedures, see Chapter 4.)

Get Enough Sleep the Night Before

If you're well rested, you'll feel more sure of yourself and be more in control of your muscles and their movements.

First-aid (On-the-spot) Treatments

Think About Other Things

Look at what's going on in the room around you. Listen carefully to what another speaker has to say. Read a magazine while you're waiting for that job interview. Think about *anything*, except your presentation. Whatever you do, *don't* engage in any last-minute practice sessions.

Pause Before You Speak

You can use that time to expend a little energy and to gather your thoughts. Stand, if possible; it's a lot easier to produce a loud, clear voice while you're standing up than while you're confined to a chair. Standing also uses more energy than sitting.

Take some time to arrange your notes. Move things so that they're to your liking. Each little task uses energy and helps you to shake the jitters.

Make sure you have an adequate supply of air before you start talking. That way you won't rush into your presentation with a low air supply and run out of steam almost immediately.

Use Energy While You Talk

Use gestures and move your body naturally. If you don't overdo it, you'll look lively, and you'll also be getting rid of useless energy at the same time. Plan some gestures in your practice sessions. You'll feel more comfortable when you use them during the actual presentation.

Look for Friendly Faces

The audience is not made up of grizzly bears. You'll see smiles of encouragement that will make you feel much better about being there.

Try the things we've suggested, but don't expect instant success. Understanding stagefright means learning to understand yourself, and that takes time. Even we, the authors of this book, have never lost our own cases of stagefright completely; nevertheless, we feel pretty confident about speaking in front of an audience. We're sure that, in time, you will too.

SUGGESTED READINGS

Adler, Ronald B. *Confidence in Communication: A Guide to Assertive and Social Skills.* New York: Holt, Rinehart and Winston, 1977.

Phillips, Gerald M. *Help for Shy People.* Englewood Cliffs, N.J.: Prentice-Hall, Inc., 1981.

Zimbardo, Philip G. *Shyness: What It Is, What to Do About It.* Reading, Mass: Addison-Wesley, 1977.

The Speech Process

When you stop to think about it, speech is really a miraculous event. You create sound by using bodily structures that were originally better suited for biological purposes, such as chewing, swallowing, coughing, and respiration. And, you don't produce just ordinary sounds, but sounds that you can use to further relationships with other people. What's more, you create these sounds almost without thinking; they are second nature to you.

We're going to examine the sounds we make and the ways in which we make them. We're also going to take a look at the structures we use to produce sound. We believe that a basic understanding of the speech process will help you develop more effective voice production (Chapter 4) and will help you learn the sounds of American English (Chapter 7) and also help you practice them. In our opinion, if you know how something works, you can use and control it more accurately.

THE NATURE OF SOUND

What Sound Is

When we talk about sound, we're *not* talking about hearing. Hearing is something that happens within your body (outer ear, middle ear, inner ear, nervous system, brain) as a result of sound. Sound is an actual physical event in which acoustic energy is generated. Hearing is the way you receive that acoustic energy from the air and eventually change it to meaningful nerve impulses in your brain.

The physical event that we call sound consists of vibratory energy that travels through the molecules of the air in ever-widening circles away from the source. To produce sound you need three things: a *force* that sets in motion a *vibrator* that generates vibrations that travel through a *medium*. When the force sets the vibrator in motion, some of the energy of the vibrations is applied to the molecules of air that surround the vibrator. These molecules send along some of their energy to the molecules next to them, and so on. Each molecule transmits some of the energy, and the process continues until there's no energy left. Since the motion of the vibrator is back and forth, waves of energy travel outward in all directions through the air (see Figure 3-1).

Characteristics of Sound

Although we can't see sound, we can observe and measure sound in a number of objective ways, and we do know a great deal about sound. Three of the ob-

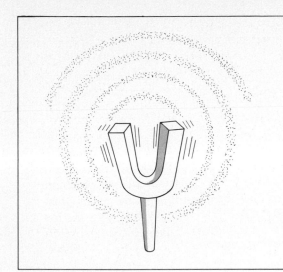

Figure 3-1.
Sound waves traveling away from
the source.

jective characteristics of sound are important for you to understand. They are *frequency, intensity,* and *spectrum.* Their subjective counterparts are pitch, loudness, and quality.

Frequency

Frequency means the number of vibrations that occur in a given period of time. The frequencies of sounds vary because some vibrating objects vibrate more rapidly than others and, in turn, cause the molecules of air to vibrate at the same rate. Humans can hear sounds that range from frequencies as low as 20 Hz. [Hz (hertz) means vibrations per second.] The upper limit of hearing is about 20,000 Hz.

How rapidly an object vibrates basically depends on three factors: the object's *mass, tension,* and *length.* In general, small, short, highly tense objects vibrate more rapidly than large, long, low-tension objects (See Figure 3-2).

Pitch

While frequency is an objective (physically measurable) characteristic of sound, pitch is subjective. That is, pitch is determined by the listener's judgment; it occurs within you. Pitch is what we call the highness or lowness of a sound. The relationship is direct: the higher the frequency, the higher the pitch we hear; the lower the frequency, the lower the pitch.

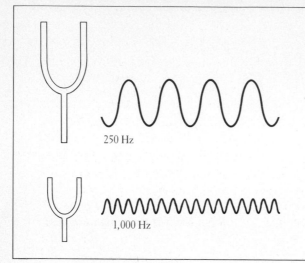

250 Hz

1,000 Hz

Figure 3-2.
The mass, tension, and
length of a vibrating object
determine its frequency of vi-
bration. Compare the fre-
quencies of the objects
above.

Intensity

Intensity is the objective measurement of the amount of energy a sound has. If you apply a greater force to the vibrating object, it will transfer more energy to the air around it. As a result, each molecule of air shoves the next one a little harder, so more energy means higher intensity. A not too pleasant example would be a minor rear-end collision in a line of cars at a toll booth. There's much more energy transmitted in a 25 mph collision than in one at 5 mph. And, as with sound, the greater the energy, the farther the sound travels.

Loudness

Just as pitch is the subjective interpretation of frequency, loudness is the subjective interpretation of intensity. We perceive high-intensity sounds as being louder than low-intensity sounds.

Spectrum

Figure 3-1 shows the way waves of sound travel away from the source, which in this case is a tuning fork. If we graphically display the movement of one molecule in any one of the waves around the tuning fork, the resulting waveform is the simple sine curve shown in Figure 3-3. That's because a tuning fork is designed and built very precisely to produce a very simple kind of sound that we call a pure-tone. By simple we don't mean easy; we mean that it's not complex. A pure-tone is a very clear, musical tone with the same movement of the molecules repeating over and over again.

INTRODUCTION TO SPEECH COMMUNICATION

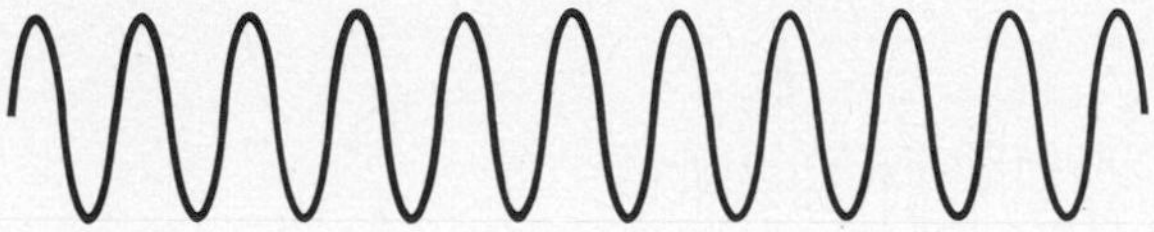

Figure 3-3.
The waveform of a
pure-tone produced
by a tuning fork (see
Figure 3-1).

Our bodies, as well as most other sound-producing objects, don't produce just one, simple pure-tone. Instead, we produce very complex tones that are made up of many pure-tones. The configuration of a complex wave that shows the relative intensities and frequencies of the component pure-tones is called the spectrum. Figure 3-4 shows the spectra of three complex sounds. Compare these with the pure-tone shown in Figure 3-3.

Quality

Your subjective interpretation of spectrum is called quality. You're well aware that sounds differ in ways other than loudness and pitch. Each complex sound is unique; there's some intangible *quality* that makes every voice, for example, different. Listen to two singers both singing the same note, and you can hear differences in their voices.

The Speech Process

Now we're ready to talk about a particular type of sound: the sound of human speech. First let's look at the body as a sound producer. You'll remember that you need three things to produce sound: a force, a vibrator, and a medium. The human body has the equipment to fill these needs and is an excellent sound producer. There are six distinct processes in producing speech sounds: *innervation, breathing, phonation, resonance, articulation,* and *audition.*

While it is not within the purview of this text to delve very deeply into two phases of speech production, audition and innervation, we feel that a simple explanation may be in order.

Audition

The auditory process begins with energy, in the form of alternating compressions and rarefactions of the molecules of air, being transmitted through the air as the result of someone speaking. These vibrations are focused by the visible portion of the outer ear, the pinna, and channeled into the external audi-

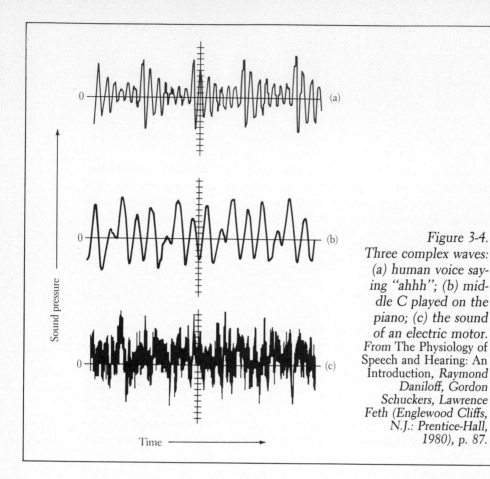

Sound pressure

Time

Figure 3-4.
Three complex waves:
(a) human voice say-
ing "ahhh"; (b) mid-
dle C played on the
piano; (c) the sound
of an electric motor.
From The Physiology of
Speech and Hearing: An
Introduction, Raymond
Daniloff, Gordon
Schuckers, Lawrence
Feth (Englewood Cliffs,
N.J.: Prentice-Hall,
1980), p. 87.

tory canal. At the end of the canal is the tympanic membrane, or eardrum, which is set into sympathetic vibration. Resting just inside and against the tympanic membrane is the malleus, or hammer, the first of three tiny bones or ossicles. Movement of the tympanic membrane sets the three ossicles, the other two of which are called the incus, or anvil, and stapes, or stirrup, into vibration. The sound energy is thus transformed from molecular energy (or variation in air pressure) into mechanical energy related to the movement of the ossicles.

The end of the ossicular chain (the footplate of the stapes) fits into an opening in the part of the inner ear called the cochlea, which is a snail-shell-like cavity in the temporal bone of the head. The cochlea is filled with fluid and a portion of it is lined with nerve endings. Pressure changes in the fluid caused by an in-and-out movement of the stapes into the opening of the cochlea cause certain of the nerve endings to be stimulated. The nerves attached to these endings gather together to form the auditory nerve, which

INTRODUCTION TO SPEECH COMMUNICATION

carries the nerve impulses to the brain where they are perceived as sound, translated into a meaningful message, and stored.

Innervation

There is a highly complex pattern of nervous impulses traveling from the brain to many parts of the body that is necessary to control and coordinate all of the functions which are involved in speech production.

First the central and peripheral nervous systems are involved in controlling the muscles of the abdomen, chest, and diaphragm (the membrane that separates the chest cavity from the stomach) so that the chest cavity is expanded to take air into the lungs, and then compressed to force that air back out again. These actions involve the rather gross movement of large muscle groups.

Next the muscles of the larynx must be controlled and coordinated to bring the vocal folds together and held under the proper tension to produce phonation at the desired pitch and loudness. Most of this control comes from a nerve called the recurrent laryngeal nerve.

In order to resonate the sound that is phonated by the larynx, nerves must control the muscles which vary the size, shape, and tension of the cavities of the head and neck which are responsible for shaping and amplifying the voice in an ever-changing pattern of movement during speech.

Finally, there are many muscles that control movements of the tongue, lips, soft palate, lower jaw, oropharynx, and nasopharynx. The nerves that are responsible for control of the movements of these muscles must exercise control and coordination of movements which are performed with a very high degree of precision, rapidity, and accuracy.

To understand the need for precision and accuracy, let us look at a short sample of speech and examine the articulatory movements just of the tongue. In Lincoln's Gettysburg Address, for example, the first words, "Four score and seven years ago . . ." involve an average of four tongue movements per word. At the average rate of conversational speech, one hundred and twenty words per minute, we would be required to perform four hundred and eighty tongue movements for each minute of speech. In addition, if we were to miss the exact place of articulation for each sound by as little as a fraction of a millimeter, the sound produced would probably come out as a completely different phoneme.

Movements of the articulators are generally controlled by the facial and trigeminal nerves, two of the eight pairs of cranial nerves, on either side of the head.

Movements of the articulators are monitored for accuracy acoustically by the hearing mechanism and kinesthetically through sensory nerves called proprioceptors, located in the muscles themselves, and which provide sensory feedback about the movements of the articulators to the brain.

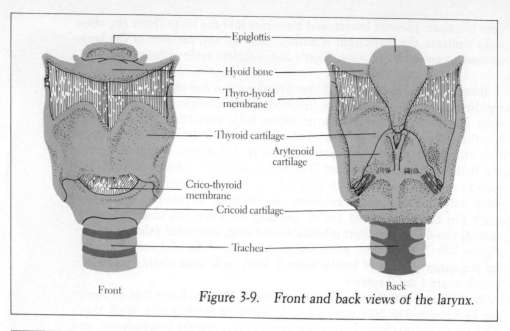

Figure 3-9. Front and back views of the larynx.

Front

Back

Epiglottis

Hyoid bone

Thyro-hyoid membrane

Thyroid cartilage

Arytenoid cartilage

Crico-thyroid membrane

Cricoid cartilage

Trachea

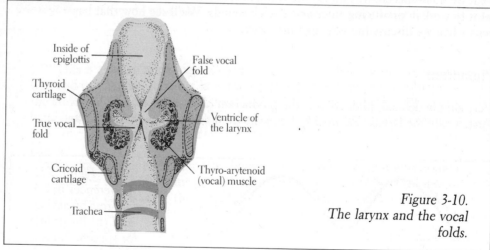

Inside of epiglottis

Thyroid cartilage

True vocal fold

Cricoid cartilage

Trachea

False vocal fold

Ventricle of the larynx

Thyro-arytenoid (vocal) muscle

Figure 3-10.
The larynx and the vocal folds.

ynx. Now take the thumb and forefinger of one hand, and very gently pinch your "Adam's apple" (thyroid cartilage). With your forefinger, trace the outline of your thyroid cartilage. This cartilage forms the outside wall of the larynx. Look at Figure 3-10. There you see the vocal folds, two bands of tissue located inside the larynx.

The larynx functions very nicely as a valve. By contracting muscles within the larynx, you're able to move the vocal folds so that they come together, entirely closing off the larynx. Why would you want to do this? Primarily to keep food and other substances out of your lungs, to build up air pressure for coughing, to hold your breath, and so on. Figure 3-11a shows you an overhead view of the vocal folds and a frontal cross-section view of the larynx during phonation. Figure 3-11b shows the same views, but during quiet breathing.

Sound Production   We said earlier that a vibrating object and a force are needed to produce sound. Well, we've got both elements here; the breathstream provides the force, and the vocal folds become the vibrating object. Here's how the process works:

1. Air is inhaled.
2. The vocal folds meet, completely closing the larynx, and stopping the air flow.
3. The diaphragm and chest muscles relax; the abdominal muscles slowly contract.
4. Air pressure builds up below the vocal folds.

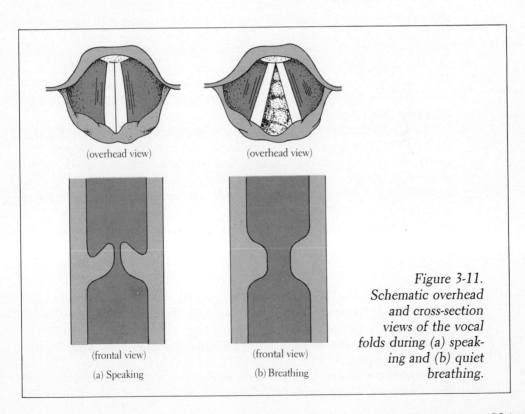

(overhead view)   (overhead view)

(frontal view)   (frontal view)

(a) Speaking   (b) Breathing

Figure 3-11.
Schematic overhead
and cross-section
views of the vocal
folds during (a) speak-
ing and (b) quiet
breathing.

5. Air pressure increases until it overcomes the muscular forces holding the vocal folds closed.
6. Air escapes in very rapid bursts, creating waves of sound in the air above the vocal folds.
7. You continue to hold the vocal folds closed, and force air between them for as long as you want to phonate.

You can demonstrate this type of sound production in other ways. Blow up a balloon, then stretch the lips of the balloon tightly by pulling the sides of the tube away from each other. You should be able to produce a high-pitched buzz or whistle. Here's another way. Stick out your tongue, lay it on your lower lip, and hold it down with your upper lip. Now, blow air beneath your tongue! You've created what's known as a "raspberry." Both it and the balloon whistle were created aerodynamically in the same way you create voice.

Pitch We said earlier that the mass, length, and tension of a vibrating object determine the frequency of vibration. These same factors determine how rapidly your vocal folds vibrate, too.

First, let's consider the normal, usual pitch of your voice. That's determined primarily by the length of your vocal folds; the longer the vocal folds, the lower the pitch of your voice. That, along with the size and shape of the resonating cavities, accounts for people having differently pitched voices. It's also the reason why, in general, women's voices are higher than men's. You have no control over how long your vocal folds grow to be or over the basic size of your resonating cavities, so you don't have much control over the fundamental pitch of your voice.

The second thing to consider is how you vary pitch to give speech the intonation patterns so necessary for meaning, as in the rising pitch at the end of many questions. Again, mass, length, and tension are the factors. Using the muscles of the larynx, including the vocal folds themselves, you vary the mass, length, and tension of the folds, and thereby change their frequency of vibration.

Resonance

A third way we vary pitch is through resonance. If you could listen to the sound of your voice *in* your larynx, you wouldn't recognize it as voice at all because, in the larynx, voice is only a buzzing noise. Something else has to happen to make that buzzing noise into recognizable voice. That "something" is resonance.

Resonance is the amplification and modification of sound by the cavities of the vocal tract. Those cavities are the larynx, pharynx, oral cavity, and nasal cavity (see Figure 3-12). First, we will explain resonance in general, then resonance in the vocal tract.

Take an empty Coke bottle. Blow across and into the neck so as to produce a low-pitched sound like a foghorn. Think for a minute about what happened; you got more sound out of that bottle than you put into it! That's right. All you did was send some air into the bottle (at just the right angle), and you got a deep, rich sound. You actually set the air inside the bottle vibrating, and the foghorn sound was produced, richer and louder than the sound you put in.

Now fill the Coke bottle about a third of the way. Blow into it again. The sound you produce this time should be higher pitched. That's because the water takes up space and reduces the volume of air that can resonate. And, if you'll remember, smaller vibrating bodies usually vibrate more rapidly than larger ones. So the pitch of the sound you hear from the bottle varies with the amount of air in the bottle. Try it. Either add some water or take some out; the pitch of the sound will rise or fall. Incidentally, the shape of the resonator also affects the way it operates. As you change the volume of air in the bottle, you're also changing the shape of the resonating cavity. So the important thing about a resonator is its size and shape.

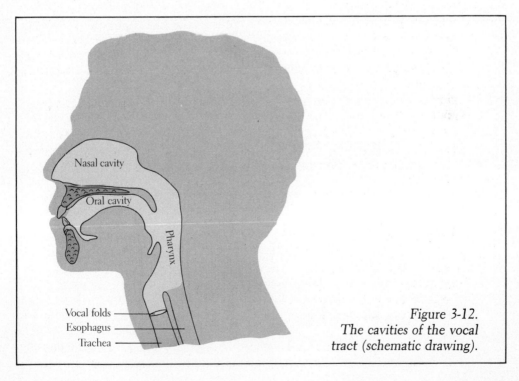

Figure 3-12.
The cavities of the vocal
tract (schematic drawing).

THE SPEECH PROCESS

Resonance in the Vocal Tract   The cavities in your head and neck are resonators; they're open chambers filled with air. They're actually very sophisticated resonators, for you can change their size and shape and, thereby, change the tones they resonate.

We use the vocal resonators to change the buzz of the vocal folds into voice. The resonators selectively amplify the buzz and not only make your voice louder but also give it its unique quality. You're using your resonators as though they were a series of Coke bottles of various sizes and shapes.

We also use resonance in the production of the different consonant and vowel sounds. Most of that production occurs in the mouth and is called articulation.

Articulation

Articulation is the production of speech sounds as a result of movement of the structures of the vocal tract. Figure 3-13 shows the articulators. They are the tongue, teeth, lips, gum ridge, hard palate, soft palate, lower jaw, and the glottis (space between the vocal folds). We use the articulators to (1) change

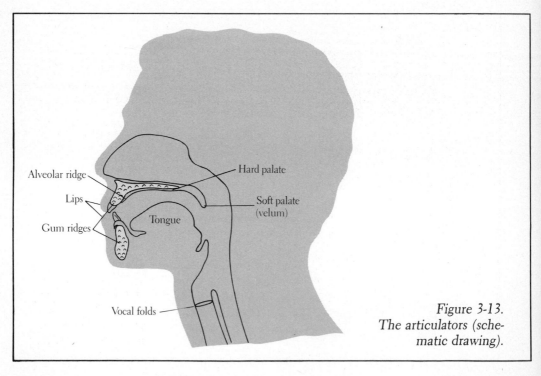

Figure 3-13. The articulators (schematic drawing).

INTRODUCTION TO SPEECH COMMUNICATION

the size and shape of the mouth for resonating vowels and (2) produce the consonants by creating sounds. You'll learn more about consonants and vowels in Chapter 7, so we'll discuss their production only briefly here.

When you produce vowels, you take the vocal buzz and put it into a different sized and shaped "Coke bottle" for each vowel. Try this: say *hee-haw*. You should be able to feel your mouth, which was almost closed for *hee*, opening wide for *haw*. By opening wider, you changed from a small resonating cavity to a large one. Look at Figure 3-14. Note that you vary your mouth's size and shape to produce different vowel sounds.

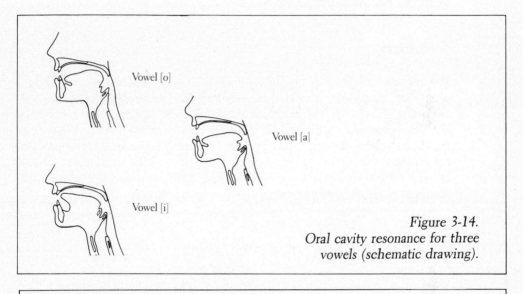

Vowel [o]

Vowel [a]

Vowel [i]

Figure 3-14.
Oral cavity resonance for three
vowels (schematic drawing).

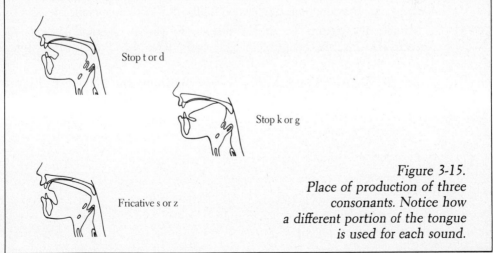

Stop t or d

Stop k or g

Fricative s or z

Figure 3-15.
Place of production of three
consonants. Notice how
a different portion of the tongue
is used for each sound.

THE SPEECH PROCESS

Consonants are an entirely different matter. Say the word *kick*. At the beginning and the end, you should feel your tongue pressing up to the soft palate, then exploding air. Try the word *pup*. With this word, you create the explosion with your lips. When producing consonants, then, the articulators are actually involved in sound production (see Figure 3-15, page 37), whereas they are not involved in producing vowel sounds.

Articulation is an amazing process. You make an incredible number of complicated movements just to produce a simple sentence. And what's more amazing, you're able to duplicate movements, returning time and time again to exactly the right spot.

Summary

We use six processes in producing speech sounds: innervation, breathing, phonation, resonance, articulation, and audition. Innervation is the neural control of the speech and breathing mechanism. Breathing is the inhalation and exhalation of air and provides the force for sound production. Phonation is the production of vocal sound by the vocal folds. Resonance is the amplification and modification of sound using the cavities of the vocal tract. Articulation is the movement of the vocal tract structures to produce speech sounds. Audition is the process of hearing (see Appendix A, "Ear Training").

SUGGESTED READINGS

Daniloff, R., Schuckers, G., and Feth, L. *The Physiology of Speech and Hearing: An Introduction.* Englewood Cliffs, N.J.: Prentice-Hall, Inc., 1980.

Minifie, F., Hixon, T., and Williams, F. (Eds.). *Normal Aspects of Speech, Hearing, and Language.* Englewood Cliffs, N.J.: Prentice-Hall, Inc., 1973.

Zemlin, W. *Speech and Hearing Science: Anatomy and Physiology.* Englewood Cliffs, N.J.: Prentice-Hall, Inc., 1968.

part two

Introduction to Nonverbal Communication

Have you ever received, from someone you know well, a letter that you misinterpreted because all there was to interpret were the written words? You probably missed all the nuances and subtle shades of meaning you usually derived from such things as the other person's facial expressions, tone of voice, and gestures. All these things, as well as others, make up what we call *nonverbal communication*. They are the accompaniments of spoken language that help make our meanings complete, help transmit the whole sense of what we want to say.

Nonverbal communication includes all the modes of communication that convey meaning *other than the actual words we use*. In the following three chapters we'll be talking about a number of different modes of nonverbal communication. In Chapter 4 you'll learn about the basics of voice production; how you control loudness, pitch, and quality. In Chapter 5 you'll learn the factors of vocal expressiveness and get a chance to put them into practice. In Chapter 6 we'll cover the other modes of nonverbal communication. You'll learn what these modes are, why we depend on them, and what kinds of messages they send. You'll also learn about mixed messages and how to avoid them.

4

Voice
Production

Voice *and* diction. You can't separate the two. Think about it; you can't get along with just one. Imagine trying to make yourself understood speaking without consonants and vowels. And, what about voice? Sure, you could whisper, but most people wouldn't be able to hear you.

Who taught you how to produce and use your voice? Not just one person, surely, and probably not in any kind of formal setting. Most of us simply learn how to use our voices by using them. We don't think about voice; we *do* it.

Your voice carries a great deal of meaning not only about what you want to say but about you. Yet most of us don't know very much about voice. As a matter of fact, a great many people have no idea that the voice they hear in their heads isn't the voice that other people hear; they have no idea what their voices sound like.

It's our purpose in this chapter to present the basics of voice production: breathing for speech, loudness, pitch, and quality. By the end of the chapter, you should know considerably more about your own voice: how you produce it and how you use it.

If you haven't read Chapter 3, we suggest that you do so before you go on with this chapter. In fact, even if you have read it, a review wouldn't hurt. Chapter 3 explains the structures used for voice production and how we physically make the sound of voice. You should be familiar with that material before you read this chapter.

BREATHING

As we explained in Chapter 3, the breathstream is the powerhouse of voice production. It's difficult to produce effective voice if you don't breathe efficiently; you'll put a strain on the entire vocal mechanism. If you're like most people, you probably don't have any real problems with breathing for speech, but don't stop reading here. If you want to be a more effective oral communicator, you can benefit from an understanding of the hows and whys of breathing for speech.

Breathing for Speech

You breathe differently when you're breathing for speech than you do when you're breathing for purely biological purposes. The difference is not that you have to breathe more deeply for speech, it's how you control your exhalations. In rest breathing, the time frames for inhalation and exhalation are usually about equal in length. In speech breathing, you take a quick breath in, then gradually let the air out, pacing the exhalation so that it lasts long enough for what you want to say. If you don't control the exhalation efficiently, you may run out of breath, sound strained or breathy, or not be loud enough.

Breath Control

You control your rate of exhalation in a couple of fairly simple ways. One form of control is by far the most important—the way you use your abdominal muscles. You could almost consider your abdominal muscles to be the pump that pushes air out of your respiratory system. And, just like a bicycle pump, the harder you push, the faster the air moves. In breathing for speech, the major part of breath control consists of contracting the abdominal muscles, but just the right amount for the level of loudness you want for the sounds you are making. The other form of control is in the use of the vocal folds; here's where they can function as a valve during phonation to help control the rate of air flow.

Not everyone uses the muscles of respiration in the same way, so perhaps you don't use the abdominal muscles in breath control. Frankly, we don't care how you breathe for speech *as long as what you're doing lets you breathe comfortably, unobtrusively, and in a way that lets you speak effectively.* If your style of breathing doesn't do all three, we recommend that you attempt to learn the central (or abdominal) style of breathing. We think it's the most efficient—the most air for the least work—style and the most effective for producing and sustaining loud, clear tones. Try the following exercise even if you're already an abdominal breather.

☐ *Abdominal Breathing Exercise* ☐

1. Lie on your back on a comfortable but firm surface.
2. Make sure your knees are supported in a slightly flexed position; your arms should be by your side, with your elbows slightly bent.
3. Place a moderately heavy weight (a book two or three times heavier than this one, for example) on your abdomen.
4. Begin breathing in and out, through your mouth, so that you push the book up when you breathe in; the book should sink down as you breathe out.
5. Keep one hand on your chest, about three inches below your neck, to make sure you are keeping chest movement to a minimum.
6. Once you are able to move your abdomen in coordination with your breathing in and out, remove the book and put your hand in its place. Continue to move your abdomen up when you inhale and down when you exhale.
7. When you feel you have abdominal breathing under control while lying

down, move to a comfortable sitting position. Continue the exercise, keeping one hand on your chest and the other on your abdomen.

8. Take a deep breath with the new breathing pattern. Exhale slowly, sighing the vowel *ahh* with each exhalation. Sustain the vowel for five seconds.

9. Take a deep breath. Exhale slowly, counting from one to five, holding each number for one full second.

10. Take a deep breath, abdominally. Exhale slowly, naming the days of the week at a rate of one per second.

11. Repeat steps 8 through 10 while standing.

Now try the following exercise. It's designed to help you develop breath control while speaking and to increase the depth of your breathing.

□ Breath Control Exercise 1: Counting □

1. Take three normal rest breaths. Make a mental note as to how much air is going in and out.

2. Take a normal breath in and count to three, holding each number for one second. Do it almost like singing. Make sure to hold each number for one *full* second and not pause between numbers.

3. Repeat step 2, but this time continue counting until you begin to run out of breath. Do it again, stopping at the same point.

4. Now take a deep breath and count again until you begin to run out of breath; you've counted as high as you can. Repeat this twice, then stop the exercise for a while.

5. Allow at least fifteen minutes after step 4 and start the whole procedure again.

The object is to increase the amount of numbers counted by at least one number each time you practice until you reach your maximum. Don't push until you feel uncomfortable, and don't do too much deep breathing all at once; you might get dizzy. Try this drill every day, and you'll soon have more efficient breath control.

Sometimes, people tend to waste so much air that their voices take on a noticeably breathy quality. This breathiness can be deliberate (an attempt to be sexy, perhaps) or simply the result of poor breath control. In any case, a breathy voice is usually hard to hear, may call considerable attention to itself, and distract the listener from the speaker's message. The exercise that follows is designed to reduce breathiness.

□ Breath Control Exercise 2: Breathiness □

You'll need a small hand mirror for this exercise. Make sure it's clean and cold enough so that your breath will condense on the surface.

1. Hold the mirror about an inch away from your mouth. Say *ahh*. Quickly

INTRODUCTION TO NONVERBAL COMMUNICATION

take the mirror away from your mouth and look at it. Check for fogging. Repeat this procedure, and try to see the pattern of fogging on the glass.

2. Hold the mirror in front of your mouth again. Say *ahh* more loudly. Check what's happened to the fogging on the glass. Repeat, and try to reduce the fogging when you say *ahh*.

3. Try the same drill with other vowels. First, see how much condensation occurs when you say the vowel the way you usually do. Then try to reduce the area of glass that gets covered.

4. Compare the breathy and nonbreathy production. Visually, the breathy production will have a large area of condensation. The nonbreathy production will result in a small area. You should also begin to *hear* the difference.

5. Now, do *Breath control exercise 1: Counting*. Make sure to use the nonbreathy voice. You can monitor your breath flow by placing your fingers about an inch in front of your mouth. You will notice a change in the number of words you can comfortably say on one inhalation.

LOUDNESS

The loudness of your voice says a lot about you. We tend to think of people with weak or soft voices as being shy and timid, perhaps afraid to speak up because they're so unsure of themselves. On the other hand, people with loud, booming voices may be thought of as overbearing, overconfident, and boorish. When a person speaks too loudly, we often pull back—both physically and mentally.

To many people, the person who doesn't talk loudly enough to be easily heard is the more annoying. It's frustrating to have to continually ask a person to speak up or, even worse, to miss much of what that person says.

Loudness problems are usually caused by a person's *inability to produce and sustain* the proper loudness or *failure to monitor* his or her own voice. The result is loudness that is inappropriate for the listeners and the environment as well as the content of the communication. Chapter 5 covers loudness in terms of monitoring your loudness level to produce a voice that fits the content, listeners, and environment. But before you can do those exercises, you must be able to produce a tone of adequate loudness. Let's work on that now.

Controlling Loudness

Have you ever gone to an exciting sporting event such as a hockey match or football game or soccer game? Remember how much you enjoyed yourself? Until the next day, that is, when your throat was so sore you could hardly talk. That sore throat may have lasted for a couple of days or longer. Your sore throat and loss of voice were probably the result of the way you were trying to produce a loud voice.

A loud voice does *not* require a lot of muscular action by the vocal folds and larynx (although that is what hurts). The force behind a loud voice should be supplied primarily by the abdominal muscles.

The vocal folds are set into vibration by the air you force out of the lungs. They don't vibrate due to muscular action of their own. So, to increase the strength of their vibrations, you must increase the force behind the breathstream. You do that by contracting the abdominal muscles.

Try this: place one hand flat against your abdomen just below your breastbone. Say "ahh" and hold it. While you're saying "ahh," hit the back of your hand with your other fist (not too hard, though). You should have heard a sudden increase in loudness. Now try this: place both hands on your abdomen. At the rate of one number per second, count to four. Start quietly but make each number louder. You should feel your abdominal muscles contract suddenly for each number. The following exercises should help you develop the proper support for a loud voice.

□ *Loudness Exercise 1: Force* □

This exercise is designed to help you increase the force with which your breathstream pushes the vocal folds apart during phonation. Practice abdominal breathing for about five minutes before you do this exercise for the first time.
1. Hold a piece of paper, about the size of this page, lengthwise just under your lower lip. Hold it by the corners closest to you, with the edge of the paper touching your skin.
2. Blow across the surface of the paper, and try to make the paper rise to a horizontal position. Do this five times, feeling for contraction of your abdominal muscles as you blow.
3. Now, use a slightly larger piece of paper. Make the paper rise five times.
4. Repeat step 3 a few times every hour for two or three days. You'll find that it will probably take less effort each day to make the paper rise.

□ *Loudness Exercise 2: Projection* □

This exercise should generate some of the same physical feelings as the previous exercise for force, but this time you'll actually be speaking. This exercise requires another person to help.
1. Have another person stand facing you, about five feet away. His or her right hand should be at shoulder height, slightly cupped, and facing you.
2. From your position, five feet away, count to five. *Try to speak into the*

INTRODUCTION TO NONVERBAL COMMUNICATION

other person's hand. Yes, you may feel a little silly, but do it anyway. Project your voice, throw it or whatever else you may call it, but speak into the other person's hand.

3. Have the other person take one step backward, and repeat step 2. Continue the procedure until the other person is about forty feet away from you.

4. Now have the other person walk back, one step at a time, reversing the procedure.

☐ *Loudness Exercise 3: Control* ☐

You don't need anyone to help you with this one. We do suggest, though, that you find a place where you won't bother other people. Again, feel for abdominal muscle contractions.

1. Pick a series of items: numbers, months, letters, and so forth. (Here we'll use numbers to describe the exercise.)

2. Count to five; start with low intensity, and increase intensity with each number. Take a breath between each number and the next. Repeat this twice.

3. Count backward, starting from five. *Start with high intensity, and gradually decrease intensity.* Again, take a breath between productions. Repeat twice.

4. On one breath, count to five. This time you should be loudest at *three.* In other words, gradually increase loudness until you reach three, then decrease. Do the entire exercise once a day.

☐ *Loudness Exercise 4: Practice* ☐

Read aloud using whatever materials you would like, but we especially recommend the "Letters to the Editor" in your local newspaper. The comedian Steve Allen used to include this as a regular feature of his late-night TV show. He would read angry letters to the editor in a loud, angry voice. As he made the writers' points for them, the audience would cheer or otherwise show their approval. Try this yourself. Ask a friend to sit across the room while you read angry letters to him or her. Make sure your voice is adequately loud and that you *project* your voice to your friend.

PITCH

The pitch of your voice—its highness or lowness—is another variable of speech that says a lot about you. As a rule, we apply certain stereotypes to our expectations of what a person's voice should sound like. For example, we have learned to expect women to generally have higher voices than men. We also expect that there will be an inverse ratio between a person's size and the pitch of his or her voice. In other words, the larger the person, the more low-pitched you expect that person's voice to be. These are just a few examples of common vocal stereotypes and, yes, many times our expectations are incorrect. Were you ever surprised to discover that someone you had only heard speaking over the phone, but had never seen in person, looked quite different than what you had expected?

We all probably know someone who attempts to influence the impression he or she makes on others by speaking in a voice that's too low or high pitched to use comfortably for a long time. By doing so, though, the person puts a strain on the vocal mechanism and also restricts the voice to a narrow pitch range. The vocal mechanism is strained because the person is using his or her vocal folds to produce a pitch they weren't designed to produce for long periods of time.

In Chapter 3 we discussed the factors that determine the frequency of vibration of your vocal folds and the pitch of your voice. You may recall that the main factors in determining the pitch of your voice are the length of your vocal folds and the size of your resonating cavities. The pitch your vocal folds and resonating cavities are naturally suited to produce is called your *optimum pitch,* and you produce it with less effort than other pitches. The pitch you use all the time is called your *habitual pitch*. It is best, for the vocal mechanism, if your habitual pitch is the same as your optimum, because using an habitual pitch that's far from your optimum can result in voice problems. Put it this way: you don't ask a trumpet to do a tuba's job.

Try the following procedure. You can use it to determine your optimum pitch.

□ *Determining Optimum Pitch* □

For this procedure, you need another person and a piano. Don't worry; neither one of you needs to know how to play the piano. The other person is there to help you confirm your judgments.

1. Pick a voice pitch near the middle of your range. Determine what that pitch is on the piano. You do this simply by playing different notes on the piano until you decide you've matched the pitch of your voice.

2. Chant down the scale to the lowest possible pitch your voice can reach. Locate that pitch on the piano. For chanting, which is really a combination of talking and singing, you can use *do, re, mi,* and so on or *me, me, me* or any vowel you like.

3. Now, chant up the scale to the highest pitch your voice can reach. Locate that pitch on the piano.

4. Count the number of notes in the range, from the lowest to the highest

INTRODUCTION TO NONVERBAL COMMUNICATION

pitch. Include both the highest and lowest pitches and count both black and white keys.

5. Divide the number of notes by four. Count this number of keys up from the lowest pitch. This should be at (or no more than one key above or below) your optimum pitch.

6. Try phonating at all three of those pitches (one above, optimum, and one below) to determine which is the most comfortable for you. The spread between the lowest and highest notes you can reach is your *pitch range*.

□ *Determining Habitual Pitch* □

Now that you know your optimum pitch, you should see if your habitual and optimum pitches are the same. You'll need the piano and a listener.

1. Read the following passage aloud, at a normal conversational loudness level. Read it three or four times, each time making it more monotonous and more like "machine" talk. Ask your listener to find the note on the piano that's closest to the average pitch of your reading. Here's the passage. It's from a booklet published by the Environmental Protection Agency.

> The decibel is the most commonly used unit to measure sound intensity at its source. The decibel level starts at 0, the hearing threshold, and goes to 180, the level heard when a rocket is launched. Brief exposure to levels over 140 decibels, however, causes pain and can rupture eardrums, resulting in permanent hearing loss. But one can suffer hearing loss or impairment at much lower levels. According to some scientific opinion, continuous exposure for 8 hours to noise levels of approximately 85 decibels can also cause permanent hearing loss.

2. Compare your habitual pitch with your optimum pitch. Are they just about the same? If they're more than two tones away from each other, you should work on changing your habitual pitch.

Changing Habitual Pitch

Essentially, changing your habitual pitch requires nothing more than ample practice speaking at your optimum pitch. You'll begin to feel more comfortable with your new pitch, and you'll also become very aware when you stray from optimum. For practicing, we suggest that you use any of the selections in Chapter 5 or other readings from literature, magazines, and so forth. You may want to check your pitch with the piano at the start to see if you're staying on pitch. Read your selections aloud at conversational loudness. Continue your practice sessions every day as long as you need them.

Extending Your Pitch Range

Often we use only a small number of the notes available from the total pitch range. We tend to stay more or less in one place on the scale; and when we do move away from that place, we tend to go up rather than down. Here are two exercises to help you extend your pitch range.

□ *Relaxation* □

Ever notice that your voice seems lower in the morning after a good night's sleep? That's because you, and your vocal folds, had a chance to relax. Before you deliberately try speaking at a lower pitch, you should be relaxed. Try the relaxation exercises on pp. 52 and 53. They'll make a difference.

□ *Singing* □

This is probably one of the best ways to extend your pitch range, especially downward. The only problem is many people think they "can't" sing or are just plain embarrassed to sing in public. That's why we suggest that you do your singing in the shower; it's a great place for it. Here's why: first, a shower's in a room that's usually square or rectangular with walls that are hard and smooth. That makes it a good resonator, so your voice sounds richer and fuller than it does outside. Second, the sound of the running water makes it hard for other people to hear you and affords you some privacy. Finally, the shower relaxes you, and you can reach those low notes more easily.

So, try singing in the shower. After a few days you should notice that your range is increasing. Then, it's time to *speak* in the shower. Try such things as Hamlet's soliloquy that begins "To be or not to be . . ." or whatever else you can have fun with.

QUALITY

It has been said of the human voice that it is the best and most accurate indicator of a person's physical and emotional state. Think for a moment of the way people you know sound when they are tired, tense, upset, angry, happy, or sad. It's likely that just by listening to the person's voice you can tell which of those emotions he or she may be feeling. The variations you hear, as well as others, are the reflections of changes in what we call *voice quality*.

Let's review the physiological processes affecting voice quality. You may

INTRODUCTION TO NONVERBAL COMMUNICATION

recall that the voice is produced by a series of puffs of air that are emitted between the vocal folds in your larynx. The complex sound created by these puffs is then bounced around (resonated) in several hollow spaces in your neck and head. This process amplifies and modifies some tones of the voice, depending on the sizes and shapes of the cavities in use.

Each person's voice quality is unique. Because no two people have resonating cavities that are exactly the same in size and shape, no two people produce voices with exactly the same acoustic characteristics. That's why it's possible for you to identify people you know when they call you on the phone. In addition, people vary the manner in which they use these resonating cavities according to their physical and emotional states. When you're tense and anxious, you generally hold your vocal folds tense, and the sound you produce has qualities that we have come to recognize as indicating tension. When you are relaxed, your voice reflects that feeling, too.

It's possible for you to assess, by the variations in voice quality, a good deal of meaning over and above what meaning is contained in the context of an utterance. Suppose you detect a note of impatience in your professor's or supervisor's voice. Even though that person's words may be telling you it's okay to be turning your work in late, you know that your next assignment had better be on time or else. Another example might be a person expressing some positive feeling toward you verbally, but there's something in the voice that tells you all is not well in the relationship. It would be difficult, wouldn't it, for a salesperson to sell a group of people on the desirability of an idea, product, or some action if he or she sounded tense or uncertain?

We've all met, at one time or another, people who told us a lot about their personalities just by the kind of voice quality they characteristically used. The person for whom all of life is one terrible catastrophe after another, for whom everything is difficult and unpleasant, will frequently have a voice quality that is petulant and complaining. Who of us has not had our nerves stretched almost to the breaking point while listening to a parent, boss, or teacher whose voice was what we call *strident?* (Stridency is a combination of a very tense quality and high pitch.) Chances are you distinctly remember people with some of these voice qualities, and the memories may not always be pleasant.

To repeat what we said earlier: your voice quality is determined, for the most part, by the size and shape of your resonating cavities. Since you can adjust those cavities and change their sizes and shapes, you can change the quality of your voice. The following sections contain a number of exercises designed to help you work on various voice qualities.

Tense, Strident, Metallic, and Hoarse Qualities

With the exception of the hoarse voice, these qualities are usually fairly high pitched and seem to be "hard hitting." The quality we call hoarseness is a combination of breathiness and harshness resulting in a voice that is very rough. Hoarseness can be associated with physical problems of the larynx, so we suggest you see your physician if you've had a hoarse voice for a long time.

Relaxation

The common denominator of these qualities seems to be tension—excess tension in the area of the larynx. Sometimes the tension may be due to inadequate breath support of loudness, so we recommend that you review and practice the Abdominal Breathing Exercise (p. 43). In addition to abdominal breathing, there are ways to physically relax the laryngeal area. Try the following exercises.

☐ *Progressive Relaxation* ☐

The purpose of this exercise is to reduce tension. You can do this alone, but it's better if someone slowly and calmly reads the directions to you.
1. Sit with your back touching the back support. Cross your legs at the ankles. Hold your hands out in front of you at chest level. Shake them energetically for about 5 seconds, then let them fall loosely into your lap. Keep them there.
2. Do the following exercise *in your mind only*, without moving any parts of your body. Concentrate on the toes of your left foot. Let the muscles go loose. Then the sole of your foot, then the ankle. Now, loosen the muscles of your right foot. When your feet have no tension left in them, move on. First to your lower legs, knees, thighs, then buttocks, back, spine, moving very slowly. Then go on to your stomach, chest, shoulders, arms, hands, and fingers, then back up to your neck, jaws, face and scalp.

As you go along, slowly and methodically untie the knots in your muscles until there is no tension left in your body. When you're finished, stand up, stretch as far as you can, yawn or take as deep a breath as you can, and then release it.

☐ *Fantasy* ☐

This is a very pleasant exercise designed to reduce tension. It can also help you fall asleep at night when you're tense and jumpy. The exercise is really quite simple. Find a comfortable position, one that you can hold for a few minutes. Close your eyes and mentally transport yourself to a place that's calm and relaxing. Don't pick a place where you'll get involved in any kind of activity. We recommend that you imagine you're sitting on a deserted beach—just clean, white sand and the ocean waves rolling in with eternal regularity, one after the other. Imagine that you're sitting there listening to the

INTRODUCTION TO NONVERBAL COMMUNICATION

waves breaking against the shore. You'll feel more relaxed after a couple of minutes of this. Just make sure that you concentrate on the waves; block out everything else.

□ *Head Rolling* □

This exercise focuses specifically on the neck.
1. Take a comfortable sitting position in a chair with a medium or low back. Holding your body erect, let your head drop forward so that your chin is resting on your chest. Keeping your face pointing forward, roll your head to the right so that your right ear is close to your right shoulder. Make sure not to raise your shoulder. Now, roll your head back and look up at the ceiling. At the same time, let your lower jaw drop. Next, roll your head to the left so that your left ear is near your left shoulder. Don't raise your shoulder. Now, roll your head forward again.
2. Repeat this exercise three times, slowly.
3. If you feel some tightness at the back of your neck during the exercise, try to relax the muscles of your neck and shoulders. The tightness should disappear. If the tightness doesn't ease or if you feel pain, discontinue the exercise.
4. Now, roll your head around as before, but this time roll it all the way around in one continuous circle. Repeat the exercise, rolling your head in the opposite direction.

□ *Sighing* □

This exercise helps relax the vocal folds and the neck during voice production.
1. Take as deep a breath as possible. Hold it for a count of three. When you release the air, all at once, sigh. That is, say the vowel *ahh* in a very breathy voice. Repeat four or five times, speaking more softly with each sigh.
2. Sigh while you count to three; then try *a, b, c.* In each case, take a deep breath, hold it for a count of three, then sigh. Repeat four or five times.
3. Make sure you monitor the quality of your voice by listening carefully.
As you sigh more softly, the amount of air expelled should decrease, and your voice should become less breathy. Even though the breathy quality leaves, it's important to keep production relaxed.

Nasality and Resonance

The way you alter and select the resonating cavities is very important in determining voice quality and in helping to support a loud tone. The following exercises should help you increase and decrease the resonance of different cavities as necessary. We're assuming that the problems in nasality and resonance we describe are not due to any physical problems. If that's the case, we advise you to discuss the condition with your instructor.

Types of Nasality

Nasality problems fall into two types—too much and too little. Let's call "too much" *excessive* and "too little" *denasal*. Sometimes excessive nasality can be characteristic of a person's entire speech pattern with all sounds having a nasal quality, or excessive nasality could occur only when there are nasal sounds in a word. In either case, the cause usually is failure to make firm contact between the soft palate and the pharynx (throat) to prevent nasal emission. Denasality is just the opposite: very close and firm contact is made, not allowing enough nasal emission.

□ *Nasality Exercise 1: Ear Training* □

1. Pinch your nostrils closed using your thumb and index finger. Read the following sentence aloud:

Robert took a good look at the spotted puppy.

Now, release your nostrils and read the same sentence. Did you hear any difference in voice quality between your first and second readings? If you're not sure, try reading each word two times, alternately pinching and releasing your nostrils.

If there is a difference, chances are your voice tends to be excessively nasal. If your voice has this quality, the likelihood of reducing the nasality depends, in part, on your being able to recognize when you are being excessively nasal and when you are not.

2. Place a clean, cool mirror directly under your nostrils in a horizontal plane and read the following sentence aloud:

Many people enjoy summer more than winter.

Immediately remove the mirror and look at it. You should notice two cloudy spots on the mirror. Now, wipe the mirror clean again, place it under your nose, and read the following sentence aloud:

The weather report calls for cloudy skies today.

Again, remove the mirror immediately and examine it. Are there any traces of cloudiness this time? If there are, you're probably using excessive nasal resonance. Repeat these two steps until you are sure you can hear when you are using excessive nasal resonance and when you're not.

INTRODUCTION TO NONVERBAL COMMUNICATION

3. This part of the exercise consists of contrast drills. Say the following pairs of words. The first word in each pair contains a nasal sound, the second does not.

ban — bat	my — high	annoy — alloy
bone — bowl	moose — loose	limit — livid
fin — fish	mouth — south	taint — taste
flame — flake	nose — rose	under — udder
roam — road	night — right	bent — bet
rent — red	nap — tap	hunt — hut

Do you hear the difference between the nasal and nonnasal sounds in each pair?

Say the following pairs of phrases aloud. Can you distinguish the one phrase of each pair that contains the nasal sound or sounds?

take a taste	— make a date
patch the book	— match the look
heap the grass	— keep the mass
rode a toad	— load the stones

4. Read the following sentences aloud. There should be no nasal emission during any of the sentences.

    a. Paul was the first of several quarterbacks to try out.
    b. Susie liked school a lot.
    c. Where will you go for your holiday?
    d. I'd like a glass of water, please.
    e. It's all right for you to stay.
    f. I hope you like the picture.
    g. Look for the girls at the beach.
    h. Take the key to your father.
    i. Write the essay at your desk.
    j. Save your cash for the right purchase.

□ *Nasality Exercise 2: Pulling* □

This exercise is designed to help you energize the area of the soft palate and pharynx.

1. Curl the fingers of both hands toward the palms. Lift your elbows to chest height. Rotate your left hand so that the curled fingers and palm are facing

outward, away from you; one thumb should be up, the other down. Hook the fingers of your left hand to the fingers of your right.

2. Begin to count aloud, slowly, from one to ten, and listen carefully to voice quality as you count.

3. At the number five, pull your arms away from each other. Use a strong pull, but make sure to keep your fingers hooked.

4. Did you notice a reduction in the amount of nasality? Did you notice a change in loudness? Most often this exercise produces an energizing effect on the entire body, including the soft palate, and increases the intensity of the voice.

5. Repeat this exercise three times, varying the number at which you begin pulling.

6. Say the names of the days of the week, starting with Sunday; but this time, pull when each day is named. Do you hear a decrease in the amount of nasal emission and/or resonance? Repeat the exercise, saying the months of the year.

□ *Nasality Exercise 3: Pushing* □

Do this sitting down.

1. Place both hands, palms down, on the front corners of your chair. Count aloud from one to ten. Listen carefully as you count. At the number five, try to push yourself off the seat by pushing down on the chair. Continue to count up to ten. Did you notice any change? What kind of change? Repeat the exercise three times.

2. Repeat the pushing exercise. First, name the days, then the months, pushing downward throughout the entire exercise. You should be able to hear a marked reduction in nasality as you go through the exercise. You can use the same exercise for practice using other words.

Denasality

Does your voice lack sufficient nasal resonance (the reinforcement of the high frequency vocal overtones that give voice its brilliance and clarity)? Do others believe that you are constantly suffering from a "stuffy nose"? The muffled, dull-sounding voice of a person whose nose is stuffed up is characteristic of the denasal voice quality. Try the following drill.

□ *Denasality Drill* □

1. Vocalize the consonant *m*. Sustain it for ten seconds, repeating it five times.

INTRODUCTION TO NONVERBAL COMMUNICATION

2. Chant the following chant at a constant pitch, prolonging the nasal consonants in the two middle syllables:

ohh – nee – hung – ahh

Repeat this five times.

3. Read aloud the following words, emphasizing and prolonging the nasal sound or sounds in each. Be careful to confine the nasality to just the nasal consonant. Don't let it move into the vowel.

no	on	sing	single
knee	in	ring	finger
my	time	song	monkey
neck	him	hand	spangle
now	hum	along	England
may	name	wing	mangle
kneel	calm	bang	mingle
more	loom	wrong	uncle
mill	moon	sting	dunking
mood	fine	fling	ringer

4. Try the drills for the nasal consonants in Chapter 8. Again, emphasize the nasals, but don't let the nasality spread to the vowels or other consonants.

Vocal or Glottal Fry

This strangely named quality supposedly sounds like bacon frying. That may be stretching the imagination, but the voice does get a rough, bubbly quality, especially at the ends of sentences or thought groups. At these times, the pitch lowers considerably, and the voice weakens. Many times this quality is indicative of a more serious ailment, so we suggest a visit to your physician. Vocal fry can sometimes be eliminated with the following exercises:

1. Use the sighing technique explained in the Hard Glottal Attack Exercise on p. 58.
2. Use the Abdominal Breathing Exercise on p. 43.

□ *Vocal Fry Exercise* □

Work on holding your pitch level at the end of the sentence or phrase. A piano can be especially helpful with this. Read phrases and sentences aloud. Find the note on the piano that is close to your pitch at the beginning of the phrase. Play the note again at the end of the phrase, and notice if your pitch has lowered. Try to keep matching your pitch to the note played all the way through your utterance. Repeat often, using various reading material.

Throaty

The throaty quality is characterized by the voice that doesn't seem to project at all, staying in the throat with a muffled sound to it. Frequently, the voice is also denasal. Exercises that help eliminate this problem are the Denasality Drill (p. 56) and the Vocal Fry Exercise (p. 57).

Hard Glottal Attack

If you have this quality, you seem to hit your vowels hard, especially when the vowel is the first sound in a word. After a long period of using this type of attack, your voice may begin to crack and may become harsh or hoarse. Do the following exercise to try to change your method of attack.

☐ *Hard Glottal Attack Exercise: Sighing* ☐

1. Sigh the vowel *ahh*, beginning it with a slight *h* sound so that it sounds like *hahhh*. Repeat three times.
2. In order, sigh the following: *ohh, aww, eee, aye* five times each, starting with an *h*: *hohh, haww, hee, haye*.
3. Repeat the previous steps, this time without the beginning *h* sound, but be careful to bring the vocal folds together gently; begin the sound without a hard attack by easing into it. *Think the "h," but don't say it.*
4. Repeat, this time gently phonating each sound, rather than sighing. Be sure to initiate each sound gently and without a hard attack.
5. Say each of the following words two times. The first time think the *h* before the vowel, but don't say it. The second time, initiate the vowel sound gently and without a hard attack.

I	own	anchor
owe	order	arson
ear	army	evening
owl	awning	over
oar	aisle	open
arm	inn	aiming
up	under	above

INTRODUCTION TO NONVERBAL COMMUNICATION

5

Vocal
Expressiveness

There's a colleague of ours whom everyone calls "Mr. Excitement." If you were in one of his classes you'd understand why. He gives his lectures in a dull, dry, and deadly tone, never changing his rate, never varying his pitch, never saying words any louder or softer, speaking in a monotone that puts his students to sleep almost instantly. Faculty members also tend to go to sleep when talking with him in a meeting or conference because his speech pattern is very much like his personality: dull, dry, and deadly.

Perhaps you know or have heard of someone like Mr. Excitement. Maybe you've dozed off in church, in class, or in a meeting. Would you want to get to know someone who speaks in such an expressionless manner? And there are worse things than just falling asleep during a monotonic delivery. We all can probably recall misinterpreting someone's remarks because the right words weren't emphasized.

Vocal expressiveness is what this chapter is all about. We're going to work on how to bring appropriate variety to the way we speak and read aloud. We think that working on vocal expression is important for the following reasons:

— Vocal expressiveness is one of the major factors necessary for gaining and keeping your listener's attention and interest. By the way, that's *your* job. You're the one with the communication purpose to be achieved.

— Vocal expressiveness can make meanings clear when the actual words leave some doubt.

— Vocal expressiveness tells your listeners what you think of them, what you think about the words you're saying, and how you feel about yourself. Listeners tend to respect and believe a person who uses vocal expression effectively.

Reading Aloud

Unfortunately, there's a little of Mr. Excitement in most of us. It usually doesn't appear when we're speaking spontaneously, although it can. It generally is noticeable when we read aloud; that's when we "put on" our reading voices. You know what we mean by reading voice; it's an artificial, unemotional, impersonal way of speaking aloud. It's usually very different from the way we speak spontaneously, and it's usually much less effective.

Why Read Aloud?

Even though you may be saying to yourself, "I really don't do much reading aloud," chances are that you will. Most of us do a considerable amount of reading aloud during the normal course of living and working. We read newspaper articles to other people; directions on how to make, build, or cook things; letters and business reports during meetings and conferences; stories and fairy tales to our children, brothers and sisters, nieces and nephews. We

INTRODUCTION TO NONVERBAL COMMUNICATION

could continue to add to the list, but we've made our point: you *do* read aloud. You do it for the same reasons that you speak spontaneously, but you may not be reading effectively.

We'll tell you first what we're *not* going to do: we're not going to teach you to be a professional radio or TV announcer, or a Broadway or film actor, or any such thing. That's beyond the scope of this text. We *do* want to help you become more effective in your everyday speaking and reading. So, we'll teach you how to use the components of vocal expression: *rate, phrasing, intonation,* and *stress.* We'll provide you with some theory and plenty of practice.

Components of Vocal Expression

Rate

Can you imagine yourself at Gettysburg listening to Abraham Lincoln deliver the famous Address at the same rate of speech as a stand-up comic in a Las Vegas nightclub act? In all likelihood, the very idea of such a rapid rate of delivery for that somber, serious message would appeal to your sense of the ridiculous rather than the sublime.

As a rule, we deliver spoken messages at a rate that is appropriate for the content. A rapid rate usually carries the unspoken message, "What I'm saying now is light, frivolous, unimportant, humorous, not meant to be taken too seriously." A slow, deliberate rate, on the other hand, implies, "This message is meant to be considered important and weighty and is to be taken seriously."

The rate of speech also reflects the speaker's physical and emotional states. When you're feeling calm or sad or tired, you'll probably speak relatively slowly. When you are in a state of physical or mental excitement, though, you'll most likely speed things up considerably.

The rate at which you speak affects understanding. The process whereby you take in and interpret messages is a highly complex one. To understand a spoken message, your brain must "hear" all the acoustic elements of the message, then translate them into the concepts or ideas they symbolize, then associate those concepts with the meanings you've attributed to them as a result of all the experiences you've had in your life. You can understand, therefore, that although you can *hear* words just as rapidly as they are spoken, it takes you longer to understand and integrate the message in some meaningful and usable form. When you are presented with a message delivered at a high rate of speed, you have more difficulty dealing with it in a meaningful way. This is especially true if the message is complex or abstract. Then you work particularly hard to understand everything the speaker is saying or you give up trying. In either case, there's a good chance that the speaker's purpose has not been successfully achieved.

If a speaker delivers a relatively unimportant message slowly and deliberately, you may become impatient or bored waiting for the message to be completed because you understood the speaker's intent long before the delivery ended. For communication to be effective, it is important for the rate of delivery to match the meaning the speaker wishes to convey.

Determining Your Own Rate

Before you practice the exercises for rate, you should have an idea of what your average rate actually is. To do this, try the exercise below. You'll need someone to act as your timekeeper and either a stop-watch or a watch with a second hand.
1. Ask your timekeeper to time you to the nearest second and to signal you when it's time to start. At the signal, read through the selection below *silently*. Don't pause to analyze. Don't struggle with the pronunciation of unfamiliar words. When you've completed the silent reading, signal your timekeeper so that you can record the silent reading time in seconds on page 63. The piece you'll be reading is from the Department of Health, Education, and Welfare Publication No. (NIOSH) 75-165.

> The basic idea behind the techniques for limiting a person's exposure to noise is very simple and straightforward. The reference frame dealt with in noise reduction is composed of a sound *source*, the sound wave *path*, and a sound wave *receiver* which, in common circumstances, is an ear or a microphone that is used for measurement.
>
> The best and most satisfying means of reducing noise levels is to reduce the source sound output. This approach may require major modifications to the noisy device. Some of these modifications include better quality control, closer tolerances on moving parts, better balancing of rotating parts, and sometimes even a complete redesign of the technique utilized to perform the job for which this machine is intended. Since something vibrating causes compression and rarefaction of the air which is observed as sound, the above-mentioned and many other modifications to a sound source are all aimed toward reducing the vibration of any part to the lowest possible level. Normally these modifications are not within the capability of the user and therefore must be left to the equipment manufacturers. Fortunately for those directly affected, manufacturers are beginning to make these changes. There is, however, one set or kind of modification that the user can perform. A particular piece of machinery may be the driving force to produce vibrations but it often is the floor, wall, or other support member that is doing much of the sound radiating. This kind of vibration problem can be effectively reduced by proper use of vibration isolation or vibration damping treatment.

INTRODUCTION TO NONVERBAL COMMUNICATION

Essentially vibration isolation means that the connection between the driving force and the driven member is such that the vibration is not transmitted through the connection. Any device which behaves as a spring can be utilized for this purpose. Vibration isolators can be made with actual steel springs, or with rubber pads. Vibration isolators are also made out of coils of cable laid on their side or even air can be used when properly contained. The selection of which vibration isolator to use depends on the forces involved, the frequency of the driving force, and the possible natural frequencies of the support member itself. If not properly selected, a vibration isolator can make a problem situation worse.

(380 words)

2. At the timekeeper's signal, read the selection *aloud*. Try to make your listener understand the contents of the passage. If you're doing this outside of class, pretend that you are addressing the entire class. Record your reading time in seconds.

3. Now use a tape recorder and give a brief extemporaneous talk. Talk about your job or your hobbies. Describe a movie you've seen or a book you've read. The subject itself isn't important as long as you can talk about it for at least two minutes. Talk to a real or imagined class. Record the speaking time in seconds. Then replay the tape and count the number of words you said.

4. To find your rate, divide the number of words read or spoken by the number of seconds. Multiply that number by 60 to find the approximate rate in words per minute (w.p.m.).

$$\frac{\text{words read silently}}{\text{seconds}} \times 60 = \text{w.p.m.} \qquad \underline{\hspace{2cm}} \times 60 = \underline{\hspace{1cm}} \text{w.p.m.}$$

$$\frac{\text{words read aloud}}{\text{seconds}} \times 60 = \text{w.p.m.} \qquad \underline{\hspace{2cm}} \times 60 = \underline{\hspace{1cm}} \text{w.p.m.}$$

$$\frac{\text{words spoken}}{\text{seconds}} \times 60 = \text{w.p.m.} \qquad \underline{\hspace{2cm}} \times 60 = \underline{\hspace{1cm}} \text{w.p.m.}$$

Enter your reading-aloud rate and spoken rate above. Compare these rates with your silent reading rate.

Appropriate Rate

If your oral reading rate falls between 150 w.p.m and 180 w.p.m. it's within the range of normal for this type of material. The middle of the range, 160 w.p.m. to 170 w.p.m. would be considered by most listeners to be the most effective, and easiest to understand. Your speaking rate should be slower, probably below 150 w.p.m. In both speaking and reading, of course, the rate will reflect the content of the material, the listener's state of mind, and so forth.

Adjusting Your Rate

If you've determined that your rate is too fast or too slow, try the following exercises for adjusting rate.

□ *Timed Readings for Rate* □

Use the following selections for either slow or fast rate. Each selection contains 160 to 170 words and should take exactly one minute for you to read aloud. Continue to read each selection (without looking at your watch) until it takes you one minute.

a.   Our shoppers bought a sample of every bicycle lock they could find. Most of the tested locks were cheap, lightweight, and insecure. More than half were rated Not Acceptable because they could be yanked, stomped, or sprung apart without the use of tools. However, we did find several locks that proved quite secure against most common assaults. Those locks were relatively expensive, though, and heavier than many bike riders would want to carry.

Types. Nearly all models tested combine a chain or a cable with a key lock or a combination lock. The two elements may be separate or attached as an integral unit. We also tested cables meant to be mounted permanently on the bike itself, and oversized shackle locks. The latter, sometimes called horseshoe locks, are essentially padlocks with shackles large enough to fit around a post. The locking devices are listed by type in the ratings.

The oversized shackle locks were generally the most resistant to assault, as the Ratings show.

(Consumer Reports Buying Guide Issue 1981)

b.   Motor behavior is basic to the human condition. In an earlier age survival and maintenance often depended upon one's ability to extract a livelihood from nature, construct shelter, and fashion clothing. Today a complex division of labor no longer requires a high degree of self-sufficiency in making provision for ourselves and the members of our immediate family. But modern technology requires a host of new skills, including operating automobiles and jet aircraft. Further, many of our leisure activities, including playing musical instruments and par-

INTRODUCTION TO NONVERBAL COMMUNICATION

ticipation in sports like skiing, golf, surfing, and baseball, demand a vast array of motor behaviors.

Within schools, motor skills are interwoven throughout the curriculum at all levels. Using a pencil, writing with chalk, making handwritten letters, drawing pictures, painting objects, employing measuring instruments, and walking from one place to another are all fundamental school activities. Similarly, playground activities and games in physical education involve complex and coordinated movements.

(From *Educational Psychology Theory and Practice*,
James Vander Zanden)

c. The manuscript should be typewritten, double-spaced, on white medium-weight paper. The sheets should be of the standard $8\frac{1}{2} \times 11$ size and of good enough quality to permit clear markings in ink. Margins should be about one inch on each side and at the top and bottom. All pages should be numbered consecutively, preferably in the upper right-hand corner, throughout the entire work. Use only one side of the sheet.

A quotation that will run four lines or more is usually set off as a single-spaced, double-indented paragraph.

It is not advantageous to submit the manuscript in any special ornamental binder. If assembled neatly in a folder, envelope, or cardboard box, the manuscript will be more in keeping with the practice of most professional writers and with the preference of most editors. The author should always retain a complete carbon copy of the manuscript, not only to facilitate correspondence between the editor and author, but to serve as insurance against the loss of the original copy.

(*The Random House Dictionary*, 1978)

It's important for you to read these passages a number of times at the rate of 160–170 w.p.m. to get the feeling in your mouth, tongue, and jaw of what that rate is like. You must also get accustomed to that rate in your mind. We'd bet that the first couple of times you read them at the desired rate, it felt awfully strange. After a while the feeling of strangeness will go.

Practice speaking spontaneously at 160–170 w.p.m. Use a tape recorder and count your words afterward, or ask a friend to listen to you and to tell you if you speed up or slow down.

Duration

Rate is partly determined by how you produce your vowels. If you sound them very quickly, they become clipped and the words become shorter. Even if you reduce the number of words you say each minute, your speech would still sound rapid. On the other extreme is prolongation. If you hold on to the vowels too long, your speech may be too slow. Use the following drill to vary duration.

□ *Duration Practice* □

Read the following words aloud at an average loudness. First, read the list and make the vowel sounds as short as possible. Then, make the vowel sounds as long as possible. Finally, give them average duration.

afraid	inch	clothing	narcotic
backache	snore	rotten	republic
ashamed	pout	total	submerging
prank	browse	creeping	polluted
grieve	doze	speaker	improvement
sleep	grunt	garden	newcomer
glib	swoop	paper	bakery
divide	girl	quarrel	saleable
voodoo	sided	nickname	commitment
fragile	shallow	dynamic	eloping

Read the following poem aloud. Decide the duration value for each vowel—long, short, or average—and mark them before you read, using the following system:——for long,——for short, and no marking for average. Here's an example:

Shall I compare thee to a summer's day?

Now you complete the rest of the sonnet:

Thou art more lovely and more temperate:
Rough winds do shake the darling buds of May,
And summer's lease hath all too short a date:
Sometime too hot the eye of heaven shines,
And often is his gold complexion dimm'd;
And every fair from fair sometime declines,
By chance, or nature's changing course untrimm'd;
But thy eternal summer shall not fade,
Nor lose possession of that fair thou owest,
Nor shall Death brag thou wander'st in his shade,
When in eternal lines to time thou grow'st;

So long as men can breathe, or eyes can see,
So long lives this, and this gives life to thee.

("Sonnet 18," William Shakespeare)

Try this same exercise with poetry and literature selections of your own choosing. Continue to be aware of overall rate while you're working on duration.

Pausing

We can't consider rate without discussing pausing. But the relationship is secondary; we use pausing for much more than simply controlling rate. Often, in fact, rate is subordinate to pausing.

We use pauses for a number of purposes: emphasis, clarity, meaning, attention, reflection, variety, change of ideas, change of mood, and last but not least, for breathing. Without pausing, you tend to lose your listener because pauses act as verbal punctuation marks. Furthermore, we use pausing to regulate the back and forth nature of conversation. If you're a listener, you wait for the speaker to pause before you begin to speak; speaking before you hear the pause is considered an interruption.

Major, or long, pauses are controlled by *thought groups*. A thought group is analogous to the written sentence; it is complete and can stand by itself. Your pause is the verbal punctuation mark. Minor, or short, pauses are used for all the purposes we listed above. Notice that of all the purposes, we listed breathing last. That's right. You should pause for meaning, not just to get air. Pausing should be frequent enough that you don't run out of breath. If you do, it means you're not pausing enough or you're not controlling your breath flow efficiently. Remember, you can only take a quick inhalation during most pauses, so breath control is very important.

☐ *Pausing Exercises* ☐

1. Read the following telephone conversation from *Come Blow Your Horn* by Neil Simon. First read it through silently, then aloud, pretending that you're actually talking on the phone. The pauses were indicated by the author (—), but he didn't indicate their length; that's up to you. Give each pause its appropriate length.

> *Alan:* Hello? — Chickie? Don't you know you could be arrested for having such a sexy voice? — Alan — How could I? I just got in from Europe an hour ago — Switzerland — A specialist there told me if I don't see you within a half an hour, I'll die — Yes, tonight — A

friend of mine is having a little party — Wonderful guy — hundred laughs — Hey, Chickie, is your roommate free? The French girl? — Wonderful. Yes. Bring her — No, I can't. I've got to get the pretzels. Can you meet me there? The Hotel Croyden, Room 326, Marty Meltzer — A half hour — Marvelous. I just love you — What? — Yes, Alan *Baker*.

2. Meaningful pauses don't have to be long. Many times we use pauses just for that little extra bit of emphasis; we can set things apart by pausing slightly before or after a word. Mark the following selections for meaningful pauses. Use / to indicate a slight pause and / / to indicate a longer pause, as in the following example:

To be / or not to be. // That / is the question.

Notice how we can change the feeling by changing the pauses:

To be or / not to be. // That is / the question.

Now, you try it.

a.   A hundred feet in the sky he lowered his webbed feet, lifted his beak, and strained to hold a painful hard twisting curve through his wings. The curve meant that he would fly slowly, and now he slowed until the wind was a whisper in his face, until the ocean stood still beneath him. He narrowed his eyes in fierce concentration, held his breath, forced one . . . single . . . more . . . inch . . . of . . . curve . . . Then his feathers ruffled, he stalled and fell.

(*Jonathan Livingston Seagull*, Richard Bach)

b.   . . . and then came, for the hundredth time, the story of his coming ashore at New York, from the *Constellation* frigate, after a cruise of four years round the Horn, —being paid off with over five hundred dollars, —marrying, and taking a couple of rooms in a four-story house, —furnishing the rooms, (with a particular account of the furniture, including a dozen flag-bottomed chairs, which he always dilated upon, whenever the subject of furniture was alluded to,) —going off to sea again, leaving his wife half-pay, like a fool, —coming home and finding her "off, like Bob's horse, with nobody to pay the reckoning"; furniture gone, —flag-bottomed chairs and all; —and with it, his "long togs," the half-pay, his beaver hat, white linen shirts, and everything else.

(*Two Years Before the Mast*, Richard Henry Dana, Jr.)

c. *Magee:* No kidding—I paint. You'd hate my work though—it's all very abstract—I stand back and splash oil all over everything and then I run all over it with my sneakers and I stick my lunch on it—in fact, my lunch came in second at a showing in Cape Cod.

(*Don't Drink the Water,* Woody Allen)

d. Our ability to design and manufacture home heating and air conditioning equipment that met the exacting performance standards of the manufactured housing industry has made us the number one supplier of these products for many years. While we have been involved to a small degree in the traditional residential housing market for many years, we believed that soaring utility bills would open an entirely new opportunity.

(1979 Annual Report, The Coleman Company)

e. Pace University holds to a philosophy that each student is the center of the institution's responsibilities: that he or she is unique, and that whatever students have in common with each other they have in varying proportions and in different ways. In this view, students can expect the University to provide them with opportunities to realize their full potential and to help them earn respect as mature adults.

(*1980–81 Undergraduate Bulletin,* Pace University)

Loudness and Stress

If someone were to say to you, in a soft, weak voice, "Pay attention; this is very important," chances are you wouldn't immediately drop what you were doing to listen. If, however, you heard the same command given in a loud, strong voice, you would probably respond immediately. As a rule, in our society, we tend to place more importance on things said loudly than we do on things said softly. This also holds true for the way we customarily *stress* (accent by loudness) the various parts of speech. Nouns, for example, are the primary conveyors of meaning, and as such, we ordinarily give them the most stress. Next come verbs, then adjectives, then adverbs. Those parts of speech getting the least amount of stress, or sometimes no stress at all, include pronouns, articles, prepositions, and conjunctions.

There are, however, certain situations for which you want to give a special twist of meaning to what you are saying. Let's take the sentence, "The boy took his dog to the park" as an example. Spoken as a simple statement, you would stress the nouns boy, dog, and park and the verb took. Using double underlining to indicate primary stress and single underlining to indicate secondary stress, we would indicate the stress pattern of that sentence as:

The boy took his dog to the park.

69

VOCAL EXPRESSIVENESS

Suppose you wished to use the very same sentence to answer a series of questions. We can predict the ways in which your stress pattern would vary. Let's ask the questions and listen to the answers:

QUESTION: Did just any boy take his dog to the park?
ANSWER: No, <u>the</u> <u>boy</u> took his <u>dog</u> to the <u>park</u>.
QUESTION: Did a girl take a dog to the park?
ANSWER: No, the <u>boy</u> took his <u>dog</u> to the <u>park</u>.
QUESTION: Did the boy take someone else's dog to the park?
ANSWER: No, the <u>boy</u> took <u>his</u> <u>dog</u> to the <u>park</u>.

A whole series of similar questions could be asked, and for each, the word receiving primary stress would change with the change of information asked for in the various questions.

Word Stress

The example above illustrates the way we use word stress, that is, make an entire word louder for emphasis or meaning.
   Try the following:

□ Word Stress Drill □

Following are some simple sentences. Read each one aloud. Begin by stressing the first word of each sentence, then move the stress to the second word, and so on, just as we did with "The <u>boy</u> took his <u>dog</u> to the <u>park</u>."

1. This is my favorite.
2. I'm buying a new car.
3. Where are you going?
4. I don't like him.
5. This is a great book.

In the following sentences, underline the words to show where you would place primary and secondary stress. Then read the sentences aloud making sure you stress the words the way you planned.

1. Please don't do that again.
2. If I've told you once, I've told you a thousand times.
3. Where are those keys of mine?
4. Which book are you going to buy?
5. I really need a rest.

INTRODUCTION TO NONVERBAL COMMUNICATION

Syllable Stress

In words of more than one syllable (polysyllabic words), one syllable will receive more stress than the others. The stress pattern is agreed to by the speakers of the language; look up a word in the dictionary and you'll see a diacritical mark indicating stress. Sometimes we stress a different syllable for special emphasis; most of the time, though, a word is considered mispronounced if the wrong syllable stress is used.

When we join two nouns to form a compound word, we usually stress the first noun more than the second. Try the following list.

☐ *Compound Word Stress Drill* ☐

Read the following words aloud. Place primary stress on the first syllable of each word:

airplane	hothouse	Sunday
flatfoot	beefsteak	downtown
bluefish	notebook	paperback
motorboat	butterfly	forestfire
rubberband	sometime	overcharge

Polysyllabic words, other than compound words, usually follow a pattern in which the stress moves farther along in the word as the word becomes longer. Try the following:

☐ *Polysyllabic Stress Drill* ☐

Read the following words aloud, reading *across* the page. Place the primary stress on the appropriate syllable.

photo	photograph	photographer	photographic
beauty	beautiful	beautification	
occupy	occupation	occupational	
excite	exciting	excitation	
subject	subjective		
object	objective	objectification	
magic	magician		
person	personify	personification	

Read the following selections aloud. It may be helpful for you to underline words for primary and secondary stress. Remember, there's no right way: interpretation of the authors' words is up to you. Just be aware of how your stress patterns may change the meaning.

a.   The idea of <u>you</u> lynching anybody is amusing. The idea of you thinking you had pluck enough to lynch a <u>man</u>! Because you're brave enough to tar and feather poor friendless cast-out women that come along here, did that make you think you had grit enough to lay your hands on a <u>man</u>? Why, a <u>man</u>'s safe in the hands of ten thousand of your kind—as long as it's daytime and you're not behind him.

(Huckleberry Finn, Mark Twain)

b.   Climb to a thousand feet. Full power straight ahead first, then push over, flapping, to a vertical dive. Then, every time, his left wing stalled on an upstroke, he'd roll violently left, stall his right wing recovering, and flick like fire into a wild tumbling spin to the right.

(Jonathan Livingston Seagull, Richard Bach)

c.   For a full day and two nights I have been alone. I lay on the beach under the stars at night alone. I made my breakfast alone. Alone I watched the gulls at the end of the pier, dip and wheel and dive for the scraps I threw them. A morning's work at my desk, and then, a late picnic lunch alone on the beach.

(Gift from the Sea, Anne Morrow Lindbergh)

d.   . . . the boat is caught by the wave and, gathering speed, begins to rush forward. The speedometer needle starts its climb—9, 10, 11 knots. Once in a while, a big one, a real graybeard comes along and we hit 12 and 13 knots. The helmsman, the wheel vibrating in his hands as the rudder is locked in a fore and aft position by the force of the water rushing by its sides, lets out a howl of triumph. It is almost an animal cry, a natural outlet, welling up in a geyser of exhilaration. He has the feeling of having harnessed the angry forces of nature to beat it at its own game. He has pulled Poseidon's beard.

(On the Wind's Way, William Snaith)

e.   Tyger, tyger, burning bright
     In the forests of the night,
     What immortal hand or eye
     Could frame thy fearful symmetry?

In what distant deeps or skies
Burnt the fire of thine eyes?
On what wings dare he aspire?
What the hand dare seize the fire?

And what shoulder and what art
Could twist the sinews of thy heart?
And, when thy heart began to beat,
What dread hand and what dread feet?

What the hammer? What the chain?
In what furnace was thy brain?
What the anvil? What dread grasp
Dare its deadly terrors clasp?

When the stars threw down their spears,
And water'd heaven with their tears,
Did He smile His work to see?
Did He who made the lamb make thee?

Tyger, tyger, burning bright
In the forests of the night,
What immortal hand or eye
Dare frame thy fearful symmetry?

("The Tyger," William Blake)

f.   The year's at the spring,
     And day's at the morn;
     Morning's at seven;
     The hill-side's dew-pearl'd
     The lark's on the wing;
     The snail's on the thorn;
     God's in His heaven—
     All's right with the world!

("Pippa Passes," Part 1,
Robert Browning)

Intonation

We spoke about pitch in Chapter 4. We also discussed it in Chapter 3. What we've talked about so far is mainly the overall pitch of your voice—pitch range and optimum and habitual pitches. Now we'll look at pitch in a different way: how you *use* pitch to bring additional meaning to or clarify or reinforce what you say.

Listen to someone who you consider to be a good speaker. Close your eyes and concentrate mainly on that person's voice, not the actual words. Begin to focus on pitch—not the overall pitch, but the changes in pitch that are occurring. After a while, you should begin to notice a pattern of pitch changes, up and down, that emerges. If you're successful in blocking out the actual words, it will almost seem as though the person is singing rather than speaking.

We *are* singing, to a certain extent, when we speak. Our language, just like every language, has its own unique melody that all native speakers learn from the beginning. We know that the melody adds a lot to the message.

We call the melody of language *intonation*. Intonation refers to the total pattern of pitch changes within an utterance. The intonation patterns we use are familiar and required by our language. For example, say the following sentence five times: *I am going to the store*. Listen closely to the pitch of your voice. You should hear that your voice started off at one pitch, rose slightly during the first couple of words, and then descended gradually during the rest of the utterance. This is a characteristic intonation pattern for a declarative statement. Now try asking some questions aloud. For example, ask "Am I going to the store?" Did you notice a different intonation pattern? You probably noted that rather than a descending pitch pattern at the end, there was a rising pitch. That pattern is characteristic of questioning utterances but not interrogatives. Notice the difference between "Are you going?" and "Why are you going?" The second question actually has a falling pitch.

It's important for you to use the appropriate intonation patterns when you speak. Otherwise, you may be sending messages using intonations that contradict what you want your words to say. Intonation patterns that disagree with the content of the utterance may indicate doubt, sarcasm, or confusion. And speech with a monotone intonation pattern may not be listened to at all. We're going to discuss the types of pitch changes that you make and give you exercises that you can use for practice. The drills and exercises should be helpful to you whether you're a native speaker or have learned English as a second language.

Key

You're most likely aware that there's a relationship between the content and purpose of your utterance and the general pitch level you use. It wouldn't be appropriate for you to, let's say, resign "regretfully" from a job and use the higher notes of your pitch range to tell your boss. Nor would it be appropriate to announce that you just won a million dollar lottery prize using the lower part of your range. Try it: say, "I'm so happy! I just won a million dollars," using a low-pitched voice. You certainly don't sound happy, do you?

What we're talking about is called *key*—the average pitch level of an utterance. Generally, we refer to three keys—*low, middle,* and *high*. The middle key should be comfortable for you because it should correspond to your optimum pitch. Here are some selections for you to read aloud using the different keys.

□ *Low Key Readings* □

a. I leaned on the gate for a moment, breathing in the sweet air. There had been a change during the last week; the harsh winds had dropped, everything had softened and greened and the warming land gave off its scents. On the lower slopes of the fell, in the shade of the pine woods, a pale mist of bluebells drifted among the dead bronze of the bracken and their fragrance came up to me on the breeze.

(*All Things Bright and Beautiful,* James Herriot)

b. "I'm afraid he's dead, Mr. Barnett."
The big man did not change expression. He reached slowly across and rubbed his forefinger against the dark fur in that familiar gesture. Then he put his elbows on the desk and covered his face with his hands.
I did not know what to say; I watched helplessly as his shoulders began to shake and tears welled between the thick fingers. He stayed like that for some time, then he spoke:
"He was my friend," he said.

(*The Lord God Made Them All,* James Herriot)

c. The sullen murmur of the bees, shouldering their way through the long, unmown grass, or circling with monotonous insistence round the dusty gilt horns or the straggling woodbine, seemed to make the stillness more oppressive.

(*The Picture of Dorian Gray,* Oscar Wilde)

d. The shell in my hand is deserted. It once housed a whelk, a snail-like creature, and then temporarily, after the death of the first occupant, a little hermit crab, who has run away, leaving his tracks behind him like a delicate vine on the sand. He ran away, and left me his shell.

(*Gift from the Sea,* Anne Morrow Lindbergh)

e. Tears, idle tears, I know not what they mean,
Tears from the depth of some divine despair
Rise in the heart, and gather to the eyes,
In looking on the happy autumn-fields,
And thinking of the days that are no more.

(from "The Princess," Alfred, Lord Tennyson)

a. Learning is finding out what you already know. Doing is demon-
strating that you know it. Teaching is reminding others that they
know just as well as you. You are all learners, doers, teachers.

(Illusions, Richard Bach)

b. There are two reasons for staining wood. The first is to enhance the
surface. In the finishing trade it's called "bringing out the natural
beauty." Actually, the idea is not too outlandish. Some fine cabinet
woods such as walnut don't look particularly rich in an unadorned
state, and so to give them a more luxurious appearance, stain is used
on the wood (for example, walnut stain on walnut wood). The grain
becomes vibrant, the richness of the wood becomes apparent, and
walnut emerges as real walnut.

The other reason for staining is to upgrade the wood. For example, some people will utilize stain in an effort to upgrade walnut so
that it resembles mahogany. In the viewpoint of other craftsmen,
this is heresy. However, some woods do make the transition fairly
easily. *(Furniture Refinishing,* W. I. Fischman)

c. Where did I learn to row? How do I know? In the *Emma* I suppose—the narrow, flat-bottomed rowboat my grandfather bought at
Macy's and stuck off the end of the dock at our summer house on
the pond, in case any of the house guests wanted to take a spin
around the lake in the evening, or Granny wanted a ride to the cove
at the far end of the pond where her old, white-haired friend lived in
the big stucco house with a red tile roof that looked as if it belonged
in Spain instead of on the eastern tip of Long Island.

(Striper, John N. Cole)

d. Use a comma only when you have a definite reason for doing so in
accordance with the guidelines below. A safe rule to follow, "When
in doubt, leave it out."

(The Random House Dictionary)

□ *High Key Readings* □

a. Realize your youth while you have it. Don't squander the gold of
your days, listening to the tedious, trying to improve the hopeless
failure, or giving away your life to the ignorant, the common, and
the vulgar. These are the sickly aims, the false ideals, of our age.
Live! Live the wonderful life that is in you!

(The Picture of Dorian Gray, Oscar Wilde)

b. If you shut your eyes and are a lucky one, you may see at times a shapeless pool of lovely pale colors suspended in the darkness; then if you squeeze your eyes tighter, the pool begins to take shape, and the colors become so livid that with another squeeze they must go on fire. But just before they go on fire you see the lagoon. This is the nearest you ever get to it on the mainland, just one heavenly moment; if there could be two moments you might see the surf and hear the mermaids singing.

(*Peter Pan*, James Barrie)

c. I spun the periscope. Nothing. Putting it down, I grabbed for the extra earphones and heard it. No doubt about it, O'Brien was right. It sounded very much the same as one of our own torpedoes—the same high-pitched whine I had heard hundreds of times. It crossed our stern, came back up the starboard side, veered to the left as if to cross our bow. That was enough. My hair tingled as I thought of the secret magnetic exploder in the warheads of our torpedoes.

(*Run Silent, Run Deep,* Edward L. Beach)

d. So let freedom ring—from the prodigious hilltops of New Hampshire, let freedom ring; from the mighty mountains of New York, let freedom ring—from the heightening Alleghenies of Pennsylvania!
     Let Freedom ring from the snowcapped Rockies of Colorado. Let freedom ring from the curvaceous slopes of California! But not only that; let freedom ring from Stone Mountain of Georgia.
     Let Freedom ring from every hill and mole hill of Mississippi. From every mountainside, let freedom ring.

("I Have a Dream," Martin Luther King, Jr.)

Inflection

Inflectional changes are those changes in pitch that occur within words while you're producing voice. You can think of them as being pitch glides or slides; they are done very smoothly. For example, say the word yes to mean, "Who is it?" You probably said that with a rising inflection. Now say the word no to mean "Absolutely not!" That word probably fell in pitch.
     In English, we generally use rising inflection to indicate:

    questions;
    incomplete series (Monday, Tuesday, Wednesday, . . .);
    doubt or uncertainty;
    that a stressed word or syllable is coming.

We generally use falling inflection to indicate:

ending or finality—positive statements;
end of a phrase;
interrogatives (Where are you?);
a greater amount of stress.

Here are some drills for inflection. Doing these with a tape recorder or a fellow student can be helpful.

☐ *Drill for Rising Inflection* ☐

Read the following sentences aloud. Read each one three times, each time making it more of a question. In other words, you're going to read them with a rising pitch at the end of the sentence, and each time you read a sentence, you're going to exaggerate the rise more than the time before.

1. Is that all there is?	6. When?
2. Are you sure?	7. Yes?
3. Up in the attic?	8. Who?
4. Want some coffee?	9. Do you?
5. Where?	10. Have you?

☐ *Drill for Falling Inflection* ☐

Read the following sentences aloud. Read each one three times, each time making it more of a definite, positive statement. Each time you read the statement, exaggerate the falling inflection.

1. That's all there is.	5. No!
2. Yes, I'm sure.	6. Yes!
3. Up in the attic.	7. Now!
4. I'd like some coffee.	8. Later.

There's another pattern of inflection that we call *circumflex*. It's a combination of rising and falling inflections. Here's an example: say the word yes to indicate a conspiracy, or say the same word to show sarcasm. You probably said it with rising and falling inflections in the same utterance.

☐ *Sentence Drill for Inflection* ☐

The following sentences have been diagrammed to indicate inflection: ⟋ means rising inflection; ⟍ means falling inflection; ⟶ means no change (level pitch). Read the sentences aloud using the inflection indicated by the marks.

INTRODUCTION TO NONVERBAL COMMUNICATION

1. Here's your coffee.
2. Did you go?
3. I want it.
4. I bought some books, pens, and paper.
5. Up, up, and away.
6. Alone?
7. How about it? Please?
8. Do you want an apple, an orange, or a pear?
9. I see.
10. Do you?

Steps

We also change pitch *between* utterances. It's an abrupt change, almost a jump, that we call a *step*. You make this type of change between syllables and words.

☐ *Drill for Steps* ☐

Read the following phrases and sentences aloud. The steps have been dia-grammed as follows: In this example the word ⌐up⌐ is said higher. In this, the word ⌐down⌐ is said lower.

1. He ⌐did.
2. What ⌐time?
3. ⌐Next⌐ week.
4. On ⌐top⌐ of the ⌐desk.
5. On top of ⌐the ⌐desk.
6. The ⌐next⌐ time.
7. This ⌐is a ⌐shift.
8. Come ⌐here ⌐right ⌐now!
9. A piece of ⌐paper.
10. ⌐Do ⌐you want it?

Integration

Now you can practice putting all the pieces of vocal expression together by integrating them for effective readings. We've provided a number of selections for you to work with. We suggest that you read a piece silently first. Consider the mood, the author's purpose. Determine how you're going to emphasize stress, rate, duration, inflection, pausing, and so on. Mark your directions with arrows, slash marks, and so on the way we've shown you in this chapter. Tape record your readings. Ask for feedback from your instructor or someone in your class.

a. When Radar O'Reilly, just out of high school, left Ottumwa, Iowa, and enlisted in the United States Army it was with the express purpose of making a career of the Signal Corps. Radar O'Reilly was only five feet three inches tall, but he had a long, thin neck and large ears that left his head at perfect right angles. Furthermore, under certain atmospheric, as well as metabolic, conditions, and by enforcing complete concentration and invoking unique extra-sensory powers, he was able to receive messages and monitor conversations far beyond the usual range of human hearing.

With this to his advantage, it seemed to Radar O'Reilly that he was a natural for the communications branch of the service, and so, following graduation, he turned down various highly attractive business opportunities, some of them legitimate, and decided to serve his country.

Before his enlistment, in fact, he used to fall asleep at night watching a whole succession of, first, sleeve stripes, and then shoulder insignia, floating by until he would see himself, with four stars on his shoulders, conducting high-level Pentagon briefings, attending White House dinner parties and striding imperiously to ringside tables in New York night clubs.

In the middle of November of the year 1951 A.D., Radar O'Reilly, a corporal in the United States Army Medical Corps, was sitting in the Painless Polish Poker and Dental Clinic of the 4077th Mobile Army Surgical Hospital astride the 38th Parallel in South Korea, ostensibly trying to fill a straight flush.

(*M*A*S*H*, Richard Hooker)

b. I looked out over the beautiful expanse, bathed in soft yellow moonlight till it was almost as light as day. In the soft light the distant hills became melted, and the shadows in the valleys and gorges of velvety blackness. The mere beauty seemed to cheer me; there was peace and comfort in every breath I drew. As I leaned from the window my eye was caught by something moving a storey below me, and somewhat to my left, where I imagined, from the lie of the rooms, that the windows of the Count's own room would look out. The window at which I stood was tall and deep, stone-mullioned, and though

INTRODUCTION TO NONVERBAL COMMUNICATION

weather-worn, was still complete; but it was evidently many a day since the case had been there. I drew back behind the stonework, and looked carefully out.

What I saw was the Count's head coming out from the window. I did not see the face, but I knew the man by the neck and the movement of his back and arms. In any case I could not mistake the hands which I had had so many opportunities of studying. I was at first interested and somewhat amused, for it is wonderful how small a matter will interest and amuse a man when he is a prisoner. But my very feelings changed to repulsion and terror when I saw the whole man slowly emerge from the window and begin to crawl down the castle wall over that dreadful abyss, *face down*, with his cloak spreading out around him like great wings. At first I could not believe my eyes, I thought it was some trick of the moonlight, some weird effect of shadow; but I kept looking and it could be no delusion. I saw the fingers and toes grasp the corners of the stones, worn clear of the mortar by the stress of years, and by thus using every projection and inequality move downwards with considerable speed, just as a lizard moves along a wall.

What manner of man is this, or what manner of creature is it in the semblance of man? I feel the dread of this horrible place overpowering me; I am in fear—in awful fear—and there is no escape for me;

(*Dracula*, Bram Stoker)

c.   The plover begin gathering in August. Small flocks of goldens and black-bellieds stand near each other at the ends of sand bars, or cluster on the mud flats at low tide. When clammers approach, the birds take wing, circling, and the crystal whistle of their calls echoes across the marsh—a pure and lonely sound that is Autumn's earliest prelude.

(*Striper*, John N. Cole)

d.   The crisis model of young people caught in a turbulent passage between their late teens and early twenties has come to be equated with the normal process of growing up. We all recognize hallmarks of this sensitive condition: kids who are at once rebellious, listless, and jumpy. Kids who are seized by sudden and riotous swings of mood. When cramped by anxiety, they cannot sleep or work. They may suffer from mysterious maladies and hold to inflexibly high ideals. Often they seem to be gripped by a negative view of themselves and by hostility to the family. They are likely to drop out of school, the job, the romance, or to stay in and be actively resentful.

In short, it's like having flu of the personality.

(*Passages*, Gail Sheehy)

e.   My son, Jaws II, had a habit that drove me crazy. He'd walk to
the refrigerator-freezer and fling both doors open and stand there until
the hairs in his nose iced up. After surveying two hundred dollars'
worth of food in varying shapes and forms he would declare loudly
"There's nothing to eat."

(*Aunt Erma's Cope Book,* Erma Bombeck)

f.   ... With tingling nerves but a fixed purpose, I sat in the dark re-
cess of the hut and waited with sombre patience for the coming of its
tenant.
    And then at last I heard him. Far away came the sharp clink of a
boot striking upon a stone. Then another and yet another, coming
nearer and nearer. I shrank back into the darkest corner and cocked
the pistol in my pocket, determined not to discover myself until I had
an opportunity of seeing something of the stranger. There was a long
pause which showed that he had stopped. Then once more the foot-
steps approached and a shadow fell across the opening of the hut.
    "It is a lovely evening, my dear Watson," said a well known voice.
"I really think that you will be more comfortable outside than in."

(*The Hound of the Baskervilles,* Sir Arthur Conan Doyle)

g.   Scientists, like other human beings, have their hopes and fears,
their passions and despondencies—and their strong emotions may
sometimes interrupt the course of clear thinking and sound practice.
But science is also self-correcting. The most fundamental axioms and
conclusions may be challenged. The prevailing hypothesis must sur-
vive confrontation with observation. Appeals to authority are imper-
missible. The steps in a reasoned argument must be set out for all to
see. Experiments must be reproducible.

(*Broca's Brain,* Carl Sagan)

h.   My Fellow Citizens: We observe today not a victory of party but
a celebration of freedom—symbolizing an end as well as a beginning—signifying renewal as well as change. For I have sworn before
you and almighty God the same solemn oath our forebears prescribed
nearly a century and three-quarters ago.
    The world is very different now. For man holds in his mortal hands
the power to abolish all forms of human poverty and all forms of
human life. And yet the same revolutionary beliefs for which our fore-
bearers fought are still at issue around the globe—the belief that the
rights of man come not from the generosity of the state but from the
hand of God.
    We dare not forget today that we are the heirs of that first revolu-
tion. Let the word go forth from this time and place, to friend and foe

INTRODUCTION TO NONVERBAL COMMUNICATION

alike, that the torch has been passed to a new generation of Americans—born in this century, tempered by war, disciplined by a hard and bitter peace, proud of our ancient heritage—and unwilling to witness or permit the slow undoing of those human rights to which this nation has always been committed, and to which we are committed today at home and around the world.

Let every nation know, whether it wishes us well or ill, that we shall pay any price, bear any burden, meet any hardship, support any friend, oppose any foe in order to assure the survival and success of liberty.

This much we pledge—and more.

(Inaugural Address, John F. Kennedy)

i.   Those who say that we're in a time when there are no heroes— they just don't know where to look. You can see heroes every day going in and out of factory gates. Others, a handful in number, produce enough food to feed all of us and then the world beyond.

You meet heroes across a counter—and they're on both sides of that counter. There are entrepreneurs with faith in themselves and faith in an idea who create new jobs, new wealth and opportunity.

There are individuals and families whose taxes support the Government and whose voluntary gifts support church, charity, culture, art and education. Their patriotism is quiet but deep. Their values sustain our national life.

(Inaugural Address, Ronald Reagan)

j.   To every thing there is a season, and a time to every purpose under the heaven:

A time to be born, and a time to die; a time to plant, and a time to pluck up that which is planted;

A time to kill, and a time to heal; a time to break down, and a time to build up;

A time to weep, and a time to laugh; a time to mourn, and a time to dance;

A time to cast away stones, and a time to gather stones together; a time to embrace, and a time to refrain from embracing;

A time to get, and a time to lose; a time to keep, and a time to cast away;

A time to rend, and a time to sew; a time to keep silence, and a time to speak;

A time to love, and a time to hate; a time of war, and a time of peace.

(*Ecclesiastes* 3: 1–8)

k.   Willie staggered out past the captain to the open wing. The wind immediately smashed him against the bridgehouse, and spray pelted him like small wet stones. He was astounded and peculiarly exhilarated to realize that in the last fifteen minutes the wind had actually become much stronger than before, and would blow him over the side if he exposed himself in a clear space. He laughed aloud, his voice thin against the gutteral "Whooeeee!" of the storm. He inched himself to the door of the radar shack, freed the dogs, and tried to pull the door open, but the wind held it tightly shut. He pounded on the wet steel with his knuckles, and kicked at it, and screamed, "Open up! Open up!"

(*The Caine Mutiny*, Herman Wouk)

l.   An eel pot or trap is a cylindrical container made of cellar window wire or hardware cloth, about thirty inches long and eight to ten inches in diameter. It has a twine head, called variously a "funnel" or "nozzle," at the front end, tied back inside and as wide open as possible. About a third of the way back is another. This one is tied so that the narrow mouth or throat can be pushed open from the front and yet leave no opening apparent when the eel has gone through into the back end or parlor. The head at the far end is tied tight with a pucker string.

(*Cape Cod Fisherman*, Phil Schwind)

m.   Engine tune-up is a procedure performed to restore engine performance, deteriorated due to normal wear and loss of adjustment. The three major areas considered in a routine tune-up are compression, ignition, and carburetion, although valve adjustment may be included.

A tune-up is performed in three steps: *analysis,* in which it is determined whether normal wear is responsible for performance loss, and which parts require replacement or service; *parts replacement or service;* and *adjustment,* in which engine adjustments are returned to original specifications. Since the advent of emission control equipment, precision adjustment has become increasingly critical, in order to maintain pollutant emission levels.

(*Chilton's Repair & Tune-Up Guide*)

n.   The gas industry continues to forge ahead. The uncertainties of supply that plagued the industry from 1974 until recently have been largely eliminated. Our industry increased gas reserves dramatically last year and the number of wells drilled in 1980 is at an all-time high. There is every reason to believe that higher wellhead prices have stimulated production activity as was anticipated. Canadian and Mexican

INTRODUCTION TO NONVERBAL COMMUNICATION

supplies of gas are increasing and more gas is available to United States users than can be marketed, primarily due to the price of these supplies. The projection of annual supply available to meet the demand by the year 2000 ranges from 23 trillion cubic feet to 33 trillion cubic feet. However, it is clear that the supply can be made available and represents the least-cost energy option for America. The variable part of the demand curve will be largely industrial and will depend a great deal upon governmental policies.

(Annual Report, National Fuel Gas Company)

o. The tide rises, the tide falls,
    The twilight darkens, the curlew calls;
    Along the sea-sands damp and brown
    The traveller hastens toward the town,
        And the tide rises, the tide falls.

    Darkness settles on roofs and walls,
    But the sea, the sea in the darkness calls;
    The little waves, with their soft, white hands,
    Efface the footprints in the sands,
        And the tide rises, the tide falls.

    The morning breaks; the steeds in their stalls
    Stamp and neigh, as the hostler calls;
    The day returns, but nevermore
    Returns the traveller to the shore,
        And the tide rises, the tide falls.

("The Tide Rises, The Tide Falls,"
Henry Wadsworth Longfellow)

p. *Birdie:* . . . Don't love me. Because in twenty years you'll be just like me. They'll do all the same things to you. . . . You know what? In twenty-two years I haven't had a whole day of happiness. Oh, a little, like today, with you all. But never a single, whole day. I say to myself, if only I had one more *whole* day, then— . . . And that's the way you'll be. And you'll trail after them, just like me, hoping they won't be so mean that day or say something to make you feel so bad— only you'll be worse off because you haven't got my Mama to remember— . . . .

(*The Little Foxes*, Lillian Hellman)

q. *Ben:* You'll tell nobody anything, because you can't, and you'll stop bargaining. You're giving me everything you've got. Is that clear? If I don't have to waste any more time with you, I'll give you enough to live on, here or wherever you want to go. But if I have to talk to you any longer, you won't get that. I mean what I'm saying, and you know I do. And it's the last time I'll say it.

(*Another Part of the Forest*, Lillian Hellman)

r.   *Sidney:* I wish you everything. I wish you luck, I wish you love, I wish you happiness. You're a gifted and remarkable woman. You've put up with me and my shenanigans for twelve harrowing years, and I don't know why. But I'm grateful. . . . You've had half a husband and three quarters of a career. You deserve the full amount of everything. . . . May the Academy of Arts and Sciences Board of Electees see the beauty, the talent and the courage that I have seen for a quarter of a lifetime. . . . I hope you win the bloody Oscar. . . . Fifty years from now I'll be able to sell it for a fortune.

(*California Suite*, Neil Simon)

s.   *Jennie:* I am sick and tired of running from places and people and relationships. . . . And don't tell me what I want because *I'll* tell you what I want. I want a home and I want a family—and I want a career, too. And I want a dog and I want a cat and I want three goldfish. I want *everything!* There's no harm in wanting it, George, because there's not a chance in hell we're going to get it all, anyway. But if you don't *want* it, you've got even less chance than that. . . .

(*Chapter Two*, Neil Simon)

t.   *Mel:* You don't know the first thing I'm talking about. . . . You don't know what it is to be in my place. . . . You've never stood on line for two hours waiting for an unemployment check with a shirt and tie, trying to look like you don't need the money. And some fat old dame behind the counter screaming out so everyone can hear, *"Did you look for a job this week?"* "Yes, I looked for a job." *"Did you turn down any work this week?"* "What the hell am I doing here if I turned down work this week?" . . . You never walked into your building and had a ninety-one-year-old doorman with no teeth, asthma and beer on his breath giggle at you because *he's* working. . . .

(*The Prisoner of Second Avenue*, Neil Simon)

u.   Economic Theory: A systematic application and critical evaluation of the basic analytic concepts of economic theory, with emphasis on money and why it's good. Fixed coefficient production functions, cost and supply curves, and nonconvexity comprise the first semester, with the second semester concentrating on spending, making change, and keeping a neat wallet. The Federal Reserve System is analyzed, and advanced students are coached in the proper method of filling out

INTRODUCTION TO NONVERBAL COMMUNICATION

a deposit slip. Other topics include: Inflation and Depression—how to dress for each. Loans, interest, welching.

(Getting Even, Woody Allen)

v.   At the age of fifteen Doug and Dinsdale started attending the Ernest Pythagoras Primary School in Clerkenwell. When the Piranhas left school they were called up but were found by an Army Board to be too mentally unstable even for National Service. Denied the opportunity to use their talents in the service of their country, they began to operate what they called "The Operation." . . . They would select a victim and threaten to beat him up if he paid them the so-called protection money. Four months later they started another operation which they called, "The Other Operation." In this racket they selected another victim and threatened not to beat him up if he didn't pay them. One month later they hit upon "The Other Other Operation." In this the victim was threatened that if he didn't pay them, they would beat him up. This for the Piranha brothers was the turning point.

(Monty Python's Big Red Book)

w.   There is no question that there is an unseen world. The problem is, how far is it from midtown and how late is it open? Unexplainable events occur constantly. One man will see spirits. Another will hear voices. A third will wake up and find himself running in the Preakness. How many of us have not at one time or another felt an ice-cold hand on the back of our neck while we were home alone? (Not me, thank God, but some have.) What is behind these experiences? Or in front of them, for that matter? Is it true that some men can foresee the future or communicate with ghosts? And after death is it still possible to take showers?

(Without Feathers, Woody Allen)

Other
Nonverbal Forms
of Communication

Remember the first day of this class, when you met your instructor for the first time? Perhaps you were already in your seat when the instructor came into the room. Do you remember the things you observed? Maybe you noticed what the person was wearing, that he or she walked in a certain way; maybe you noticed hair color, height, weight, the way he or she looked out over the class, the sound of the person's voice, the way the words were pronounced. You took in all this information, then your mind started to interpret it, and you formed an opinion about your instructor on the spot.

Or, have you ever noticed the conversation that goes on between the pitcher and the catcher in a baseball game? The pitcher looks at the catcher. The catcher makes a sign with his hands. The pitcher shakes his head. The process repeats itself until the catcher makes a sign that's followed by the pitcher nodding his head.

Both the baseball game and the classroom game are examples of nonverbal communication. By nonverbal communication we mean all the communication forms we use other than the actual words themselves.

Most of the modes of nonverbal communication were in existence before the human race developed speech and language. Such things as gesture and facial expressions were commonly used to transmit messages long before humans developed the system of sounds and noises, or the written symbols representing these sounds and noises, that we call language. Because these nonverbal forms of communication have become an innate part of the language system, we tend to derive a great deal of meaning from them, and to respond to them on a deep, often unconscious level. Often the specific meanings of individual nonverbal behaviors vary from culture to culture. For example, a gesture meaning "This is important; you'd better listen to me" in one culture might mean "I give up" in another. So deeply ingrained are nonverbal behaviors in our interpersonal relationships that we place a high value on them.

Mixed Messages

Think back in your experience. Have you ever met someone for the first time and, even though your conversation with that person went smoothly and pleasantly, you came away with a certain amount of dislike for him or her? If so, you may have blamed your dislike on "bad vibes" or some similar expression. In all likelihood, what you were responding to was discordance between the pleasant words that that person used and various physical or vocal behaviors.

In other words, you reacted to a *mixed message*, a segment of communication in which the nonverbal message differs from or contradicts the verbal message. In situations like this, where there is a conflict between what a person's words say and what his or her nonverbal behavior says, you will tend to

INTRODUCTION TO NONVERBAL COMMUNICATION

believe the nonverbal message. The result: the listener often either ends up confused or reacts unfavorably.

For you to be a more effective communicator, you should know about the meanings transmitted by various forms of nonverbal behavior and be sure that all the ways you transmit a message are in harmony with one another. Let's take a look at some of the most common areas of nonverbal communication.

Paralanguage

There's more to words than just their symbolic meanings. In spoken communication you can use variables such as loudness, stress, pitch, rate, and rhythm to add to or even completely change the symbolic meanings of words. We call these variables the paralinguistic elements of speech. Chapters 4 and 5 cover the paralinguistic elements pretty thoroughly, so we won't repeat that topic here.

Kinesics

Just as you respond to the many auditory cues in a speaker's message through what you hear (paralanguage), you also respond to a multitude of visual cues. All the behaviors you can observe visually make up the category of nonverbal communication called *kinesics*. Your response to the kinesic elements of communication is probably more unconscious than your response to paralanguage. Yet the role kinesics plays is just as important, if not more important, in your reception and interpretations of others' communicative efforts with you. Remember the "bad vibes" mentioned earlier? If you developed an almost instant dislike to a person, really without knowing why, you were probably responding unconsciously to the other person's kinesics.

Kinesics usually includes gestures, movements of the body or its extremities, facial expressions, the states of muscle tension or relaxation in body parts, postural attitudes, and behaviors involving the eyes, such as winking, blinking, and the direction and duration of eye contact and gaze.

Social and behavioral scientists who make an intensive study of nonverbal behavior have developed a system for examining nonverbal behaviors, including kinesics, in such a way that we can group certain behaviors together into categories. One such system, developed by Ekman and Friesen, includes the categories of *emblems, illustrators, affect displays, regulators,* and *adaptors.*

Emblems

Behaviors that, although not verbalized, can be directly translated into a very specific verbal entity are called *emblems.* Any football fan knows immediately that when an official raises both arms directly overhead, he is indicating that one of the teams has scored; when he stands with his hands on his hips, elbows out, we know that one team was offside. Another example in sports includes the umpire's raised hand, with fingers flexed and thumb extended, meaning "You're out!" And, of course, you know that the very same emblem used outside of the ball park can mean something else when used by a hitchhiker.

We also display emblems on a less formal basis during our everyday communication situations. You may frequently show dislike or displeasure by wrinkling your nose; you may tell someone to approach you by holding out one hand with the palm up and the last three fingers flexed, curling the index finger. These are only a couple of the many emblems we use as individuals and as a culture.

Illustrators

Illustrators are behaviors that *accompany* speech and are directly related to it. They are used for emphasis or to clarify or illustrate an idea through the use of body movements. Try to describe, in words alone, a spiral staircase. It's hard, isn't it? It is much easier to use illustrators, gestures with your body and hands, to help your verbal communication.

Affect Displays

Affect displays are the elements of nonverbal communication to which we probably respond most directly and consciously. If you have ever smiled warmly at an attractive member of the opposite sex and received a warm smile in return, you didn't need very much verbal communication to realize that there was a mutuality of feeling between you. We can express affect displays facially or bodily. The droop of the head and shoulders, for example, can express sadness, weariness, or depression.

Regulators

During any conversation, be it a dialogue between two close friends or a conversation among several people at a party, signals are passed from one person to another or to the group as a whole. We call these signals, or cues, *regulators*. These signals regulate, or control, the back-and-forth flow of the conversation, governing its rate and duration. You give someone permission to speak, encouragement to continue, or a message to stop talking through some nonverbal behavior such as making or avoiding eye contact or head-nodding or head-shaking.

Adaptors

An *adaptor* is a nonverbal behavior we use to manifest some of our unconscious needs or drives. Some of these behaviors, such as scratching our heads, rubbing our noses, covering our mouths, or chewing our glasses, are ways of handling anxiety, hostility, or other negative feelings. Most people are not aware of displaying adaptors. Look around your classroom before the next quiz or before a class presentation is to be made. What kind of adaptive behaviors do you see? Probably a lot of foot-tapping, playing with pencils, hand-rubbing, and so on.

In addition to looking at the type of behavior displayed, we can examine the body part we used for the communication, and what we mean to "say." For example, facial expressions may indicate a wide variety of feelings, ranging from depression and anger, on one hand, to such emotions as joy, delight, and exaltation on the other. Specific organs of the face may also play a part in transmitting messages.

Eyes

The eyes play a very important role in communication. The length of time that you hold eye contact with another person is generally an indication of the degree and quality of your relationship with that person. Your eye contact with a total stranger or a casual acquaintance is likely to be considerably shorter than eye contact with one of your close friends or family members. If you are angry with someone fairly close to you, you are likely to make your eye contact with that person either very short or much longer than usual. When you're forced into uncomfortably close quarters with someone you don't know intimately, you'll usually compensate by avoiding eye contact. Recall the behavior of people on crowded elevators. Where do they look? Usually at the numbers that indicate the floors. What about on crowded buses or trains? There, people generally look up at the advertising signs or down at their feet.

The eyes may play a role in discouraging relationships. When you avoid eye contact with an acquaintance or friend, you may be saying, "I don't wish to recognize you now or spend time with you." Literature is full of expressions that relate to the wide variety of meanings a person can express in a glance. As Ben Jonson said, "Drink to me only with thine eyes,/And I will pledge with mine."/

Eye pupil size expresses another aspect of meaning. When you look at something you find pleasant, your eye pupils tend to enlarge. When you look at something you find unpleasant, your pupils contract. You don't consciously control the size of your pupils, though, and your response to the eye pupil size of others is also largely unconscious. Many experiments have shown that people generally prefer to relate to, be friends with, and work with, people with large eye pupils.

Arms and Legs

The arms and legs also play an important part in conveying either specific meaning or some indication of the communicator's feelings and attitudes.

On one occasion, one of the authors was participating in a group interview of a candidate for a position as counselor. The candidate was very opinionated and outspoken as to her views on a number of subjects and gradually antagonized several of the interviewers, especially the author. After he addressed a couple of questions toward the candidate and received what, to him, were highly unsatisfactory answers, the author's attention was embarrassingly called to his posture by one of the other interviewers. To his surprise and consternation, he found himself leaning way back in his chair, with his arms and legs tightly crossed. Any one of these behaviors would have indicated the interviewer's negative attitude toward the candidate. Together, all of them meant "You don't stand a ghost of a chance with me." The candidate very shortly took the hint, and left. (P.S.: She didn't get the job.)

□ *Attending and Nonattending Exercise* □

Pair off with another student or a friend. Pick a subject you can discuss for about five minutes. (Possibly what each of you wishes to do to improve your communication effectiveness.) Have one person sit in an *attending position:* leaning slightly forward, arms and legs unfolded but comfortable, with gaze fixed on the other person's face. The other person should sit in a *nonattending position:* slouched back in the chair, arms and legs crossed, gaze averted from partner. Discuss the topic you selected.

At the end of five minutes, reverse your roles so that the former *attender* becomes the *nonattender* and vice versa. Continue to discuss the same topic, or another topic, for another five minutes.

Now discuss with your partner the feelings each of you experienced, both as an attender and as a nonattender, as well as your feelings about being attended to and not being attended to.

What were your feelings about yourself? Were they different in each role? Were your feelings toward your partner different when your partner was assuming a different role with respect to you? Which posture encourages better

INTRODUCTION TO NONVERBAL COMMUNICATION

communication? Which posture encourages better interpersonal relationships? Which role did you find to be more comfortable?

Proxemics

Imagine waking up in the morning, getting out of bed, washing, and dressing. In addition to your usual clothing, this morning you are going to enclose yourself in a transparent plastic bubble. You can see through this bubble, hear through it, smell, touch, and taste through it. As you go through your daily activities, the bubble expands and shrinks, sometimes fitting as tightly as your skin. Most of the time you are quite comfortable with the size of the bubble. Sometimes, though, the bubble is either larger or smaller than you would like it to be, and you feel quite uncomfortable and begin to behave differently than usual.

This imaginary plastic bubble is actually your *personal space*—the distance from another person at which you feel comfortable and at ease. You probably realize that this distance varies considerably depending on the situation and the relationship between the people involved. Generally, as far as communication goes, we can divide personal space into four categories of distance.

Public Distance

This is the longest distance, usually ranging anywhere from twelve to about twenty feet or more. Public distance is appropriate for highly impersonal situations such as the movies, theatre, or sports events such as football or baseball games. At these events, the distance between the spectators and participants indicates that there is little or no *personal* relationship between them. (Except, perhaps, during the World Series, when the wives of the baseball players are frequently shown in the stands. They, however, usually sit in the first row, box seats, as close to the players as possible.)

Social-consultative Distance

The limits for social-consultative distance range between four feet and twelve feet. This is the range of distance at which impersonal business between two people, or one person and a group, is usually carried out. If you were in a class in which the instructor did some lecturing and spent some time leading class discussions, you would most likely feel more comfortable at a distance between four and twelve feet from the instructor. Closer than four feet, you might feel somewhat threatened and uncomfortable. Farther away than twelve feet, you might feel separated and lose interest in the lecture or discussion.

Casual-personal Distance

This distance may range from one-and-one-half feet to four feet. At this distance, we usually hold conversations with friends, members of our family, and acquaintances with whom we have some sort of working relationship. If you were being interviewed for a position, the interviewer and you would probably sit at a distance in this range. Most of your everyday communication situations take place within this range.

Intimate Distance

This is the closest distance, ranging from actual physical contact to about one-and-one-half feet. This distance is usually maintained by two persons who have a very close, personal relationship, and usually is used in a private situation. Husbands and wives, lovers, and close family members are the types of pairs who maintain the intimate distance in their communication. If you were forced to be at this distance with a stranger or casual acquaintance in a crowded public situation, you would probably feel a good deal of discomfort and would either avoid eye contact with the other person or use a variety of adaptor behaviors.

□ *Distance Exercise* □

1. Pair off with a partner. Stand facing one another about twenty feet apart. Start a conversation and continue it for about two minutes. What was your comfort level? What was the topic of conversation? Was it very personal or impersonal? You were at *public distance* during this exercise.
2. Move to a distance of about ten feet from your partner. Continue your conversation for another two minutes. Did your conversation topic change? If so, to what? Was your comfort level any different from the first situation? You were at *social distance*.
3. Move to a distance of three feet from your partner. Continue your conversation for another two minutes. For this distance, answer the same questions asked above. You are now at *personal distance*.
4. Now move close enough to your partner so that you are directly face-to-face, practically touching. Continue your conversation, if you can. Observe your own physical behaviors.

INTRODUCTION TO NONVERBAL COMMUNICATION

5. Discuss with your partner, or the class, the following questions for each distance:

> What is the effect of distance on feelings of comfort or discomfort?
> What effect does distance have on the topic of conversation and vice versa?
> Does the sex of your partner affect the distance at which you feel comfortable? You may wish to repeat the exercise with a partner of the opposite sex to your original partner and take note of your reactions.

Other Aspects

Space and human relationships can influence communication situations in other ways, too. Think back to your childhood days and remember, if you can, a situation in which you may have been the only child present in a gathering of adults. The likelihood is that you felt small, insignificant, and unimportant in contrast to all those "giants" surrounding you. Some of that feeling may persist into adulthood when you encounter someone who is considerably taller or at a greater height than you. If you attend a conference or a banquet, you will probably find that the "important" people there, speakers and "honored guests," are seated at tables on a raised platform or dais to indicate their importance in regard to the "ordinary people" seated at a level below them.

In most large organizations that occupy offices on more than one floor in a building, the people with the higher status job titles will occupy offices on the higher floors. An example you may relate to more easily can be found in the classroom. Most of the time the students are seated while the instructor stands and lectures or leads discussion; this is a way of indicating that the teacher is the most important person (has more power) in that classroom and that the seated students should pay close attention.

These are only some of the intentional devices we use to communicate importance in our culture; these devices indicate that we generally associate height directly with importance.

☐ *Height Exercise* ☐

Pair off with a partner. One of you will be the "persuader" and the other the "persuadee." The persuader will stand and talk to the persuadee, who will be seated. Try to persuade your partner to accept some belief. After two minutes or so, reverse positions but do *not* reverse roles. (The persuader is now seated, the persuadee, standing.) Continue for another two minutes. Now reverse roles and repeat the exercise.

What different feelings did each of you have as persuader when you were standing, as opposed to sitting? What different feelings did each of you have as the person being persuaded while standing as opposed to sitting?

If you were seriously engaged in a persuasive activity, would you choose to be higher or lower than the person or persons you were attempting to persuade?

Location

You can also indicate status or importance through location. If you were to visit a member of a large organization, you would find that the distance to that person's office depends on the person's status within the organization, that is, the higher the status, the farther away the individual would be from "the center of things." In addition, you would find that higher-status persons have larger offices (more personal space) and more barriers separating them from others.

Even through the subtle use of space, humans communicate some piece of information. Space not only plays a part in *what* we communicate, it plays a part in *how* we communicate.

Touch

Our understanding of how we use touch as a form of communication is not as clear or complete as it is of some of the other nonverbal forms, yet there are some principles involved in touch that are important to understand.

We know, for instance, that touch is one of the most important ways for parents to communicate feelings of love and caring to a young child. In fact, children who do not receive a good deal of touching during their early childhood usually show some delays in their emotional development and may develop into adults who are incapable of sensing or expressing very much in the way of feelings. In addition, children who experience little touching behavior usually are found to have very low self-concepts.

In many American cultures, touching is discouraged more and more as we grow older, except in certain formalized, stylistic ways, until we experience very little touching in our daily lives as adults. There are some exceptions, to be sure. If you watch sports you can't help but be aware of all the vigorous touching athletes do to one another. Watch to see what happens to the wide receiver on a professional football team after he catches a long pass and scores a touchdown.

During discussions held in the authors' classes about what makes people feel good about themselves, one of the actions students mentioned most often as a morale booster is a pat on the back (literally!). Another action that makes

INTRODUCTION TO NONVERBAL COMMUNICATION

them feel good is a hug from someone they feel close to. Yet, at the same time, they report that they are reluctant to touch others in the same way they themselves would like to be touched. Unfortunately, as adults we generally associate touching with sexuality and tend to be inhibited about it.

□ *Touching Exercise* □

(One member of the class may read the directions as the others perform the exercise.)
1. Sit in a circle with other members of your class.
2. Hold hands with your neighbors so that your right hand *is clasping* the left hand of the person on your right, and your left hand is *being held* by the person on your left.
3. *Close your eyes,* and focus on the feelings in your left hand. How does that hand feel being held? What messages, if any, are you receiving from the person holding that hand? How do you feel about the person holding that hand?
4. Now focus on your right hand. How does that hand feel holding someone else's? What message is being sent to you by the person whose hand you're holding? How do you feel about that person?
5. When you are in touch with all these feelings, open your eyes. (Notice the metaphor—"in touch with"—that we frequently use in regard to being aware of our feelings.)
6. As a group, discuss what you experienced during the exercise. Did you feel differently about holding as opposed to being held? Why? Did you feel differently about the two persons next to you after the hand-holding? Did it matter whether your hand was being held or doing the holding? How comfortable were you while holding hands with your classmates? Was there a difference between touching a member of the same sex as compared to touching a member of the opposite sex? Can you communicate through touch?

Time

There's an old story about a psychiatrist's secretary who informed her boss that she was quitting her job because she didn't want to suffer a nervous breakdown. When her boss asked her why she would have a breakdown on the job, she said that she never knew what time to report to work. Her boss then assured her that she was due at work at 9:00 A.M. every morning. She replied, "Yes, I know that. But when I get here early, you tell me I'm anxious. When I get here late you tell me I'm being hostile. And when I get here on time, you tell me I'm compulsive. There's no way to win!"

Although something of an exaggeration, this anecdote does reflect how people manage and use time to express feelings toward others. Although most of us sit patiently waiting to be seen by doctors or dentists (Did you ever wonder about the derivation of the medical use of the term "patient?"), very few of us would casually appear significantly late for an appointment with one of them. Similarly, in job interviews, you'd be more likely to expect that the interviewer might keep the applicant waiting rather than the other way around. We usually think that the person of lower status waits for the person of higher status.

What is your sense of time like? Do you have on-time arrivals and departures? Or, perhaps, do you arrive "fashionably late" to parties and meetings? Do you sometimes punish people by making them wait? What messages do you send through the medium of time? In any case, let us observe a moment of silence in honor of the psychiatrist's secretary in all of us.

Clothing

Imagine that you are a young man or woman preparing for an interview for a position as a junior accountant in a large accounting firm. Which of the following outfits would you be more likely to wear?

1. jeans, T-shirt, sneakers
2. a well-tailored suit, white shirt (blouse), tie, conservative shoes

At many colleges and universities, the faculty always knows when on-campus job interviews are being held, just by the change in attire worn by many students. The reasons are obvious. Outfit #1 says its wearer is casual, relaxed, informal. Outfit #2, on the other hand, says its wearer is business-like, serious, mature, hard-working, conforming. The old expression, "Clothes make the man" is not strictly true, but clothes certainly contribute heavily to the impression you make on the rest of the world. Your attire conveys a general impression about you before you have a chance to *say* a word about yourself.

Other Nonverbal Modes

In the morning when you splash on a dab of perfume or aftershave lotion, you may not be consciously thinking about how other people will react to that particular scent. The odds are, though, that someone has spent some time thinking about that very question. It could be the person who blended the fragrance, the person who named it, the person who planned the advertising campaign, the person (either you or someone else) who purchased it. All those people attempted to associate that perfume or aftershave with a very specific, attractive image, probably one that is attractive to the opposite sex.

INTRODUCTION TO NONVERBAL COMMUNICATION

Our senses of smell and taste do provide additional channels of nonverbal communication. We don't now know a great deal about those channels, about which research is currently being carried on, but we'll know a lot more in the future.

Caution

At this point, we feel it is important to point out a few cautions. When you interpret and respond to nonverbal behaviors, now that you have become more sensitized to them, try to remember that individual bits of behavior may mean different things in different cultures, in different contexts, and in different people. In interpreting nonverbal behavior, the experienced observer will observe, make a tentative hypothesis about what the behavior means, and observe further to test the hypothesis before arriving at a definite conclusion. We can generalize, however, to the extent that "people watching can be both fun and profitable."

SUGGESTED READINGS

Birdwhistell, Ray L. *Kinesics and Context.* Philadelphia. University of Pennsylvania Press, 1970.

Ekman, Paul, and Friesen, Wallace. "The Repertoire of Nonverbal Behavior: Categories, Origins, Usage and Coding." *Semiotica I* (1969), pp. 49–98.

Knapp, Mark L. *Non-verbal Communication in Human Interaction,* 2nd Edition. New York: Holt, Rinehart and Winston, 1978.

Leathers, Dale. *Non-Verbal Communication Systems.* Boston: Allyn & Bacon, 1978.

Kronkhite, Gary. *Communication and Awareness.* Menlo Park, Calif.: Cummings Publishing Co., 1976.

Rosenfeld, Lawrence, and Civikly, Jean. *With Words Unspoken: Non-verbal Experience.* New York: Holt, Rinehart and Winston, 1976.

part three

Diction

We think it's a good idea to say a few things here that are meant to help you get the most out of this section of the book. Not so much Chapter 7 (Chapter 7 provides a certain amount of theory that leads into the next two chapters). We are, rather, concerned with Chapters 8 and 9, in which you'll put theory into practical application in your own speech.

Chapters 8 and 9 present each of the individual sounds of American English starting with a sample sentence, typical spellings, a description of the sound, and, in many cases, drills to help you to produce the sound accurately. Then, we present drills on the single word, the phrase, and the sentence levels. These practice exercises are arranged according to levels of difficulty. Level 1 drills contain the sound under study in contexts that are fairly easy to produce. Level 2 drills present the sound in slightly more difficult sound contexts. Don't start Level 2 drills until you are sure you have mastered Level 1. Level 3 drills are the most difficult, usually dealing with troublesome sound combinations and contrasts. You absolutely should not try Level 3 until you feel you have mastered Level 2. In the lists of "Practice Words" sections you will notice the headings "Beginning" "Middle," and "End." These headings indicate where in the word the sound being discussed is located.

We have tried to avoid the use of "tongue twisters" and other overly difficult practice sounds. The drill sentences are not overloaded with words containing the particular sound you are working on. We feel that such drills make it easier for you to fail than to succeed.

How to Do It

Unless your instructor specifies a different procedure, we recommend that you use the following routine for working on sounds you may have difficulty articulating correctly.

1. FOLLOW THE EAR TRAINING GUIDE PRESENTED IN APPENDIX A. You'll find that having a clear, accurate auditory perception of the sound is an essential first step in mastering the production of that sound.

2. TRY PRODUCING THE SOUND BY ITSELF. Have someone check your production. Once you are able to produce the sound consistently correctly, go on to the drill words.

3. TRY THE SOUND IN SINGLE WORDS. Take your time with each word. Listen carefully, and don't go on until you're satisfied that you've said the word correctly.

4. TRY THE SOUND IN PHRASES AND SENTENCES. Again, take your time. You're not trying to be perfectly fluent the first time around. And, it's okay to exaggerate the sound in practice; not all of what you do in practice will come out in conversational speech.

5. BECOME AWARE OF THE POSITION AND MOVEMENTS OF YOUR ARTICULATORS. As you are working on Step 2, try to experience the feeling of what is happening to your tongue, your lips, your hard and soft palates. This can be helpful in stabilizing the correct production of the sound.

You'll probably find it helpful to monitor yourself visually with the aid of a mirror, particularly when you're working on the sounds produced at the front of the mouth. You may want to buy a small compact or shaving mirror to use in practice and to take to class with you.

6. DON'T BE DISCOURAGED. Remember, you may be trying to change habit patterns of long standing, so there's a good chance that your first efforts won't be immediately successful. Frequent practice is often necessary to achieve the results you're after.

7. PRACTICE FOR A SHORT PERIOD EVERY DAY. Twenty minutes a day, *every day*. You won't tire as easily, and you won't forget as much between practice sessions.

8. GATHER YOUR OWN PRACTICE MATERIALS. Make word lists from the words *you* use everyday. Read articles from newspapers and magazines or dialogues from plays. The idea is to become proficient in contexts that are usable to you.

9. USE APPENDIX B FOR ADDITIONAL HELP. In Appendix B you'll find procedures outlining more ways to correct misarticulations of some of the more difficult sounds. If you are working on any of those, be sure to refer to these procedures. They will probably help you work more efficiently and effectively.

Warm-ups

Now you're almost ready to start learning about and working on the sounds of American English. To help you progress more rapidly, we suggest you try some warm-up exercises before each practice session (even though you may feel slightly ridiculous).

□ *Sensitizing Exercise* □

This exercise should help you become more aware of your articulators and how you use them in speaking.

1. Place the tip of your tongue between your upper lip and the upper tooth farthest back in your mouth on the right side. Now, slowly slide your tongue tip forward to the front teeth, then all the way back on the left side. Now, reverse the movement; first forward to the front teeth, then back to the teeth on the right side. Repeat, placing the tongue tip between the lower lip and the lower teeth.

2. Touch the inside of the upper front teeth with the tongue tip. Slowly slide the tip upward. The first soft tissue you feel is the gum. Next, you will feel a bump extending backward inside your mouth. This is the gum ridge or alveolar ridge. Several consonant sounds are produced with the tongue tip touching this ridge.

Now, drop the tip of the tongue to the floor of your mouth, open your mouth, and alternately raise the tongue tip, touch the alveolar ridge, and drop the tongue again.

3. Starting with the tip of your tongue at the gum ridge, slowly curl the tip upward and backward along the roof of your mouth. You should encounter a concave area. This is the hard palate. In case you have difficult locating it, it's the place where peanut butter always gets stuck.

Now drop your tongue. Raise it so that the front third is touching the hard palate. With your mouth open, alternately raise the tongue to the hard palate and lower it. Do this a few times as rapidly as you can.

4. Hold a mirror in front of your mouth so that you can see the back of your mouth. With your mouth wide open, say, *ga-ga-ga*. You should be able to see the back of your tongue rising up and the back part of the roof of your mouth dropping down to meet it. This part of the roof is called the soft palate or velum. Alternate raising and lowering the tongue and soft palate, first by repeating *ga-ga-ga,* then by performing the sound movement but without making any sound.

Now you're ready to begin learning the sounds of American English.

7

The Sounds of American English

SPEECH COMES FIRST

Each of you now reading this book has been given a great and wondrous gift. It's a gift that has been given to only a very small fraction of all the people who have ever lived on this planet. In fact, only two-thirds of the people alive today have it. What is this gift? Literacy—the ability to read and write.

Literate people are fortunate in many ways; but when they begin to study speech, they are often placed at a disadvantage. They have been given, as Marshall McCluhan said, "an eye for an ear." In other words, literate people frequently confuse speech with writing. Illiterate people, on the other hand, know something that few literate people are aware of: *language is speech, and writing is only its reflection.*

Writing attempts to do what the tape recorder does, to capture and make available something that has been said (or thought) in another place and at another time. Of course, the tape recorder does a much better job.

Imagine that instead of reading the sentences on this page, you were listening to a tape recording of the authors speaking these sentences. You would hear many "things" that can't be put in print, things that make up the total spoken content of our words. You would hear qualities of voice as well as rate and emphasis. You could make fairly accurate guesses as to the age of the authors and their emotional states at the time. Certainly you would know whether the voice belonged to a male or female. But what do you know about the authors as a result of *reading* the words? Unless it is a description of him or her, what can you know of an author's age or sex from reading? Nothing! Because we strip speech of its qualities when we reduce talk to the medium of writing. Communication that began as something designed for our ears is, finally, transmitted to our eyes.

Sounds, Not Letters

There's a lot of confusion about writing and speech. Most people don't seem to be aware that letters and sounds are different in fundamental and important ways.

Speech and Writing Confusion

Most of us are unable to deal with words other than in writing, and it's hard to understand why. You probably wouldn't say that you had heard a picture or that you had seen music. Nor would you claim to smell a flavor or taste an aroma. But this confusion of the senses—*synesthesia*, it's called—affects most people in their beliefs about language. Somehow, they find it hard to grasp the fact that *speech consists of sounds that come out of your face* and *writing is marks you make with your hand*. It's because of this mix-up between visual and auditory reflections of language that many people believe speech consists of "saying letters." For example, if you say *thinkin'* or *goin'* in place of *thinking* or *going*, you are said to be "dropping the g." But you know that the *l* of *almond*, the *t* of *listen*, and the *ch* of *yacht* are all "silent letters," so although you're not producing them, you're not dropping them, either. Or perhaps you've heard a person pronounce his name and later saw it spelled and wondered, "Why would he pronounce it *that* way when he spells it *this* way?" We really *do* depend on our eyes to translate what we hear with our ears.

Why do we have these mix-ups between the auditory and the visual? Mainly because the system that educated us supports the belief that talking is subordinate to writing. The reason for that belief is inherent in the long, arduous, and formal process by which we learn to write as compared to the casual, easy, and seemingly automatic way we learn to speak. Think about it. Someone had to teach you how to write; years and years of study, great feats of memorization, hours upon hours of practice, and most of this occurring within the atmosphere of the classroom. Did any one teach you how to speak your native language? Or did your speech develop without the classroom, without books, without exams, without conscious learning? That's why you use the written word as the point of reference for the spoken; you have been taught to depend on letters instead of sounds.

The Problem with Letters

The difference between sounds and letters is a fundamental one and is really indispensable to you if you want to understand spoken language. Writing is a passive medium. It reflects what we say in a subtle and mysterious way. The written word *cat* is a good example of this. It is composed of a series of marks—*c*, *a*, and *t*—that allow us to recapture the utterance *cat*. But the marks are not the same as the utterance. When we say aloud the word *cat*, we produce speech sounds by movements of structures within the head, throat, and chest. Our spelling of the word *cat* cannot reflect those movements with any great degree of accuracy.

English Spelling and English Speech

The alphabet we use today was first designed about 1,300 years ago. When it was new, it accurately reflected the movements of speech because it adhered to the underlying principle of all alphabets. This principle has two conditions: (1) each written symbol will represent one spoken sound; (2) no spoken sound shall be represented by more than one symbol. In other words, there would be one, and only one, symbol for every sound in the language.

Today the situation is, to put it mildly, not quite what it was. English spelling no longer accurately reflects English speech sounds. The reason is, speech is dynamic, personal, and transitory while writing is static, institutionalized, and permanent. Language changes over time, but writing is frozen. The written language you learned was out of date 1,300 years ago!

How many English languages are there? If you're talking about *written* languages, the answer is one. (With the exception of a few minor spelling differences—color/colour, for example—every English writer uses exactly the same symbols in exactly the same way.) If you're talking about *spoken* English languages, the answer is thousands! Does an English speaker from Boston speak the same way as someone from New York City? Does someone from Atlanta sound the same as someone from San Francisco? On hearing them, would you mistake the words of a native of Trinidad for the words of someone born and raised in Quebec? Speakers all over the world write English in the same way, but their letters would give you no clue as to the way they sound.

At this point in time, English has strayed so far from the alphabetic principle that it's a miracle we can pronounce from spelling at all. For example, George Bernard Shaw's often quoted spelling of "fish" as *ghoti*, with the *f* from enou*gh*, the *i* from w*o*men, and the *sh* from na*ti*on. Or how about this: take the *mn* from autu*mn*, the *ai* from pl*ai*d, and the *c* from *c*ello and you can write *mnaic* for "match." Try another. Take the *k* of *k*iss, the a-sound of m*e*ringue, and the t-sound of de*b*t for an unusual spelling of "cat": *kibt*.

We could give you lots more examples, but we've made our point: there is enough duplication and overlap in our spelling to allow any word to have more than one "logical" pronunciation. And that gives us, in this speech class, a problem.

You're going to be spending a lot of time talking about speech sounds. But because of the inadequacies of English spelling, you don't have any accurate means of taking notes in such a way that your notes can tell you about sounds. Here's an example: The vowel sound in the word *do* is also in all the following spellings: *ewe, beauty, crew, shoe, cool, group, rude, fruit, true, rheumatism,* and *Sioux!* At the same time, the letter "e" has all of the following pronunciations: *pet, few, sew, eye, women, mete, serve, sergeant,* and *Jones!* You may know what you mean at the time you write your notes, but what about hours later? Do you think you'll remember which sound you meant when you wrote, "Work on 'e' tonight"?

I.P.A.

Fortunately, we do have a tool that will help us out of our dilemma: the International Phonetic Alphabet (I.P.A.). This alphabet (*not* a language) was designed almost one hundred years ago for the purpose of writing down the sounds of a language. I.P.A. is international, meaning it can be applied to any language; it is phonetic, meaning it is based on observed speech sounds; it is an alphabet, meaning it adheres without exception to the alphabetic principle of one sound per symbol. Although you may not have heard of I.P.A. until now, it is in widespread use today by people who wish to accurately record spoken language. In addition to linguists, I.P.A. is used by actors, radio and TV announcers, speech pathologists, teachers, and anthropologists, to name a few.

I.P.A. can be very useful to you as you learn more about speech. First, by learning the I.P.A. symbols, you will be learning to distinguish all the sounds of spoken English. In other words, we'll use I.P.A. as an ear training tool. Second, as you become familiar with I.P.A., you'll begin to associate the symbols with actual movements of the speech mechanism, which will reinforce the sounds as you learn them. Third, I.P.A. solves the problems created by English spelling; it provides us with a common framework for understanding.

I.P.A. Transcription

When you write something in I.P.A. you have *transcribed* it. If you are new to I.P.A. you may be tempted to regard transcription as merely being a weird version of English spelling, and you may spend your time trying to find equivalents between written English spelling and this new, unfamiliar alphabet. If you do that, you're trying to move from one written form to another without the intervening awareness of the *sounds* of speech. This practice will only slow down your learning of I.P.A. Remember, you only use I.P.A. symbols to record speech; it is not for writing.

To help distinguish between I.P.A. transcription and traditional English spelling, I.P.A. symbols are always enclosed in brackets. For example, *k* is the eleventh letter of the English alphabet, but [k] is the I.P.A. symbol used in transcribing the first sound in the English words *king, queen, cool,* and *choir* and the last sound in *rock* and *antique.*

Mostly I.P.A. uses the familiar symbols derived from the Latin-origin alphabets, including English, in use in western European languages. But even if the symbols look familiar to you, don't confuse them with the English letters whose names you've known for years.

The list of symbols shown in Table 7-1, given with key words and dictionary symbols, is completely adequate to transcribe just about any utterance spoken in American English and show accurately the phonetic (sound) content of that utterance. You'll also find practice materials at the end of this chapter that will help you learn phonetic transcription.

Table 7-1. The Phonemes of American English (I.P.A. Alphabet)

Phonetic Symbol	(I.P.A.) Dictionary Symbol	Key Words	Description
p	p	pat–pen–Paul	voiceless bilabial plosive
b	b	boat–bad–buy	voiced bilabial plosive
t	t	top–tea–ten	voiceless lingua–alveolar plosive
d	d	dog–day–duck	voiced lingua–alveolar plosive
k	k	key–kick–cake	voiceless lingua–velar plosive
g	g	go–game–guess	voiced lingua–velar plosive
f	f	four–feel–fine	voiceless labio–dental fricative
v	v	very–vine–vat	voiced labio–dental frictative
θ	th	thin–thick–thanks	voiceless lingua–dental fricative
ð	~~th~~, ~~ph~~, th	the–those–them	voiced lingua–dental fricative
s	s	snake–see–sue	voiceless lingua–alveolar fricative
z	z	zoo–zap–zip	voiced lingua–alveolar fricative
ʃ	sh	she–shoe–shore	voiceless lingua–palatal fricative
ʒ	zh	beige–pleasure	voiced lingua–palatal fricative
h	h	hot–hat–head	voiceless glottal fricative
hw	hw	where–which–why	voiceless bilabial glide
w	w	wet–wear–weather	voiced bilabial glide
r	r	red–roses–right	voiced lingua–palatal glide
j	y	yes–yellow–young	voiced lingua–palatal glide
l	l	left–loose–lick	voiced lingua–alveolar lateral
m	m	man–me–mitt	voiced bilabial nasal
n	n	no–knee–north	voiced lingua–alveolar nasal
ŋ	ng	sing–hang–king	voiced lingua–velar nasal
tʃ	ch	chair–cheat–choke	voiceless affricate
dʒ	j	judge–Jane–jump	voiced affricate
i	ē	see–east–free	high front tense vowel
ɪ	ĭ	sit–in–pit	high front lax vowel
e	ā	ate–pay–able	mid front tense vowel
ɛ	ĕ	bet–bed–end	mid front lax vowel
æ	ă	pat–flat–Adam	low front tense vowel
a	ā	ask (Boston "a")	low front vowel
ɑ ɒ	a	calm–honest–car	low back lax vowel
ɔ	ô	awful–often–all	mid back lax vowel
o	ō	so–open–hotel	mid back tense vowel
ʊ	o͞o	book–push–wood	high back lax vowel
u	oo	too–pool–food	high back tense vowel
ʌ	ŭ	up–uncle–usher	low mid stressed vowel
ə	ə	banana–sofa–about	low mid unstressed vowel (schwa)

Table 7-1. Cont.

(I.P.A.) Phonetic Symbol	Dictionary Symbol	Key Words	Description
ɝ—ɜ	ur	early–urn–pearl	mid central stressed vowel
ɚ	ər	father–perhaps	low mid unstressed vowel
aɪ	i	ice–light–time	diphthong
aʊ	ou	how–out–ouch	diphthong
ɔɪ	oi	coin–boy–oyster	diphthong

The Phoneme

Each of the I.P.A. symbols represents one *phoneme* of American English. A phoneme, though, is not exactly one sound. Instead, it is better described as a *sound family*. Let's look at it this way: the word *dog* refers to a type of animal that includes many different subtypes ranging from Great Danes to Chihuahuas with all sorts of dogs in between. The word *dog,* although it doesn't tell you exactly what kind of dog, fits any type in the dog family. Well, we have sound families, too. Take the phoneme [k], for example. It doesn't sound exactly the same in *keep* as it does in *peek,* but it's still in the family of [k].

The Allophone

Say the following sentence aloud: *I can open a can of beans.* Now say it again, and this time listen to the two utterances of the word *can.* The vowel seems to change slightly, doesn't it? Now reverse the *cans,* saying the noun as if it were the verb. It may sound strange to you, but it doesn't change the meaning. That's because both those sounds are *allophones* of the phoneme [æ]. An allophone is a *variation of a phoneme.* You can hear that it's slightly different, but not different enough that you would call it another phoneme. So remember, even though we say we're using one sound per symbol, each I.P.A. symbol really respresents a family of sounds that are so similar, it's hard to hear the differences among them.

Foreign Accents

If you've learned a second language, chances are you learned to speak it not like a native but, rather, with an accent that reflected your first language. For example, if your first language is American English, you learned to speak Spanish, say, with an American accent. Conversely, if your first language is Spanish, you probably speak English in a way that indicates that fact to your

113

listeners. Why do these accents exist? They come about as a result of the pho-nemic differences between languages. Let's use English and Spanish as exam-ples. In English, the words *seat* and *sit* are pronounced with two very distinct phonemes, [i] and [ɪ]. Very distinct, that is, to someone whose native lan-guage contains those sounds. Since Spanish does *not* have the [ɪ] of sit, the native Spanish speaker doesn't hear that there are two separate sounds pro-duced, and he says, "I will seat down on the seat." *Sit* and *seat* probably sound the same to him; the difference must be taught.

Standard Speech and Dialects

Up to now we've been talking as though there were but one spoken American English. But you know from your own experience that there are varieties, or *dialects,* spoken across the nation.

Dialects

A dialect is a variation of a language; it is spoken by a subgroup of speakers. This subgroup differs geographically or socially or ethnically, and so on, from the rest of the speakers of the language. The dialect can differ in pronuncia-tion, vocabulary, and grammar. For example, how do you say *Florida?* Do you use the vowel in *oar* or the vowel in *are?* Do you call the paper container you use for groceries a *sack* or a *bag?* Do you say "I be going" or "I am going"? These are just a few examples of dialectical differences.

Standard Speech

Is there any one standard way to speak American English? Any one standard dialect that doesn't vary across the country? We don't think so. When the au-thors speak of "standard," we are referring to the speech of a relatively large geographical area, such as New England or the Middle Atlantic region. Within that area, we view the standard as the following: *standard speech de-scribes the language usage of the majority of the educated people in the area.*

Nonstandard

If you live in Massachusetts and say the word *greasy* so that it rhymes with *fleecy,* your production would be considered standard. Should you use the same pronunciation in North Carolina, your production would be *nonstan-dard.* Why? Because in North Carolina, most people say *greasy* so that it rhymes with *breezy.* So what's standard in one place may not be standard in another. And what's standard for one social subgroup may be nonstandard in another.

Notice that when we say "nonstandard," we simply mean "different." We don't believe that any region has a "better" dialect than another region. Is there any advantage to speaking "standard" for an area? We think so. It has to do with the way listeners may judge you simply by the way you speak. The standard of an area usually carries more prestige for the speaker simply because it reflects the way the highly educated speak. It also provides a more formal way of speaking that is probably more versatile than the way you speak with your family and friends.

CLASSIFICATION OF SOUNDS

Take a look at Table 7-1. You'll see that the phonemes of our language have been placed in three general categories: *consonants, vowels,* and *diphthongs.* Each category differs from the others in the way its sounds are produced, particularly in the way the articulators modify the breathstream. Let's examine them individually.

Consonants

The consonant sounds are produced when the articulators obstruct the breathstream either completely or partially. Make the first sound in the word *kiss.* You produce it by holding the back of the tongue firmly against the soft palate, which shuts off the breathstream completely. Then you build up air pressure and suddenly explode the air past the point of obstruction. The last sound in *kiss,* though, only needs a partial obstruction. You force the breathstream through the narrow opening between your tongue and teeth, making a hissing sound.

Classification of Consonants

We classify the consonant sounds according to three factors: *voicing, place of articulation,* and *method of articulation* (see Table 7-2).

Voicing

If you produce voice at the same time that you produce a consonant sound, the consonant is said to be *voiced.* If there is no voice with the consonant, it is *voiceless.* The difference is usually fairly easy to hear, but if you have trouble telling if a consonant is voiced or voiceless, try this: gently rest your fingers on either side of your thyroid cartilage (Adam's apple) and hum. You should be able to feel vibrations with your fingertips. Now say the first sound in the word *gap.* Again, there should be vibrations. Now say the first sound in the word *cap.* You shouldn't feel vibrations because the word *cap* begins with a voiceless sound.

Table 7-2.   Consonants: Method of Articulation

Place of Articulation	Plosives		Fricatives		Nasals		Glides		Lateral		Affricates	
	vs	v	vs	v	vs	v	vs	v	vs	v	vs	v
Bilabial (both lips)	b	p			m		hw	w				
Labio-dental (lip-teeth)			f	v								
Lingua-dental (tongue-teeth)			θ	ð								
Lingua-alveolar (tongue-gum ridge)	t	d	s	z	n				l		tʃ	dʒ
Lingua-palatal (tongue-palate)			ʃ	ʒ			r	j				
Lingua-velar (tongue-soft palate)	k	g				ŋ						
Glottal (vocal folds)			h									

Look at Table 7-2. You'll see that a number of the consonant sounds are in pairs on the chart. We call these pairs *cognates.* Cognate sounds are sounds produced in the same place, in the same way, using the same articulators; the only difference is one sound is voiced, the other is voiceless.

Place of Articulation

The point at which we obstruct the breathstream is an important factor in consonant classification. To identify the physical place of articulation, we use the names of the articulators involved. Look again at Table 7-2. The places of articulation of the various consonants are listed down the left side of the chart. The listings are (1) bilabial (both lips); (2) labio–dental (lip–teeth); (3) lingua–dental (tongue–teeth); (4) lingua–alveolar (tongue–gum ridge); (5) lingua–palatal (tongue–palate); (6) lingua–velar (tongue–soft palate); (7) glottal (the space between the vocal folds). The first sound in the word *pet*, for example, is a bilabial sound—you make it with both lips.

Method of Articulation

Method of articulation means the physical process used to produce the sound. The various methods of articulation are listed from left to right in Table 7-2. Let's take the time now to explain each method briefly.

1. *Plosives* are sounds you make by blocking off the breathstream entirely for a very short period of time, just long enough to build up some air pressure behind your articulators. You then suddenly "explode" this air to produce the sound. The first sound in *pet* is a plosive.

2. *Fricatives* differ from plosives in that you don't have to block off the breathstream as completely. All you need is a very narrow opening through which you can squeeze some air. The first sound in the word *see* is a fricative.

3. *Glides* are consonant sounds you make while you're moving your articulators from one position to another. You can hear and feel the motion. The first sound in the word *yes* is a glide. Say it slowly to feel the gliding motion.

4. *Nasals* are just as the name suggests. You produce the nasals by lowering the soft palate and blocking the oral cavity with the lips or the tongue. You then let the air go out the nostrils. The first and last sounds in the word *man* are nasals.

5. *Lateral* sounds (English has only one) are produced by dropping the sides of the tongue and allowing the air to leave by the sides of the mouth. The first and last sounds in the word *lull* are laterals.

6. *Affricates* are really consonant combinations. The two English affricates are formed by joining together a voiceless plosive with a voiceless fricative, and a voiced plosive with a voiced fricative. The first and last sounds in the word *charge* are affricates.

You'll learn the method of articulation in more detail when you read Chapters 8 and 9 on consonants and vowels.

Vowels

What are the vowels of spoken English? Your first impulse is probably to say that the vowels are "a, e, i, o, u, and sometimes y." Wrong! Those are, unfortunately, the vowels of *written* English. We don't name the vowels of spoken English to separate them from the consonants; instead, we define them by how they are produced. *The vowels of spoken English are speech sounds produced without obstruction of the breathstream by the articulators.* Here's an example: open wide and say *ahhh.* You'll notice that the breathstream is not blocked at all.

Classification of Vowels

We'll also use three factors to classify the vowels. They are *height of the tongue, the place of production,* and *muscle tension.* Let's briefly explain each one, and you can look at the vowel chart (Figure 7-1) as we go along.

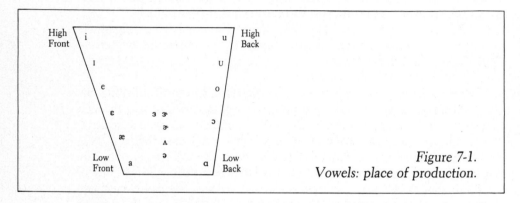

Figure 7-1.
Vowels: place of production.

Height of the Tongue

You raise your tongue to different heights to create different vowel sounds. Say the words *see* and *saw.* You should be able to feel your mouth opening for the word *saw.* That's because *saw* has a lower tongue position than *see.*

Place of Production

"Place" really refers to the part of the tongue primarily responsible for producing a particular vowel—the front, middle, or back. The vowel in *see* is made with the front of the tongue; the vowel in *saw* is produced with the back of the tongue.

Muscle Tension

The tension of the tongue muscles also affects vowel production. Try this: place the thumb and forefinger of one hand lightly on your neck above the larynx. Swallow. You should be able to feel muscle contractions. Keeping your fingers in the same place, say the words *see* and *sit*. The vowel in *see* is tense, so you can probably feel the tongue muscles contracting. The vowel in *sit* is lax (no tension) so you won't feel the muscles contracting as much.

Diphthongs

A diphthong is a *vowel blend;* two vowels are blended together and said in such a way that the sound begins with one vowel and ends with the other. You use a smooth, gliding motion, and although two vowels are used, the resulting diphthong is perceived as one sound. The sound that follows the initial consonant in the word *time* is an example of a diphthong.

Phonetic Transcription

Now it's time for you to begin practicing phonetic transcription. At the beginning you'll frequently feel frustrated; it will take a while for you to train yourself to hear the fine differences between sounds and to stop thinking of sounds as being letters. After all, you never had to do it before. Start with the basic transcription list that follows. Have someone read the words aloud to you, or listen to a tape recording. Transcribe what you actually hear, not what you think *should* be said. Don't write what you hear in English spelling; you'll only confuse the visual and auditory inputs. When you're ready, move on to short phrases and simple sentences and, finally, complex sentences and longer utterances.

WORDS FOR PHONETIC TRANSCRIPTION

STANDARD	WORD	ANSWER
[pæt]	1. pat	
[bot]	2. boat	
[flæt]	3. flat	
[rop]	4. rope	
[tu]	5. two	
[ist]	6. east	
[rum]	7. room	
[dɔg]	8. dog	
[fɛd]	9. fed	
[snek]	10. snake	
[græs]	11. grass	
[foʊn]	12. phone	
[θɔt]	13. thought	
[ðɪs]	14. this	
[baðɚ]	15. bother	
[θɪŋk]	16. think	
[ɔfʊl]	17. awful	
[reɪz]	18. raise	
[bʊk]	19. book	
[taɪɚ]	20. tire	
[tʃɝtʃ]	21. church	
[dʒʌdʒ]	22. judge	
[ɛmbəsi]	23. embassy	
[ʍiəl]	24. wheel	
[jɛloʊ]	25. yellow	
[læfɪŋ]	26. laughing	
[frɛnd]	27. friend	
[θʌm]	28. thumb	
[pɛnz]	29. pens	
[keɪdʒ]	30. cage	
[vɪʒən]	31. vision	
[beɪʒ]	32. beige	

Fold left side of page over to meet dashed line.

WORD	ANSWER	STANDARD
33. machines	_____	[məʃinz]
34. cruise	_____	[kruz]
35. shouted	_____	[ʃaʊtəd]
36. Chicago	_____	[ʃɪkɑgo]
37. relative	_____	[rɛlətɪv]
38. boiler	_____	[bɔɪlɚ]
39. oyster	_____	[ɔɪstɚ]
40. English	_____	[ɪŋglɪʃ]
41. laundry	_____	[lɔndri]
42. downtown	_____	[daʊntaʊn]
43. calm	_____	[kɑm]
44. upper	_____	[ʌpɚ]
45. hamburger	_____	[hæmbɚgɚ]
46. early	_____	[ɝli]
47. arrive	_____	[əɹaɪv]
48. rather	_____	[ræðɚ]
49. under	_____	[ʌndɚ]
50. foil	_____	[fɔɪl]
51. sound	_____	[saʊnd]
52. shave	_____	[ʃeɪv]
53. jumbojet	_____	[dʒʌmbodʒɛt]
54. shoes	_____	[ʃuz]
55. choice	_____	[tʃɔɪs]
56. flounder	_____	[flaʊndɚ]
57. difficult	_____	[dɪfəkʌlt]
58. exit	_____	[ɛksət]
59. balance	_____	[bæləns]
60. underneath	_____	[ʌndɚniθ]
61. Olympics	_____	[əlɪmpəks]
62. basketball	_____	[bæskətbɔl]
63. magazine	_____	[mægəzin]
64. computer	_____	[kəmpjutɚ]
65. tournament	_____	[tɝnəmənt]
66. carwax	_____	[kɑɚwæks]

Fold right side of page over to meet dashed line.

Diction:
The Consonants

On the following pages you'll find all the exercises you'll need to work on the consonant sounds. We've arranged them in the following order:

		PLOSIVES		
		vs	v	
Bilabial (both lips)		[p]	[b]	page 124
Labio-dental (lip-teeth)				
Lingua-dental (tongue-teeth)				
Lingua-alveolar (tongue-gum ridge)		[t]	[d]	page 131
Lingua-palatal (tongue-palate)				
Lingua-velar (tongue-soft palate)		[k]	[g]	page 143
Glottal (vocal folds)				

[p]   [b]
pat   boat

Sample: [p] PAT WAS VERY HAPPY.
        [b] THE BOY WAS IN THE RUBBER BOAT.

Spellings: *p* as in *pat*   *b* as in *boat*
            pp as in *happy*   *bb* as in *rubber*

Description

[p] and [b] are cognate sounds; [p] is a voiceless plosive, [b] is voiced. You produce them by stopping the airstream with your lips, building up pressure, and suddenly releasing the air.

☐ *Production:* [p] ☐

1. Put your lips together; press them fairly firmly closed.
2. Build up air pressure in your mouth; don't let any air escape through your nose. Keep your teeth slightly apart.
3. Allow the air pressure to force your lips apart making an audible explosion of air.

☐ *Production:* [b] ☐

1. Follow all the steps for [p], but start to produce voice at the same time that your lips close.
2. Don't press the lips as firmly or hold them together as long as you did for [p].

Problems

[p] and [b] are sounds you learned to produce with very little difficulty. The problems that exist with these sounds are usually minor and are corrected quite easily.

Problem 1. Confusion of [p] and [b]

Sometimes people, especially nonnative speakers, may voice the voiceless sound, and vice versa. This turns the [p] into a [b] and the [b] into a [p]. Check your production by trying the following contrast drill.

☐ *Contrast Drill for* [p] *and* [b] ☐

Say the words in the following lists aloud. First read down the list of [p] words, making sure you don't feel or hear voice. Then read down the list of [b] words, this time listening and feeling for voice. For the last step, read across, contrasting pairs of words—the first word voiceless, the second voiced.

[p]	[b]	[p]	[b]
pat	bat	lap	lab
pet	bet	rope	robe
pie	by	rip	rib
pen	Ben	staple	stable
pond	bond	rapid	rabid
cap	cab	napped	nabbed

Problem 2. Fricative [p]

If you don't press your lips together firmly enough, [p] loses its explosive quality and sounds rather like an [f]. To avoid this, make sure your lips touch each other firmly and completely, leaving no gaps that can let air escape. Also, don't let the air out until you've built up sufficient pressure to make a strong, sudden sound. As you read the Level 1 drills, feel for lip pressure and closure.

Problem 3. Fricative [b]

This problem occurs most often with people whose first language is Spanish. Their pronunciation of *berry* may sound like *very*. This is because Spanish has a phoneme that is a bilabial fricative that sounds rather like [v]. If you make this substitution, feel for firm lip pressure when you read the practice words.

Problem 4. Stress

When [p] and [b] are followed by stressed vowels, you must make a strong plosive sound. You should be able to feel the air on your hand if you hold it about two inches in front of your mouth and say *pie*. But when an unstressed vowel follows, the [p] and [b] won't be as strong. They are also weaker when they are followed by [l], [r], [s], and [t]. The Level 2 practice words will give you some of these combinations to work on.

Level 1 Drills for [p]

□ *Practice Words for* [p] □

Say the words in the following lists slowly and clearly. Listen carefully, and also feel for the right degree of lip pressure. Don't voice the [p]; there are no

[b] words in this list. The words in the Middle list all have a stressed [p]. Don't overdo the final [p].

Beginning	Middle	End
pea	Japan	seep
pin	unpaid	tip
pig	appear	dip
pen	upon	step
pay	upend	tape
pat	apology	tap
punt	superior	up
pearl	appoint	cup
pot	impact	top
paw	repel	mop
poke	teapot	hope
push	opponent	stop
pool	opinion	loop

□ *Practice Phrases for* [p] □

Say the following phrases slowly.

pig pen	stop sign
stew pot	pay day
step up	tea cup

□ *Practice Sentences for* [p] □

Say the following sentences slowly but easily. Don't overdo it. Read them a number of times, and, if you can, have someone listen to you.

1. They were like two *peas* in a *pod*.
2. I *hope* you'd like a *piece* of *pie*.
3. *Stop* the *tape* when you reach the *loop*.
4. The *pen* had a *poor* writing *point*.
5. The *plumber* had to let the water *seep* out of the *pipe*.
6. *Step up* the *pace*.
7. I *put* my money in the *pot* on *pay* day.
8. My *opponent apologized* for *pushing* me.
9. *Pat* tried to *tip-toe* home after his *nightcap* at the *party*.
10. In my *opinion*, *pearls* come from *superior* oysters.

Level 2 Drills for [p]

At this level you'll find words that are slightly more difficult to say, usually because they are blends of [pl], [pr], or [pt]. Make sure to produce the [p], but be aware that the stress will vary; emphasize the [p] only slightly in [pl] and [pr], and don't give any emphasis to the [p] in [pt]. Notice that when *ed* follows *p*, it's pronounced [pt]. For example, *wrapped* is pronounced the same as *rapt*.

□ *Practice Words* □

Try saying the words in the following lists slowly and clearly.

[pl] (All Positions)	[pr] (Beginning and Middle)	[pt] Middle and End)
please	priest	crept
place	praise	except
pleasant	press	slept
plastic	prank	rapt
plow	proud	wrapped
hopeless	progress	concept
explicit	repressed	hoped
staple	represent	popped
apply	appropriate	leaped
ample	opera	topped
		soaped
		optical
		cryptic
		mapped
		septic
		peptic

□ *Practice Sentences for* [p] □

Follow the directions given for Level 1 Sentences.

1. I was pleased to represent the opera company.
2. We planted plastic tulips in the spring.
3. You must display your pool pass.
4. There was an ample supply of press cards.
5. He plowed the pea patch under this spring.

6. It was hopeless to try to repair the stapler.
7. Practical jokes are not appropriate in this place.
8. The patient dropped his toothpaste in the water pitcher.
9. The zookeepers opposed the sheepshearing.
10. He unwrapped all the presents except one.

Level 1 Drills for [b].

☐ Practice Words for [b] ☐

Say the words in the following lists slowly and carefully. Listen closely and correct your production until you are sure you have a clear and correct sound. Remember that the [b] should have slightly less pressure than the [p]. Remember, too, that [b] is a voiced sound.

Beginning	Middle	End
beam	about	rib
beat	abound	fib
bed	above	cab
bake	cabin	ebb
bait	maybe	web
bad	obey	nab
bag	fabulous	tab
band	nobody	tub
bond	hobby	tube
Boston	abdomen	swab
bull	ribbon	stab
boon	webbing	mob

☐ Practice Phrases for [b] ☐

Say the following phrases slowly.

bunch of bananas	bed and board
black innertube	big hot tub
bank book	fabulous backhand

☐ Practice Sentences for [b] ☐.

Say the following sentences slowly but easily. Don't overdo it. Read them a number of times, and, if you can, have someone listen to you.

DICTION: THE CONSONANTS

1. *Debbie* rode her *bike* to the *bank*.
2. *Bob's cabin* had a *beamed* ceiling.
3. I couldn't get the *bass* to take the *bait*.
4. The *band* won the red *ribbon*.
5. I went on *board* the *banana boat* in *Boston*.

Level 2 Drills for [b]

□ *Practice Words* □

The [b] words in the following lists contain various blends and combinations. Also, some of the words will have [p] for contrast. Try the words, saying them slowly.

Beginning	Middle	End
breathe	nimble	crab
bridge	abbreviate	bib
bleak	cheeseburger	describe
blend	December	icecube
belt	labor	sparerib
balloons	mailbox	disturb
because	observing	prescribe
billion	strobelight	scrub
bundle	subterranean	curb
bump	probable	probe
blimp	pebble	crib

□ *Practice Sentences for* [b] □

Read the following sentences slowly. Read them a number of times.

1. They made a billion balloons in December.
2. The biscuits were served with a bowl of butter.
3. They had barbecued ribs on the boat.
4. There's a bundle of mail in the box by the curb.
5. The view from the bridge was very bleak.

Level 3 Drills for [b]

Now you can try sentences that combine difficult blends and also offer [p] and [b] words for contrast.

Read the sentences that follow. Don't overdo it; read them slowly but easily a number of times.

1. They probably had icecubes in the tub.
2. The party at Pebble Beach disturbed the neighbors.
3. We had crab cakes and boiled lobster at the clambake.
4. All the parrot could say was, "Pretty boy, pretty boy."
5. Overall, probing questions were asked by the Labor party.

[t]   [d]
top   dog

Sample: [t] <u>T</u>HOMAS LIKE<u>D</u> <u>T</u>O WALK <u>TW</u>O <u>T</u>IGH<u>T</u> ROPES.
[d] THE <u>D</u>OG <u>D</u>IGS FOR BONES IN THE YAR<u>D</u>.

Spellings: *t*   as in *top*   *d* as in *dog*
tw as in *two*   *dd* as in *ladder*
th as in *Thomas*   *ed* as in *poured*
ed as in *liked*
ght as in *tight*
tt as in *tattoo*
pt as in *ptomaine*

Description

[t] and [d] are cognate sounds. [t] is a voiceless plosive. You produce it by blocking the airstream with the tongue and upper gum ridge, building up air pressure and suddenly releasing it. [d] is produced in the same way. Just add voice as you produce it.

□ *Production:* [t] □

1. Narrow the tongue and place it against your upper gum ridge. Make sure the sides of the tongue touch the sides of the upper molars. Lower your jaw slightly, keeping your teeth apart.

2. Hold your tongue firmly in place against the gum ridge. Force some air from your lungs and allow pressure to build up behind your tongue.

3. Let the air pressure overcome your tongue and force it away from the gum ridge. This way, the air escapes quickly and goes over the dropped tongue and between the teeth.

☐ *Production:* [d] ☐

Follow Steps 1 and 2, and start Step 3. As the air pressure begins to force your tongue away from the gum ridge, add voice. Try to time your voicing so that it begins at exactly the same time that your tongue starts to leave the gum ridge.

☐ *Contrast Drill for* [t] *and* [d] ☐

Slowly read the following pairs of words aloud. Remember, [t] is voiceless and [d] is voiced. Try to feel and hear the difference.

[t]	[d]	[t]	[d]	[t]	[d]
tea	– dee	kitty	– kiddy	feet	– feed
tip	– dip	rated	– raided	hit	– hid
ten	– den	writing	– riding	let	– led
tan	– dan	butted	– budded	sat	– sad
tie	– die	knotted	– nodded	right	– ride
tuck	– duck			cot	– cod
toe	– doe			shoot	– shooed

Problems

Problem 1. Dentalization

[t] and [d] are tongue–gum ridge sounds. Some people tend to dentalize the sounds, that is, they make the sounds on the back of the upper front teeth. Look closely at your mouth in a mirror while you say the word *tea.* If you can see the sides of your tongue peeking around your upper incisors, you're probably dentalizing. You can hear a difference, too. A dentalized [t] sounds hissy and slightly "wet."

Place the tip of your tongue lightly on the upper gum ridge. (The exact spot is where you burn yourself when you bite into a piece of steaming hot pizza.) Don't press too hard; if you do, the tongue spreads out and overlaps onto the teeth. Now say the following words aloud, reading across the page. Alternate saying the words, first dentally and then nondentally. (Say the words in parentheses dentally.)

(tea)	tea	(tea)	tea	(tea)	tea	(tea)	tea	(tea)	tea
(tap)	tap	(tap)	tap	(tap)	tap	(tap)	tap	(tap)	tap
(top)	top	(top)	top	(top)	top	(top)	top	(top)	top
(toe)	toe	(toe)	toe	(toe)	toe	(toe)	toe	(toe)	toe
(too)	too	(too)	too	(too)	too	(too)	too	(too)	too
(die)	die	(die)	die	(die)	die	(die)	die	(die)	die
(day)	day	(day)	day	(day)	day	(day)	day	(day)	day
(do)	do	(do)	do	(do)	do	(do)	do	(do)	do
(dog)	dog	(dog)	dog	(dog)	dog	(dog)	dog	(dog)	dog

Use a light touch with your tongue, and return it precisely to the same place each time. Listen carefully as you say the words. Try to eliminate the "wetness."

Problem 2. Fricative [t]

When you make the [t], don't press your tongue too tightly against the gum ridge. Sometimes this may result in the normally plosive [t] sounding like a fricative or, more accurately, like a combination plosive and fricative. For example, the word *too* [tu] might sound like [tsu]. So when you make the sound [t], make sure there is a clean, sharp break that you can feel as your tongue leaves the gum ridge.

The same problem occurs when [t] and [d] are blended with [r], as in *drew* and *true*. We'll cover that in the Level 3 drills.

Problem 3. Omission of [d] and [t] in the Middles and Ends of Words

This problem is most common when [d] or [t] are preceded by other consonant sounds. For example, if you omit the final [t], the word *past* becomes *pass*. This generally occurs simply because your tongue doesn't get up quite high enough to produce the sound; you *under*articulate. You can work on this problem when you have progressed to Level 2 drills. Say the words slowly and carefully. Make sure you hear every sound that's supposed to be there.

Problem 4. Substitution of [d] for [t]

This substitution occurs most often in words like *city, butter, metal,* in which the [t] receives secondary stress. It's very easy, in words like those, to simply carry over your voicing from the vowel that precedes [t] to the vowel that follows. This is one of the most pervasive nonstandard substitutions in our language. We'll cover it in Level 3.

Level 1 Drills for [t]

☐ *Practice Words for* [t] ☐

Say the words in the following lists slowly and clearly, reading down each column. Start with the Beginning words. These are short, precise sounds; don't hold them longer than necessary. Listen carefully, and correct your production until you are satisfied that the sound is clear and correct.

Beginning	*Middle*	*End*
team	guitar	eat
tin	after	pit
tame	enter	gate
ten	attack	bet
tank	alter	fat
ton	utter	but
top	until	pot
talk	autumn	caught
toe	atone	coat
took	intend	put
too	entire	cute

Now read the End column again. Make sure not to overcorrect the [t]. When this sound is the last in a word, it usually is not aspirated. That is, you don't make it with a puff of air.

☐ *Practice Phrases for* [t] ☐

Say the following phrases slowly.

ten cats	took a coat
two tons	tin pot
until autumn	top team
took a bet	a top in the pit
until we eat	after he was caught

□ *Practice Sentences for* [t] □

Say the following sentences slowly, but easily. Don't overdo it. Read them a number of times, and, if you can, have someone listen to you.

1. I saw *ten cats* sleeping on his *coat.*
2. Worry *about* the *tip* of the iceberg *later.*
3. He was *caught after* the *attack.*
4. They *took ten tons* from the *pit.*
5. *It* was *fate that* we *met.*
6. I *don't want to talk* now.
7. I *put* the *fishtank* away *until later.*
8. His car was *towed* away from the *meter.*
9. The girl who plays the *guitar* is *cute.*
10. The *team took bets* as they *left* the *gate.*

Level 2 Drills for [t]

Words that end in *ed* such as *raced, banned,* and *feasted* can sometimes cause confusion as to whether the last sound should be a [t] or a [d] and whether it should be part of a separate syllable or just added to the previous one. Here are some general rules that may help:

• If the sound preceding *ed* is voiceless, pronounce the *d* as a [t]. **Example:** *wrapped* [wræpt]

• If the sound preceding *ed* is voiced, pronounce the *d* as [d]. **Example:** *banned* [bænd]

• If the sound preceding *ed* is a [d] or a [t], the *ed* is pronounced as a separate syllable, [əd]. **Example:** *patted* [pætəd]

□ *Practice Words for* [t] □

Say the words in the following columns slowly and clearly, reading down the columns starting with Beginning. These words have slightly more difficult combinations to produce; also, you'll have to remember the rules about "ed."

Beginning	Middle	End
telephone	sister	raced
tweezer	faster	fished
twins	forester	trust
term	rotate	passed

(*Lists continue on p. 136*)

Beginning	Middle	End
tall	brighter	brushed
tongue	western	receipt
tangle	sooty	roofed
terrain	footing	brought

□ *Practice Sentences for* [t] □

Say the following sentences carefully, but don't exaggerate the [t].

1. The sun grew brighter in the western sky.
2. His sister sent the guitar by air freight.
3. The tangle of wires brushed against the telephone pole.
4. The forester called after the storm had passed.
5. He lost his footing on the loose stones.
6. He brought his receipt to the store.
7. The twins fished until twilight.
8. Sometimes the tongue is faster than the eye.
9. I placed a lot of trust in the system.
10. It was a twelve-week term.

Level 3 Drills for [t]

Sometimes the combination of [t] plus [s] or the [sts] combination can be difficult. If you have problems with these, see [s], Level 3, page 176.

Problem 1. Substitution of [d] for [t]

The most common problem with [t] is the tendency for people to voice it when it is not in the syllable receiving the primary stress, as in the words *batter, butter, bitter, sitting,* and *party.* The result is a substitution of [d] for [t]. To avoid this, use a light touch of your tongue on the gum ridge, and be sure to stop voicing for the brief instant that it takes for you to produce the [t]. Try the following:

□ *Production Drill* □

Read the words in the following lists, reading across the page. Gradually close the gap between the syllables, and reduce the amount of [h].

bat . . . her	bat . . her	bat . her	bat her	batter
but . . . her	but . . her	but . her	but her	butter
bit . . . her	bit . . her	bit . her	bit her	bitter
kit . . . he	kit . . he	kit . he	kit he	kitty
let . . . her	let . . her	let . her	let her	letter

□ *Contrast Drill for* [d] *and* [t] □

Say the following pairs of words slowly. Try to feel and hear the difference between the [d] and [t].

batter	— badder	bitter	— bidder
writing	— riding	wetting	— wedding
rating	— raiding	heating	— heeding
shutter	— shudder	latter	— ladder

□ *Practice Words for* [d] *for* [t] *substitution* □

batter	bitter	butter
writing	rating	wetting
shutter	latter	heating
sitting	pretty	city
letter	suited	pity
twenty	thirty	forty
fifty	sixty	seventy
patted	petting	kitty
sooty	smarter	litter

Now take the words above and others you can find to practice with, and make up short, simple sentences. Ask your instructor or a member of your class to listen to you and to be especially aware if you are overcorrecting.

Problem 2. [t] Followed by [n] or [l]

This is an especially difficult combination of sounds to deal with because it occurs so frequently. There's no mystery about it, though, and it's not hard to correct. Typical words are *little, bottle, kitten.*

The trick is this: don't let your tongue move away from the gum ridge after making the [t]. When it's followed by an [l], you simply hold up the tip and let the sides drop, exploding the air laterally. When it's followed by an [n], drop the soft palate and let the air come out the nose. Be careful not to substitute [d] for [t]. Here are some practice words:

little	bottle	tattle
battle	cattle	rattle
petal	metal	kettle
glottal	scuttle	total
kitten	mitten	bitten
button	mutton	cotton
mountain	fountain	certain

Make sure you're not producing a *glottal stop* instead of a [t]. A glottal stop is not really a sound at all. You make it simply by stopping the air flow momentarily with the vocal folds. Try it with the word *little*. Leave out the [t] in the middle and say "li/le." That's a glottal stop. It's not a [t] but our minds perceive it as one.

Problem 3. [tθ] or [tð] Combinations

There is a time when the standard way to produce the [t] is on the teeth instead of the gum ridge. That's when it's followed by [θ or ð], as in *hit the ball* or *at the game*. Just make sure you say the [θ/ð] after the [t].
  Try these phrases:

hit the ball	at the game	at third
bright thought	put out the light	sent that
went through	eight-thirty	sit there

Problem 4. [kt] Combination

When the [kt] combination occurs at the end of a word, we sometimes tend to omit the [t]. Try the following words. Make sure to say the [t].

correct	attract	tricked
precinct	direct	fact
select	licked	blocked

Problem 5. [tr] Blend

We mentioned the [tr] blend in Problem 2. Fricative [t] (p. 133). If you let your tongue slide back off the gum ridge on its way to making the [r], it sounds as though you're adding [tʃ], and making the plosive [t] into a fricative. Say the following words slowly and carefully. Do you hear a [t] or a [tʃ]?

treat   trip   true   trap   train

□ *Production Drill* □

Read the words in the following lists aloud, from left to right. Gradually close the gap between the syllables as you go.

tuh . . . rue	tuh . . rue	tuh . rue	tuhrue	true
tuh . . . rip	tuh . . rip	tuh . rip	tuhrip	trip
tuh . . . rap	tuh . . rap	tuh . rap	tuhrap	trap

□ *Practice Words for* [tr] □

true	entrust
trip	detract
trap	entrap
treat	entreat
troop	entropy
track	actress
train	electric

□ *Practice Sentences for* [tr] □

1. The electric train went off the track.
2. She was a true actress.
3. I trust you had a safe trip?

Level 1 Drills for [d]

Remember, almost all the misarticulations that can happen with [t] can also happen with [d]. This might be a good time to reread Problems 1 through 3 at the beginning of this section. Do the contrast drill and the drill for dentalization.

Here are Level 1 practice words. Take your time with them; say them slowly and clearly. Listen carefully and correct your production until you are satisfied that the sound you are making is correct. These are short, precise sounds; don't hold them too long.

□ *Practice Words for* [d] □

Beginning	Middle	End
deep	body	and
date	candy	reed
den	under	bid
dip	cider	add
damp	wedding	red
dog	bidding	ride
day	bedding	rod
dumb	India	code
doctor	adding	hood
dive	radio	food

□ *Practice Phrases for* [d] □

dead dog	wedding day	red riding hood
bed and board	dive under	damp dock

□ *Practice Sentences for* [d] □

1. They *had cider* on their *wedding day.*
2. Her hair was *damp under* her *hood.*
3. The *doctor ended* the *bidding* for the *dog.*
4. It was *dumb* to *dive under* the *dock.*
5. They broke the *code* by *adding* the *dates.*

□ *Practice Drills for* [d] □

It's very easy to omit [d] when it follows another consonant or comes at the end of a word. When you read the following list of words aloud, make sure you put a [d] every place it should be. Be especially careful at the ends of words; make an extra effort to voice the sound so you don't substitute [t] for [d], but at the same time, don't overcorrect it.

□ *Practice Words for* [d] □

Beginning	Middle	End
diesel	building	leaned
dare	louder	old
darn	padlock	seemed
dawn	hydrant	played
dank	headlight	poured

□ *Practice Sentences for* [d] □

Say the following sentences slowly and carefully, but don't exaggerate the [d].

1. Don ordered a padlock for the barn door.
2. Dawn poured oil in the old pan.
3. I turned off the headlights at the end of the road.
4. He dared to say it louder.
5. I found some diesel fuel after daybreak.

Level 3 Drills for [d]

The difficulties at this level occur primarily with the [dr] blend and omitting [d] before [z], as in *hands.* Let's take the omission problem first.

□ *Practice Words for* [dz] □

Say the words below carefully. Try to produce one sound that combines [d] and [z] together.

hands	bands	stands
reeds	heeds	beads

Notice that these words all end in [z]. Make sure you're saying the [d] firmly and pronouncing the [z]. Let's try some more.

seeds	feeds	leads
bids	kids	lids
raids	maids	fades
lends	bends	sends
woods	hoods	shoulds

□ *Production Drill for* [dr] □

Use the same technique you used for the [tr] blend. Read the words below aloud, from left to right. Make a clean break between the tongue and the gum ridge. Don't slide the tongue along the palate. As you read, gradually close the gap between the syllables.

duh . . . rue	duh . . rue	duh . rue	duhrue	drew
duh . . . rip	duh . . rip	duh . rip	duhrip	drip
duh . . . raw	duh . . raw	duh . raw	duhraw	draw

□ *Practice Words for* [dr] □

dream	adrift	draw	hundred
drip	adroit	drain	droop
drape	hydrant	drop	drag

Another problem occurs frequently when [n] follows [d]. Use the same technique you used for [tn], and leave your tongue tip touching the gum ridge for [n]. This technique also works for [d] followed by [l].

□ *Practice Words for* [dn] *and* [dl] □

hidden	student	rodent
sudden	sadden	shouldn't
ridden	widen	hadn't
riddle	middle	paddle
dwindle	idle	poodle

[k]　　[g]
key　　　go

Sample:　[k] THE QUIET LOCKSMITH WAS THE PLAY'S KEY CHARACTER.
[g] YOUR GRADES GO DOWN WITH VAGUE GUESSES ON EXAMS.

Spellings:　*k*　as in *key*　　　　*g*　as in *go*
c　as in *cat*　　　　*gg*　as in *egg*
ck　as in *lock*　　　*gu*　as in *guess*
cc　as in *occur*　　*gue* as in *plague*
ch　as in *echo*　　*x*　as in *exam* (with [z])
qu　as in *queen*
que as in *plaque*

Description

[k] and [g] are cognate sounds; [k] is voiceless, but [g] is voiced. They are plosives that you produce by blocking the breathstream with the tongue and soft palate, building up pressure, and suddenly releasing it.

□ *Production:* [k] □

1. Open your mouth slightly, keeping your teeth apart.
2. Raise the back of your tongue and press it against the soft palate.
3. Build up air pressure behind the tongue. Don't let any air escape through your nose.
4. Let the air pressure force your tongue away from the palate. Make sure the release is sudden—an explosion.

□ *Production:* [g] □

1. Follow the same steps as for [k]. Produce voice as the tongue begins to block the airstream.

Problems

Problem 1. Confusion of [k] and [g]

This is really a problem in voicing. It usually occurs as a simple error of pronunciation, or it could be due to failure to voice the [g]. The following contrast drill should help you distinguish between the two sounds.

□ *Contrast Drill for* [k] *and* [g] □

First read down the column of [k] words. Then read down the column of [g] words. The last step is to read pairs of words across. Read slowly and carefully, and make sure to hear and feel the difference between voiceless [k] and voiced [g].

[k]	[g]	[k]	[g]
Kate	gate	sacking	sagging
came	game	lacking	lagging
cape	gape	lock	log
cap	gap	tuck	tug
cash	gash	pick	pig
cut	gut	duck	dug
coast	ghost	rick	rig
coat	goat		

Problem 2. Weak or fricative [k] and [g]

These two sounds require a firm and complete closure between the back of the tongue and the soft palate. If you don't have complete closure, you produce a weak or almost fricative sound. In a similar problem, people sometimes allow air to enter the nasal passages, nasalizing the sound. If you have either of these problems, try the following Production Drill.

□ *Production Drill* □

[k] and [g] need strong, active articulation. Say the following sounds, reading across. Say them forcefully. Try to get as much air out on [k] and [g] as you do on [p] and [t].

[p . . . t . . . k . . . g]
[p . . . t . . . k . . . g]
[p . . . t . . . k . . . g]

Now try the following. Say [k] three times as strongly as you can, then say the word that follows.

[k k k] cat [k k k] cat [k k k] cat
[k k k] cap [k k k] cap [k k k] cap

Now try the same thing with [g].

[g g g] gap [g g g] gap [g g g] gap
[g g g] gab [g g g] gab [g g g] gab

Problem 3. Pronunciation of the letter x

Many people become confused about how to pronounce *x*; whether it's a [ks] or a [gz]. Usually they fail to voice the [gz]. This won't happen if you know a couple of simple rules:

- When *x* is followed by a stressed vowel, it's pronounced [gz]. **Example:** *exam* [ɛgzæm]. (In the word *exit* you say pronounced [ɛksɪt].)
- When *x* is followed by a pronounced consonant or an unstressed vowel, it's pronounced [ks], as in *extra* [ɛkstrə] and *exit*.
- When the word ends in *x*, it's pronounced [ks], as in *wax* [wæks].

In other words, the only time you pronounce *x* as [gz] is when it's followed by a stressed vowel. Here are some words in which the *x* is a [gz]:

exact	examine	example
exist	exert	exempt
executive	exuberant	exhaust

Here are some words in which the *x* is a [ks]:

ax	exit	except
mix	experiment	explain
box	exciting	excellent

Problem 4. Omission of [k] in the cc spelling

Don't omit [k] in words such as *accept*. Although *cc* can be pronounced [k], as in *occur*, in words like *accept* the *cc* indicates a [k] followed by an [s]. Try these words:

accept   accident   access
accessory   accent   accelerate

Level 1 Drills for [k]

□ *Practice Words for* [k] □

Say the words in the following lists slowly and carefully. Correct your production until you are satisfied that you are producing a firm, clear sound. Start with the Beginning words.

Beginning	Middle	End
key	because	beak
kit	picking	pick
cape	aching	make
chemistry	beckon	neck
cattle	backhand	pack
come	ducking	buck
chorus	talking	walk
common	knocking	dock
coat	hokey	broke
cushion	hooking	took

□ *Practice Phrases for* [k] □

atomic attack	common cause
back ache	echo echo
Cape Cod	a buck a book

□ *Practice Sentences for* [k] □

1. I left the *cookbook* in the *car.*
2. Put on your *pack* and *take* a *walk* to the *dock.*
3. I *called* about the *duck decoys.*
4. I nearly *broke* my *neck* surfing at *Cape Cod.*
5. The *key* nearly *broke* in the *lock.*
6. She needed a *cushion* for her *aching back.*
7. The engine *knock* was *caused* by the low *octane* gas.

Level 2 Drills for [k]

☐ *Practice Words for* [k] ☐

Say the words in the following lists carefully and slowly. Make sure you don't omit the [k] at the end position, but don't overdo it.

Beginning	Middle	End
cool	basket	look
call	looking	milk
car	blacken	thank
catch	locker	like
calf	liquor	park
couch	raccoon	work
Kansas	Alaska	fork
carnival	lucky	shook
kilowatt	flicker	jerk
collision	tracking	historic

☐ *Practice Sentences for* [k] ☐

1. The broken bottle was in the liquor locker.
2. The carnival traveled from Kansas to Alaska.
3. I was lucky the milk didn't spill on the couch.
4. There's a lot of work for marketing consultants.
5. The road was blackened by the oil from the truck collision.
6. The cashier shook with fear after he caught the raccoon.
7. We had a continental breakfast in the park before work.

Level 3 Drills for [k]

Many people have problems with [k] when it is blended with certain other consonants such as [l], [r], and [s]. When you read the following words, try to produce the [k] blends as one sound; mesh them together, don't separate them.

☐ *Practice Words for* [k] ☐

[kl]	[kr]	[ks]
claim	crash	box
clasp	crate	ax

(*Lists continue on p. 148*)

[kl]	[kr]	[ks]
clash	crisp	hoax
cleared	crew	fix
cloth	crush	flex
clock	cross	Bronx
incline	concrete	excellent
enclose	recruit	fixture
inclement	democrat	mixture
buckle	sacrifice	expand
sickle	incredible	express
ankle	increase	axiom
circle	microfilm	excuse
icicle	incriminate	exercise
bicycle	accrue	exhale

□ *Practice Sentences for* [k] □

1. Excuse me, is this the express train to the Bronx?
2. He broke his bike when it didn't clear the curb.
3. His insurance rates increased after he filed his claims.
4. A cycle of breathing consists of one inhalation and one exhalation.
5. He hid the incriminating microfilm in the camera.
6. I couldn't close the clasp on the buckle.
7. Biking is an excellent form of exercise.
8. The new recruits made incredible sacrifices.
9. They cleared a circle on the incline.
10. The mixture expanded and spilled on the cloth.
11. I couldn't break through the crowd to the box seats.
12. He fixed the clock so that it worked fairly accurately.
13. He flexed his muscles as he picked up the ax.

Level 1 Drills for [g]

□ *Practice Words for* [g] □

Say the words in the following lists slowly and clearly. Listen carefully and correct your production until you are satisfied that the sound is clear and strong enough, but don't overdo it. Start with the Beginning words.

Beginning	Middle	End
go	again	beg
gave	began	big
get	dignify	bug
game	disgust	egg
gift	ignite	wig
gone	misguided	bag
guide	engage	fatigue
guess	navigate	vague

□ *Practice Phrases for* [g] □

begin again	going, going, gone
engagement gift	dog days
get a guide	guess what you get

□ *Practice Sentences for* [g] □

1. The *fog* made it difficult to *navigate*.
2. The *goat began* to butt the *dog*.
3. Please *give* me a soft-boiled *egg*.
4. He threw the *disgusting bug* in the *bag*.
5. I had to *beg* her to *go* to the *game*.

Level 2 Drills for [g]

□ *Practice Words for* [g] □

Say the words in the following lists carefully and slowly. Make sure to produce the [g] in each word. Be careful not to overdo the [g] in the end position.

Beginning	Middle	End
garden	figure	flag
gale	forget	leg
gauze	organ	snag
gear	sugar	smog
guilt	legal	vague
girth	regard	league

(*Lists continue on p. 150*)

Beginning	Middle	End
guard	buggy	frog
gamble	trigger	intrigue
garlic	hugging	monologue
gasket	vigorous	epilogue
gainful	elegant	smug
going	vagrant	underdog
gallon	signature	lug

□ *Practice Sentences for* [g] □

1. The vague statement of guilt had no legal standing.
2. He gambled that he wouldn't hit the trigger guard.
3. The garden was full of elegant forget-me-nots.
4. They shifted into first gear when the guard waved the yellow flag.
5. Their efforts against the smog began to bog down.

Level 3 Drills for [g]

Here are practice words for the blends [gl], [gr], and [gz]. Say them slowly as blends, not separating consonants.

□ *Practice Words for* [gl], [gr], *and* [gz] □

[gl]	[gr]	[gz]
gleam	grow	eggs
glass	gripe	nags
glitter	grass	tugs
glimpse	gross	rigs
anglo	agree	exact
aglow	engrave	exist
igloo	aground	example
angle	angry	exhausted
single	ingrate	executive

□ *Practice Words for* [gd] □

bagged	tagged	flagged
fatigued	shrugged	begged
snagged	bugged	rigged

□ *Practice Sentences for* [g] □

1. From this angle it was hard to see the gleam of light from the igloo.
2. You need fertile ground to grow grass.
3. I was exhausted from hunting for exact examples.
4. He shrugged even though his shirt was snagged.
5. The engraving glittered under the glass.

□ *Practice Sentences for* [k] *and* [g] □

1. I begged her not to put all her eggs in one basket.
2. They asked the guard to show them the executive quarters.
3. The angry captain let the boat go aground.
4. The rig was controlled by a single lever.
5. I asked for the exact name of the vanilla extract.
6. I flagged down a cab to go from the Bureau of Engraving to the Department of Agriculture.
7. Are you going to the groundbreaking ceremony?
8. A clove of garlic goes a long way.

FRICATIVES			
	vs	v	
Bilabial (both lips)			
Labio–dental (lip–teeth)	[f]	[v]	page 152
Lingua–dental (tongue–teeth)	[θ]	[ð]	page 160
Lingua–alveolar (tongue–gum ridge)	[s]	[z]	page 168
Lingua–palatal (tongue–palate)	[ʃ]	[ʒ]	page 180
Lingua–velar (tongue–soft palate)			
Glottal (vocal folds)	[h]		page 185

[f] [v]

four   very

Sample: [f] FOUR PHONE CALLS ARE ENOUGH.
             [v] IT WAS VERY HOT, OF COURSE.

Spellings: *f* as in *four*   *v* as in *very*
              ff as in *affair*   *f* (only in the word *of*)
              gh as in *enough*   *ph* (only in *Stephen*)
              ph as in *phone*
              lf as in *half*

Description

[f] and [v] are cognate sounds. [f] is voiceless, but [v] is voiced. They are fricative sounds that you produce by forcing the breathstream between your upper teeth and lower lip.

☐ *Production:* [f] ☐

1. Very lightly, rest the cutting edge of your upper front teeth against your lower lip.
2. Let your tongue rest against the floor of your mouth.
3. Start the breathstream moving, and force it between your lower lip and upper teeth. Don't allow any air to escape through your nose. Make sure you use a light touch. If you press too hard, not enough air comes through.

☐ *Production:* [v] ☐

1. Follow the same steps you used for [f]. As soon as you feel your teeth and lip touch, add voice.

Problems

Problem 1. Confusion of [f] and [v]

Native-born speakers of American English usually don't have many production problems with [f] and [v]. Some nonnative speakers, especially native

German speakers, may frequently confuse [f] and [v] or substitute [w] for [v]. The contrast drills below will help you eliminate such confusion.

☐ *Contrast Drill for* [f] *and* [v] ☐

Say the following words aloud. First read down the list of [f] words, making sure you don't hear or feel voice. Then read down the list of [v] words, this time listening and feeling for voice. For the last step, read across, contrasting pairs of words—the first word voiceless, the second voiced.

[f]	[v]	[f]	[v]
feel	veal	proof	prove
fine	vine	half	have
fast	vast	leaf	leave
fail	veil	surface	service
fan	van	rifle	rival
fat	vat	shuffle	shovel
safe	save		

☐ *Contrast Drill for* [v] *and* [w] ☐

Say the following words aloud. First read down the list of [v] words, making sure that you feel the contact between your upper teeth and your lower lip. Then, read down the list of [w] words, making sure that you can feel the pursing movement of the lips; you shouldn't make lip–teeth contact. For the last step, read across, contrasting pairs of words.

[v]	[w]	[v]	[w]
vest	west	vent	went
vet	wet	vie	why
vine	wine	vane	wane
veil	wail	verse	worse
vaults	waltz		

Problem 2. Substitution of [b] for [v]

This occurs most often with native Spanish speakers. For example, the word *very* would become *berry.* Try the contrast drill below if you have this substitution.

Say the following words aloud. First read down the list of [b] words, feeling the plosive quality of the sound. Next, read down the list of [v] words, making sure to feel that there is not a buildup of air resulting in a plosive sound. You should feel your teeth touching your lip, not both lips touching each other. For the last step, read across, contrasting pairs of words.

[b]	[v]	[b]	[v]
ban	van	bend	vend
berry	very	saber	saver
beer	veer	dub	dove
bile	vile	robe	rove
best	vest	curb	curve
bow	vow	curbing	curving
boat	vote		

Problem 3. Omission of [v]

This is a problem shared by many native speakers. There is a tendency to omit the [v] in the word *of* or to assimilate it into the next word. There is also a tendency to omit the [v] when it's followed by a word beginning with a consonant. You'll work on this problem in the Level 2 Phrases.

Level 1 Drills for [f]

□ *Practice Words for* [f] □

Say the words in the following lists slowly and clearly. Listen carefully and correct your production until you're satisfied that the sound is clear. Remember, [f] is voiceless. Start with the Beginning words.

Beginning	Middle	End
feet	effect	beef
fee	infect	chief
fit	confident	if
fin	infection	miff
fate	headphone	laugh
fare	defend	safe
fine	jiffy	puff

(*Lists continue on p. 155*)

Beginning	Middle	End
finger	offend	cough
foot	confide	cuff
photo	benefit	wife
funny	coffee	off
four	café	life

☐ *Practice Phrases for* [f] ☐

fifty-five	funny photos	face the facts
fine beef	off the cuff	safe by a foot

☐ *Practice Sentences for* [f] ☐

1. He was *six feet, four* inches tall.
2. My *life* story will make you *laugh*.
3. His *chief* complaint was that the *coffee* tasted *funny*.
4. I wonder *if* he paid the *photo fee*.
5. The loud *coughing offended* the singer.

Level 2 Drills for [f]

☐ *Practice Words for* [f] ☐

Beginning	Middle	End
face	afford	brief
fall	befall	bluff
fast	effort	grief
fault	breakfast	strife
first	wishful	giraffe
fold	default	strafe
Philip	daffodil	shelf
female	refuse	relief

☐ *Practice Phrases for* [f] ☐

Fran will forget	famous females	foolish Fred
fold first	fast fault	steadfast effort

1. The first fall went to Frank.
2. I put the daffodils on the shelf.
3. The female giraffe fell for the bluff.
4. I couldn't refuse a fast breakfast.
5. He could afford to make the effort to be brief.

Level 3 Drills for [f]

Here are practice words for four blends that can cause difficulty. They are [fl], [fr], [fs], and [ft]. Say them carefully, as one sound. Don't let any vowel sound creep in between the consonants in the blends.

□ *Practice Words for* [f] □

[fl]	[fr]	[fs]	[ft]
flake	free	beliefs	raft
floor	frog	skiffs	reefed
flunk	friend	reefs	laughed
flame	frost	graphs	beefed
flush	frenzy	laughs	left
inflexible	infringe	safes	staffed
cauliflower	afraid	chefs	after
sniffle	Afro	chafes	shafted
raffle	refreshment	calfs	rafted
			laughter
			safety

□ *Practice Sentences for* [f] □

1. His face grew flushed when he won the raffle.
2. I'm afraid I infringed on my friend.
3. He laughs at others' beliefs.
4. We reefed the sail on the raft in complete safety.
5. I left the snowflakes on the frosty shelf.

Level 1 Drills for [v]

□ *Practice Words for* [v] □

Say the words in the following lists slowly and clearly. Listen carefully and correct your production until you feel sure that the sound is clear and accurate. Try to start your voicing at the same time that your teeth touch your lip. Start with the Beginning words.

Beginning	*Middle*	*End*
vee	even	weave
victor	evict	give
vacate	paving	move
view	devote	wave
void	given	native
vent	event	pave
vitamin	avoid	effective
veto	heaven	deceive
voice	having	have
vine	nova	cave
visit	seven	save
vendor	invent	concave

□ *Practice Phrases for* [v] □

heaven above	save the tiger	voice vote
concave paving	even Stephen	seven vines
visiting native	vitamin invention	move over

□ *Practice Sentences for* [v] □

1. The *veto* was *overridden, seven* to one.
2. He was a *devoted saver.*
3. After the *eviction,* the apartment was *vacant.*
4. The *vines* were *woven* in the *cave.*
5. The *vent* blocked my *view,* so I *moved.*

Level 2 Drills for [v]

□ *Practice Words for* [v] □

Beginning	Middle	End
veal	evil	leave
veer	ravel	rave
violent	gravel	glove
vase	adverse	achieve
verse	civic	cleave
vaccine	crevice	strive
verbal	nonverbal	positive
vibrate	driver	relative
volunteer	prevent	passive
value	devil	starve
vulture	clover	naive

□ *Practice Phrases for* [v] □

The preposition *of* contains the sound [v], but people often omit it or assimilate it into the following word. Say the following phrases, making sure to put the voiced sound [v] in the word *of.* Don't overdo it, though, especially when the consonant that follows is voiceless. In that instance, it's normal to "devoice" the [v] slightly.

loaf of bread	can of beans	nick of time
pair of shoes	one of hers	best of it
two of them	ace of spades	one of the boys
barrels of fun	hill of beans	glass of water
cup of coffee	jug of wine	some of us

Many people tend to omit the [v] when it comes at the end of a word. They also omit it or assimilate it into the next word if that word begins with a consonant. Say the following phrases, making sure to produce a moderately strong [v].

five dollars	five times	five more
five hundred	five thousand	five months
pavement	have many	live wire
have one on me	I've done it	give me
give them	save me	leave me
love me	have some	save some

1. I tried to save five dollars.
2. Give me the vial with the vaccine.
3. I have one of them at home.
4. The driver tried to save some time.
5. Love me, love my dog.

Level 3 Drills for [v]

☐ *Practice Words for* [v] ☐

Here are some practice words for three blends that can be troublesome: [vl], [vz], and [vd]. Say them carefully, as one sound. Don't let any vowel sound creep in between the consonants of the blend.

[vl]	[vz]	[vd]
evil	halves	saved
shovel	shelves	loved
marvel	leaves	received
rival	loves	proved
snivel	hooves	lived
grovel	heaves	revolved
gravel	curves	curved
gavel	shoves	shoved
oval	moves	moved
level	carves	carved
hovel	deceives	deceived
weevil	slaves	slaved
survival	grooves	grooved

☐ *Practice Sentences for* [v] *and* [f] ☐

1. They proved that the levels were uneven.
2. He deceived us in the way he moved on the curves.
3. It's the best work of fiction I've read in five years.
4. Speaking for myself, I've never been happier.
5. I was positive there was a live wire on the pavement.
6. I've told you at least five thousand times never to do it.
7. Half of the shelf was overflowing.
8. I haven't received the load of concrete yet.
9. Make sure to leave some of it for me to give away.
10. I lost the chance for victory in only seven moves.

$$[\theta] \qquad [\eth]$$

thin   the

Sample: [θ] I THOUGHT IT WAS A THIN SLICE.
[ð] MY MOTHER SAID THEY WERE THE BEST.

Spellings: *th* and final *the* are the only spellings.

Description

[θ] and [ð] are cognate sounds. They are fricatives that you produce by squeezing the breathstream between your tongue and teeth.

□ *Production:* [θ] □

1. Open your mouth until your teeth are slightly apart.
2. Round the tip of your tongue; don't try to point it too sharply.
3. Place your tongue so that it protrudes very slightly between your upper and lower front teeth.
4. Force the breathstream to come out between your tongue and teeth. Don't press too tightly; you'll end up forcing the sound. Don't let any air through the nose.

□ *Production:* [ð] □

1. Follow the steps for [θ]. Add voice as soon as you feel your tongue touch your teeth.

Problems

[θ] and [ð] are sounds that cause trouble for both native and nonnative speakers. They're very weak sounds (hard to hear) and are two of the last sounds children acquire. Since these sounds exist in only a few languages, most nonnative speakers have difficulty with them.

Problem 1. Tongue placement

Most misarticulations of [θ] and [ð] result in sounds that are similar to [t] and [d]. That's because you are placing your tongue too close to the gum ridge behind your upper front teeth or because you're putting your tongue too firmly on the teeth to produce a fricative. Instead, you produce a plosive. If you are misarticulating these sounds, try the following.

□ *Production Drill* □

1. Review the production notes on [θ] and [ð].
2. Look in a mirror and say the [θ] sound.
3. Make sure you can see the edge of your tongue protruding between the teeth. Say [θ] again. It may feel unusual and uncomfortable, but don't let that bother you.
4. Say the [θ] sound over and over again. Don't move your tongue between sounds. Try the following:

> [θ] ... [θ] ... [θ] ... [θ] ... thin
> [θ] ... [θ] ... [θ] ... [θ] ... thanks
> [θ] ... [θ] ... [θ] ... [θ] ... thought

Monitor your production visually with the mirror and by listening carefully. If you're unsure of your production, ask your instructor or another student to help.
5. Once you're satisfied with [θ], try the same exercise with [ð].

> [ð] ... [ð] ... [ð] ... [ð] ... the
> [ð] ... [ð] ... [ð] ... [ð] ... those
> [ð] ... [ð] ... [ð] ... [ð] ... them

□ *Contrast Drill for* [θ] *and* [t] □

If you're satisfied that you can produce the [θ] sound correctly in the previous drill, you can go on. In the following drill, contrast the words in the first column, which contain [t], with the [θ] words in the second column.

[t]	[θ]		[t]	[θ]
tin	thin		tread	thread
tick	thick		true	through

(Lists continue on p. 162)

[t]	[θ]	[t]	[θ]
tanks	thanks	boat	both
taught	thought	bat	bath
tie	thigh	oat	oath
tinker	thinker	bet	Beth

Now try contrasting [d] words with [ð] words.

[d]	[ð]	[d]	[ð]
day	they	ladder	lather
doze	those	wordy	worthy
dough	though	load	loathe
den	then	laid	lathe
dine	thine	seed	seethe
dare	there	breed	breathe
udder	other	ride	writhe
mudder	mother	fodder	father

Problem 2. [θ] and [ð] Confusion

Since both [θ] and [ð] sounds are spelled in exactly the same way, many times people don't know which sound to use. Even if English is your native language and you know instinctively, most of the time, how a word is pronounced, you can still become confused. Maybe these general rules (which have exceptions) can help:

- Use the voiced sound [ð] when the word ends in *ther*. **Example:** *bother* [baðɚ]
- Use the voiced sound [ð] when the word ends in *the*. **Example:** *breathe* [brið]
- Use the voiceless sound [θ] when the *th* follows a pronounced consonant. **Example:** *month* [mʌnθ]

So *rather* uses [ð], *lathe* uses [ð], and *fifth* uses [θ].

Problem 3. Substitution of [f] for [θ]

Sometimes people attempt to make the [θ] and [ð] without protruding their tongue. If the lower jaw comes forward and up at the same time, a fricative sound is produced with your lip and teeth instead of with your tongue and teeth. Try the following Contrast Drill.

First read down the column of [f] words. Then read down the column of [θ] words. Finally read across, contrasting pairs of words. Feel for contact between your tongue and teeth on the [θ] words. You shouldn't feel any contact between your lip and teeth on those words. Complete the drill and then do it again, this time using a mirror to control your lip movement.

[f]	[θ]	[f]	[θ]
fin	thin	free	three
fink	think	miff	myth
fought	thought	sheaf	sheath
first	thirst	reef	wreath
Fred	thread		

Problem 4. Substitution of [s] for [θ] and [z] for [ð]

These substitutions are commonly made by nonnative speakers. If you make this substitution, try the following.

□ *Contrast Drill for* [θ] *and* [s] □

Read down the list of [s] words first. Use a mirror, and make sure your tongue stays behind your teeth. Next read down the list of [θ] words. Use the mirror again, and this time, make sure your tongue protrudes slightly between your teeth. For the last step, read across, contrasting pairs of words.

[s]	[θ]	[s]	[θ]
sink	think	miss	myth
sought	thought	pass	path
sick	thick	mouse	mouth
seem	theme	moss	moth
sin	thin	mass	math
saw	thaw	worse	worth
sing	thing	face	faith
sigh	thigh	truce	truth
sank	thank		

DICTION: THE CONSONANTS

□ *Contrast Drill for* [ð] *and* [z] □

Read down the list of [z] words first. Use the mirror, and keep your tongue behind your teeth. Then read down the list of [ð] words, saying each word carefully. Use the mirror again, and this time make sure your tongue protrudes slightly between your teeth.

[z]	[ð]	[z]	[ð]
Zen	then	breezing	breathing
zee	thee	close	clothe
razzer	rather	seize	seethe
teasing	teething	tease	teethe
closing	clothing	laze	lathe

Level 1 Drills for [θ]

□ *Practice Words for* [θ] □

Say the words in the following lists slowly and clearly. Listen carefully, and correct your production until you are satisfied that it is accurate and clear. You may want to use a mirror so that you can see if your tongue is far enough between your teeth. Remember, [θ] is a voiceless sound. Start with the Beginning words.

Beginning	Middle	End
theme	atheist	faith
thief	nothing	myth
thin	bathtub	mouth
thing	birthday	teeth
thanks	bathmat	Judith
thud	Athens	math
thought	Kathy	both
thicken	Matthew	zenith
think	toothache	booth
thigh	anything	Beth
theft	Anthony	youth
thaw	mouthpiece	oath
thimble	toothpick	path

□ *Practice Phrases for* [θ] □

    thick thumb   think thin   thief thought
    thud in the bathtub   birthday thanks   Athens theme

□ *Practice Sentences for* [θ] □

1. *Math* is not my *thing*.
2. I had *faith* in a spring *thaw*.
3. *Kathy* was on a *path* to *tooth* decay.
4. He used a *thick mouthpiece*.
5. He *thought* of *both thefts*.

Level 2 Drills for [θ]

When [θ] is surrounded by other consonants in a cluster, the result is a "tongue-twister." Such clusters are [θs] as in *myths*, [ksθ] as in *sixth*, [pθ] as in *depth*, and [nθ] as in *ninth*. You'll find these words mixed in with the other Level 2 words. Take them slowly. When [θ] is followed by [s], combine the two into one sound. Don't stop production between the two; keep the breathstream going while you are moving your tongue back. Remember, these words have the voiceless [θ].

Beginning	*Middle*	*End*
third	athlete	breath
thirst	bathtowel	seventh
three	Kathleen	growth
throw	lethal	wealth
thorough	ruthless	fifth
thread	Southport	sixth
thrifty	mouthful	ninth
thwart	something	length
threat	synthetic	warmth
Thursday	ethyl	worth
thrive	truthful	earth
thrush	earthy	fourth
threw	fourths	north
therapy	fifths	mirth
thrash	sixths	girth

1. She was thoroughly ruthless.
2. A sixth share was nothing to throw away.
3. Southport is a thoughtlessly wealthy town.
4. I've got a thirsty synthetic bath towel.
5. A person of girth needs a lot of earth for growth.
6. Two fifths equals four tenths.
7. Thrushes thrive in the north.
8. Truthfully, they go to great lengths to be thrifty.

Level 1 Drills for [ð]

□ *Practice Words for* [ð] □

Say the words in the following lists slowly and clearly. Listen carefully and correct your production until you are satisfied with it. You may want to use a mirror so that you can check your tongue to make sure it is far enough out between your teeth. We suggest that you start with the Middle words first. It's easier to produce [ð] when it's preceded by a vowel. Remember to start your voicing early enough.

Beginning	*Middle*	*End*
thee	either	bathe
these	other	with
they	bother	breathe
this	mother	soothe
thus	father	lathe
those	clothing	writhe
that	together	seethe
then	rather	scathe
there	weather	

There are two blends that are difficult; [ðd] and [ðz]. Here are some words for them:

[ðd]	[ðz]
bathed	bathes
breathed	breathes
clothed	clothes

[ðd]	[ðz]
soothed	soothes
mothered	mothers
fathered	fathers

Level 1 and 2 Sentences for [ð]

Note: the word *the* is one of the most frequently used in the English language. Yet many people are confused as to how to pronounce it, especially when they see it in print. Here are rules you can use to help you when you read aloud:

- The word *the* is pronounced [ðʌ] or [ðə] when it's followed by a consonant.

- The word *the* is pronounced [ði] when it's followed by a vowel.

So it's [ðʌ] beginning and [ði] end.

1. The weather was rather bad.
2. Either one is okay with me.
3. I'd like to bathe in those cooling waters.
4. That's the way it is with my father.
5. It was soothing to soak in a cool bathtub.
6. The critic made a scathing attack after the opening.
7. My mother said that was the end.
8. She was clothed in cotton that breathed.
9. We can move this together.
10. I knew without a doubt that it was they.

Level 3 Sentences for [θ] and [ð]

1. Descartes said: I think, therefore I am.
2. I threw a blanket over the leather couch.
3. I think they weathered the storm together.
4. Neither one liked to think about it.
5. I have three exams this Thursday.
6. They hired her at the clothing store.
7. They sailed south by southeast.
8. There are three other ways you can do that.
9. I thanked him for the birthday present.
10. I thought there were going to be three fifths, not two thirds.

[s]   [z]

snake   zoo

Sample: [s] THE DOG LOST THE SCENT OF THE SNAKE IN
THE GRASS.
[z] THEY HOSED OUT THE CAGES AT THE ZOO.

Spellings: s as in *snake*   z as in *zoo*
ss as in *grass*   s as in *hose*
sc as in *scent*   x as in *Xerox*
c as in *cent*
ps as in *psychology*
tz as in *waltz*

Description

[s] and [z] are cognate sounds. They are fricatives that you produce by forcing
air between your tongue and the upper or lower front teeth.

□ *Production:* [s] □

1. Place your tongue in the position to say [t], but don't say it.
2. Drop the tip of your tongue down and slightly back, but keep the sides
lightly pressed against the middle and back upper teeth. Your tongue should
now be pointing at the cutting edges of your front teeth or toward the gum
ridge.
3. Make a shallow groove lengthwise along the midline of your tongue. Keep
the sides up.
4. Blow the breathstream at the cutting edge of the teeth; create a "hissing"
sound. [s] is voiceless.

□ *Production:* [z] □

1. Follow the steps for [s]. Start voicing as soon as the air begins to move.

Problems

[s] and [z] are sounds that can cause you a lot of trouble. They are difficult sounds to produce—they require precision actions by the articulators, especially accurate movements, and fine auditory discrimination to produce just the right amount of "hiss." And, if you don't get it exactly right, people notice.

Although you can correct minor distortions fairly easily, major distortions, such as a frontal or lateral lisp, take more time and usually require trained guidance. If you have a frontal or lateral lisp, your instructor will probably refer you to Appendix B.

Problem 1. "Whistling" [s] or [z]

If the sound you make is too sharp or too high in pitch, you're probably holding your tongue tip too high and too close to the teeth. Gradually lower the tongue tip a millimeter at a time, and, at the same time, draw it back ever so slightly. Listen carefully as you produce an [s] with each adjustment. You'll probably notice that the pitch of the sound drops. Ask your instructor or another student to tell you when you've reached the right pitch. Keep practicing the sound until you're sure you can remember it.

Problem 2. Excessive Sibilance

This is a high-pitched hissiness that seems to pervade a person's entire speech pattern. It usually results from overemphasizing and prolonging the [s]. Many times it's coupled with a whistling [s] and [z]. Try to make the [s] and [z] as short as you can, without actually omitting them when you practice the word lists.

Problem 3. "Broad" [s] and [z]

In this problem, the sounds are too low in pitch or too broad. This happens when you let the air go out to one side of the mouth instead of down the central groove or when you fail to make a groove at all.

Problem 4. Unvoicing of [z]

This occurs frequently at the ends of words and less frequently in other positions by starting the voicing halfway through production. Try the following contrast drills.

Read down the list of [s] words first. Notice the absence of voice. Then read down the list of [z] words, feeling for voice. Make sure to start voicing at the start of the sound. The last step is to read across, contrasting pairs of words.

[s]	[z]	[s]	[z]
sue	zoo	busing	buzzing
sap	zap	loose	lose
sip	zip	fuss	fuzz
racer	razor	spice	spies
lacer	laser		

Level 1 Drills for [s]

□ *Practice Words for* [s] □

Say the words in the following lists slowly and clearly. Listen carefully, and adjust your tongue to produce the clearest, strongest [s]. Don't overdo it. Use moderate air pressure. Start with the Beginning words.

Beginning	*Middle*	*End*
see	acid	bets
seam	aside	pets
sit	basic	bats
sift	cassette	cats
sin	decent	pats
sing	decide	rats
safe	essay	plates
sane	icing	rates
saint	kerosene	oats
set	Tennessee	pass
send	medicine	place
sack	baseball	pace
sag	guessing	bless
sand	passing	mass
Sam	racing	kiss
sign	busing	bus
sight	fantasy	miss
soon	foster	mess

(*Lists continue on p. 171*)

Beginning	Middle	End
suit	pester	hiss
soup	rooster	grass
soak	east	juice
soar	west	menace
soft	also	purchase
sauna	mist	price
soot	racer	goodness
sound	price	cactus
sun	bossy	caps
supper	blossom	tips
Sunday	presser	tops
someday	messy	pups

☐ *Practice Phrases for* [s] ☐

sad sack	soft soap	cats and rats
cactus flower	purchase price	new suit
set aside	sing song	pass the soup
kiss me	safe and sound	out of sight

☐ *Practice Sentences for* [s] ☐

1. *It's* hard to *see cats* in the *grass*.
2. The heavy *safe* made the floor *sag*.
3. I *sent* the package *last* week.
4. He didn't *pass* the *salt*.
5. I'm going to *sign* the *lease* on the *house*.
6. He bought the *suit* at a low *price*.
7. The *sand* made a *mess* on the *seat*.
8. *It's* the tip of the *iceberg*.
9. *That's* your *basic racing* car.
10. *Set aside* a bottle of battery *acid*.

Level 2 Drills for [s]

☐ *Practice Words for* [s] ☐

Beginning	Middle	End
sell	assemble	actress
sail	worrisome	address

(*Lists continue on p. 172*)

Beginning	Middle	End
salt	assign	blouse
search	icicle	endless
certain	saucy	release
circle	sissy	press
central	sister	furnace
sorry	policy	nauseous
soil	proceed	depress
solve	taste	lettuce
cycle	jealousy	breathless
solar	essential	thoughtless
spite	courtesy	police
sold	classic	worse
Sarah	bicycle	hearse
ceiling	deceive	verse
sulk	blister	curse
solemn	recent	nurse
soccer	thermostat	

□ Practice Sentences for [s] □

1. Sarah lowered the thermostat on the furnace.
2. The soccer game proceeded in spite of the rain.
3. They sent the blouse to the wrong address.
4. The police found the stolen classic car.
5. The actress had to rehearse the role of the nurse.
6. That's the worst lettuce I ever tasted.
7. They searched in an endless circle.
8. Send me a press release.
9. My sister sold her new bicycle at a loss.
10. Problem solving is an endless cycle.

Level 3 Problems and Drills

[s] is most difficult to produce when it occurs in *blends* with other consonants. Some blends that can be troublesome are [sw], [sp], [str], [skr], and [sts].

Problem 1. [sw] and [ʃ] confusion

Sometimes people may substitute [ʃ] as in *shoe* for [s] as in *sue*. Try it. See what happens when the [ʃ] is substituted for the first sound in the word *swim*. This substitution happens when you drop your tongue tip too soon before the [w].

□ *Production Drill* □

1. Produce a long [s], stop completely, then say the rest of the word.
2. Read across each line. Gradually shorten the [s] and bring the parts together.

sss . . . weet	ss . . weet	s . weet	sweet
sss . . . wing	ss . . wing	s . wing	swing
sss . . . way	ss . . way	s . way	sway
sss . . . well	ss . . well	s . well	swell
sss . . . wine	ss . . wine	s . wine	swine

□ *Practice Words for* [sw] (*Beginning Position Only*) □

sweet	sweat	swan
sweep	swept	swallow
Sweden	swell	swarm
swim	swear	swollen
swill	suede	swoosh
swift	swam	swoon
sway	swag	swamp
swing	swine	swum

Problem 2. [sp] and [ʃ] confusion

The same thing that happens with [sw] can happen with [sp] if you lower your tongue too soon.

□ *Production Drill* □

1. Produce a long [s], stop completely, then say the rest of the word.
2. Read each line across. Gradually shorten the [s] and bring the parts together.

sss . . . peak	ss . . peak	s . peak	speak
sss . . . pit	ss . . pit	s . pit	spit
sss . . . pare	ss . . pare	s . pare	spare
sss . . . pool	ss . . pool	s . pool	spool
sss . . . pry	ss . . pry	s . pry	spry
sss . . . print	ss . . print	s . print	sprint

□ *Practice Words for* [sp] □

Beginning	*Middle*	*End*
speak	respect	lisp
speed	teaspoon	hasp
spit	desperate	clasp
spin	despair	grasp
spill	perspire	cusp
Spain	respond	rasp
spare	Mr. Spock	
spat	respite	
span	inspire	
spackle	desperation	
spot	respiration	
spawn	cuspidor	
spore	rasping	
spoke		
spool		
spoon		
spunky		
sponge		
spry		
spurt		
spring		

Problem 3. Tongue shaping

With [str], the trouble occurs when you prematurely flatten your tongue to make the [t]. This results in [ʃtr] instead of [str].

1. Produce a long [s], stop completely, then say the rest of the word.
2. Read across each line. Gradually bring the two parts together, shortening the [s] at the same time.

sss . . . treet	ss . . treet	s . treet	street
sss . . . trip	ss . . trip	s . trip	strip
sss . . . tray	ss . . tray	s . tray	stray
sss . . . trap	ss . . trap	s . trap	strap
sss . . . truck	ss . . truck	s . truck	struck
sss . . . tripe	ss . . tripe	s . tripe	stripe

□ *Practice Words for* [str] □

For this set of words, we'll group Beginning and Middle separately. There is no End group for this set.

Beginning

straddle	street	stream
streak	strip	string
strict	stray	straight
strain	stranger	stretch
stress	strap	strand
strangle	strontium	strop
structure	struck	struggle
strung	straw	strong
stripe	strike	stride

Middle

instrument	construction	frustrate
instruct	restrict	restrain
downstream	Main Street	constrict
destroy	distress	distract

Problem 4. Anticipation

Problems with [skr] are usually the result of anticipating the [k]. You raise the back of the tongue too early, and, as a result, the tip lowers. You then substitute [ʃkr] for [skr].

1. Produce a long [s], stop completely, then say the rest of the word.
2. Read each line across. Gradually shorten the [s] and bring the parts together.

sss . . . creen	ss . . creen	s . creen	screen
sss . . . cript	ss . . cript	s . cript	script
sss . . . crape	ss . . crape	s . crape	scrape
sss . . . cratch	ss . . cratch	s . cratch	scratch
sss . . . crew	ss . . crew	s . crew	screw
sss . . . crub	ss . . crub	s . crub	scrub

□ *Practice Words for* [skr] □

For this set, too, we've grouped Beginning and Middle separately.

Beginning

screen	scream	screech
script	scribble	scrimmage
scrape	scratch	scrap
scrabble	scramble	scrub
scruffy	scrunch	screw

Middle

describe	discreet	discretion
discrimination	unscrupulous	unscrew

Problem 5. Omission of [t]

The most common problem with this blend is omitting the [t].

□ *Production Drill* □

Think of the [sts] blend as being *two* sounds, not three. It's composed of [s] followed by a [ts] blend. The [ts] is the same sound as the last sound in the word *cats*.
1. Make a long [s], stop completely, then make a [ts] sound:

sss . . . ts   sss . . . ts   sss . . . ts   sss . . . ts

Read across.

beas . . . ts	beas . . ts	beas . ts	beasts
wris . . . ts	wris . . ts	wris . ts	wrists
gues . . . ts	gues . . ts	gues . ts	guests
cas . . . ts	cas . . ts	cas . ts	casts
rus . . . ts	rus . . ts	rus . ts	rusts
coas . . . ts	coas . . ts	coas . ts	coasts

☐ *Practice Words for* [sts] (*End Position Only*) ☐

beasts	feasts	priests
fists	wrists	mists
bastes	pastes	pests
bests	rests	guests
casts	masts	blasts
rusts	busts	dusts
firsts	bursts	costs
rousts	jousts	roasts
boasts	hosts	boosts

Level 1 Drills for [z]

☐ *Practice Words for* [z] ☐

Say the following words slowly and clearly. Listen carefully, and adjust your tongue for the clearest [z] possible. Don't overdo it; use moderate air pressure. Start with the Beginning words.

Beginning	*Middle*	*End*
zebra	benzine	bees
zinc	busy	buzz
zip	easy	choose
zone	daisy	fizz
zodiac	music	gaze
zany	noisy	has
zinnia	Tuesday	was
zoo	using	is
zoom	teasing	nose
zeal	design	days

□ Practice Phrases for [z] *□*

zigzag	buzzing bees	was his
zodiac zone	is a zoo	zany days
noisy music	busy Tuesday	using his nose

□ Practice Sentences for [z] *□*

1. I *zigzagged* on my way to the *zoo*.
2. The *zany music* was *noisy*.
3. I *was* only *teasing*.
4. *Is* that the right *zip* code *zone*?
5. I didn't *choose* the *zodiac design*.

Level 2 Drills for [z]

□ Practice Words for [z] *□*

Don't unvoice in End position.

Beginning	*Middle*	*End*
zeal	blazer	bruise
zero	Brazil	draws
zillion	buzzer	flows
zircon	cleanser	lies
zoology	clumsy	prize
Zanzibar	crazy	cars
Zurich	causing	bars
zestful	result	fours

□ Practice Sentences for [z] *□*

1. She was crazy to wear that blazer.
2. Zoology was a zero for me.
3. The bruise was due to my clumsy move.
4. The river flows zestfully over the bars.
5. There are a zillion cars in Brazil.

Level 3 Drills for [z]

Sometimes people have a tendency to unvoice [z] and turn it into an [s] when [z] is blended with other consonants. Say the following words, making sure to voice the [z]. Also, make sure that the two consonants blend into one sound.

[dz]	[nz]	[vz]
reeds	beans	believes
bids	bins	gives
fades	rains	waves
reds	tens	shelves
dads	cans	halves
rods	barns	gloves
cords	lawns	stoves
codes	loans	loves
woods	groans	wolves
foods	spoons	grooves
floods	buns	shoves
rides	lines	hives

☐ *Practice Sentences for* [s] *and* [z] ☐

1. He really shovels in the junk foods.
2. She paints green lawns and red barns.
3. As the saying goes, the race is to the swift.
4. He goes with the flow and rides with the tides.
5. Wood stoves are my answer to the energy crisis.
6. I can't stand long bus lines in the mornings.
7. Deposit cans are worth five cents apiece.
8. She fought her way through the wolves standing outside.
9. My sister groans when she lends me money for school.
10. Sometimes this is an exercise in patience.

[ʃ] she   [ʒ] beige

Sample: [ʃ] SHE DREAMED THAT HE LIVED IN A MANSION MADE OF SUGAR NEAR CHICAGO'S RUSSIAN EMBASSY.
[ʒ] SHE WAS A VISION IN BEIGE AND AZURE AT THE GARAGE.

Spellings:
sh as in *she*
c as in *ocean*
s as in *tension*
ss as in *fissure*
ch as in *Chicago*
t as in *nation*
sch as in *schnapps*

s as in *measure*
ge as in *beige*
z as in *azure*

Description

[ʃ] and [ʒ] are cognate sounds. They are fricatives. You produce them very much like the [s] and [z], except the tongue is farther back.

□ *Production:* [ʃ] □

1. Open your mouth slightly so that your teeth are apart and your lips are separated.
2. Round your tongue slightly, and raise the sides so that they are against the upper molars.
3. Raise the front of the tongue so that it points to the area just behind the gum ridge.
4. Keep the sides of the tongue up and start the breathstream flowing. Force the air against the front teeth, but make sure to keep the front of the tongue elevated. [ʃ] is voiceless.

□ *Production:* [ʒ] □

1. Follow the same steps as for [ʃ]. This time add voice at the same instant that the air starts to move.

5. *Washing* the *dishes*
6. *She* had a *notion* to

Level 2 Drills for [ʃ]

□ *Practice Words for* [ʃ] □

Beginning	Midd
shield	leashi
shale	foolis
shell	glacie
shawl	comm
shore	flashli
sheer	crush
shower	crashe
shovel	brush
shelter	relaxa
schnapps	inflec
schwa	insura
shrink	croch
shrank	racial

□ *Practice Sentences for* [ʃ

1. I relished the thou
2. He shrank back fro
3. The flashlight was
4. She is a commercia
5. It's hard to establi
6. Don't brush agains
7. Are you sure you g
8. The boat shook as
9. She used her shawl
10. The commercials r

Level 1 Drills for [ʒ]

□ *Practice Words for* [ʒ] □

Say the following words slov
Correct your production ur

Problems

[ʃ] and [ʒ] are fairly easy to articulate, and most people don't have many problems with them. The most frequent problems are confusion of [ʃ] and [ʒ], lateral emission, and substitution of [tʃ] as in *chip* and [dʒ] as in *huge*.

Problem 1. Confusion of [ʃ] and [ʒ]

□ *Contrast Drill for* [ʃ] *and* [ʒ] □

First read aloud the column of [ʃ] words. You shouldn't feel voice. Then read the column of [ʒ] words. This time feel and listen for voice. The last step is to read across, contrasting pairs of words.

[ʃ]	[ʒ]
assure	azure
pressure	pleasure
shack	Jacques
shallot	jabot
vicious	vision
glacier	glazier
Aleutian	illusion

Problem 2. Lateral emission

If you don't press your tongue firmly against the upper side teeth, the air can escape from the sides of your mouth. Hold your hands with the forefingers touching the corners of your mouth, as though you were making a megaphone with your hands. Say the sound [ʃ] very forcefully. Do you feel any air on your fingers? If you do, you're emitting the air laterally. Make the sound again, and make sure the sides of your tongue are up and touching the teeth. Hold two fingers about one inch in front of your mouth. Try to direct the stream of air at your fingers. If you have great difficulty directing the air out the front of the mouth, you should read Appendix B.

Problem 3. Confusion of [tʃ] and [ʃ]

The following contrast drill should help you with this problem.

□ *Contrast Drill for* [ʃ] *and* [tʃ] □

Read the words in the following lists aloud, slowly and clearly. First read down the list of [ʃ] words, then read the list of [tʃ] words. You should not feel

181
DICTION: THE CONSONANTS

any plosive c
read the wor

[ʃ]
sheet
sheep
ship
shin
shoe

Level 1 Dri

Say the word
correct your ƒ
If you're not
help. Start wi

Beginnii
she
sheep
ship
shed
shout
shook
shock
Chicago

□ *Practice Ph*

machine
push anc

□ *Practice Se*

1. *She* voi
2. They w
3. I *ment*
4. What's

182
DICTION

□ *Production Drill* □

The following words begin with [h]. Say the [h] three times, then say the word. Make sure you hear the h at the beginning of the word.

[h . . h . . h . .] home
[h . . h . . h . .] him
[h . . h . . h . .] hum
[h . . h . . h . .] ham

Now try the same drill with the Practice Words below.

□ *Practice Words for* [h] □

There are only a few words that contain the letter [h] in which it isn't pronounced, for example, *hour, heir, honest, honorary,* and *herb,* so you're usually safe pronouncing it. Incidentally, there are no English words that end with the [h] sound. Because you can produce this sound so easily, we've only provided Level 1 words and sentences.

Beginning	*Middle*	*Beginning*	*Middle*
heat	unheated	heed	behind
hat	ahead	happy	behave
head	cowhide	hurt	anyhow
humid	Ohio	hungry	rehearse
human	perhaps	who	lighthouse
humor	somehow	house	overhaul
huge	unharmed	health	White House
help	exhale	here	coherent

□ *Practice Sentences for* [h] □

1. It isn't the heat that bothers me, it's the humanity.
2. Somehow, I think that lighthouse is beyond help.
3. They were happy, but hungry, after the rehearsal.
4. Perhaps it's not as humid in the western half of Ohio.
5. Too huge a helping can be hazardous to your health.

186
DICTION

	vs	v	
Bilabial (both lips)	[hw]	[w]	page 187
Labio–dental (lip–teeth)			
Lingua–dental (tongue–teeth)			
Lingua–alveolar (tongue–gum ridge)			
Lingua–palatal (tongue–palate)		[r] [j]	page 191 page 199
Lingua–velar (tongue–soft palate)			
Glottal (vocal folds)			

[hw]   [w]
where   wet

Sample: [hw] THE   WHEEL   OF   THE   WHETSTONE WHIRRED.
[w] WANDA DROPPED ONE OF THE WATCHES IN THE LIQUID.

Spellings: *wh* as in *where*   *w* as in *wet*
w after *t* in *twelve*   *o* as in *one*
w after *s* in *swim*   *u* as in *liquid*
w after *k* in *quit*

Description

[hw] and [w] are glides you make by moving your lips while you're producing the sound. The air is emitted between the lips. They are cognate sounds; the [hw] is voiceless, while the [w] is voiced.

□ *Production:* [hw] □

1. Round your lips and purse them. Raise the back of your tongue toward the soft palate, but don't let it touch. Keep your mouth slightly open.
2. Blow air out of your mouth with enough force to make an audible rush of air.
3. As you create the sound, open your mouth slightly. Keep this sound very short, and don't add voice.

□ *Production:* [w] □

1. Follow the same steps used for [hw]. This time add voice as soon as you purse your lips. Continue to voice it as your lips open slightly.

Problems

Problem 1. The disappearance of [hw]

Chances are you don't know very many people who use the [hw] sound consistently. As a matter of fact, the [hw] sound seems to be going out of our language fairly rapidly. Listen to your pronunciation of these words: *what, why, when, where, anywhere.* Do you use [hw] or [w]? How about other people around you? What do they say?

So the question is, what's the standard way to pronounce those words? Should we use [hw] or [w]? Well, it's up to you to decide which one you like; either one is acceptable. Here are some words to help you determine which one you use.

□ *Contrast Drill for* [hw] *and* [w] □

Say the words in the following lists aloud, reading across. Contrast the word pairs. The left column should contain the sound [hw] and the right column, the sound [w].

[hw]	[w]	[hw]	[w]
where	wear	whirred	word
which	witch	whetstone	wet stone
whether	weather	while	wile
whale	wail	whey	way
whine	wine	when	wen

This contrast drill is the only one we've included for the [hw]. Since the decision to use that sound is a matter of choice, we'll avoid using that sound in the drills that follow for [w]. That way there will be less confusion.

Problems

Problem 1. Substitution of [v] for [w]

Nonnative speakers sometimes have this problem. Try the Production Drill first, then try the Contrast Drill.

□ Production Drill □

This drill is designed to help you learn to produce the [w] sound. First say the sound [u] (as in cool), then say the word that follows. Read across, and gradually shorten the spacing between [u] and the word.

[u] . . . air	[u] . . air	[u] . air	wear
[u] . . . itch	[u] . . itch	[u] . itch	witch
[u] . . . end	[u] . . end	[u] . end	wend
[u] . . . ache	[u] . . ache	[u] . ache	wake
[u] . . . aid	[u] . . aid	[u] . aid	wade

You can try this same production drill with other [w] words, too.

□ Contrast Drill for [w] and [v] □

Once you can produce the [w] correctly, you're ready to try contrasting [w] and [v]. Say the following words aloud. First read down the list of [w] words. Use a mirror, and check to see that there is no lip–teeth contact. Then read the list of [v] words. Finally, read the pairs across. Try to feel and hear the difference between the [w] and the [v].

[w]	[v]		[w]	[v]
wine	vine		we	vee
wet	vet		wane	vane
wail	vail		waltz	vaults
west	vest		wiser	visor
wend	vend		wiper	viper
worse	verse		wow	vow
went	vent			

Level 1 Drills for [w]

Since the [w] is so easy to produce, all the practice exercises are at Level 1.

□ *Practice Words for* [w] □

Say the words in the following lists slowly and clearly. Note that there are no words in English that end with the [w] sound.

Beginning	*Middle*		*Beginning*	*Middle*
we	awake		woman	quack
wake	byway		woods	reward
witty	cobwebs		weird	unwise
wave	midweek		waffle	backward
weak	thruway		wash	dwarf
wife	highway		welcome	dwindle
wide	everyone		weld	seaweed
window	quick		walk	quiz
with	quiet		wedding	required

□ *Practice Sentences for* [w] □

1. The thruway was closed for one hour due to high winds.
2. I was late for the quiz because I woke up at twelve.
3. The supply of wood had dwindled by Wednesday.
4. Grapes are really wine on the vine.
5. Young men in the West frequently wear vests.
6. It was the last waltz at the wedding.
7. It takes me until midweek to brush away the cobwebs.
8. I rewarded the dog with a sandwich.
9. The weather has been wetter than usual.
10. We walked through the seaweed in the backwash.

[r]
red

Sample: THE RED FERRY WENT IN THE WRONG DI-RECTION.

Spellings: *r* as in *red*
rr as in *ferry*
rh as in *rhythm*
wr as in *wrong*

Description

[r] is a voiced sound that can be produced in two ways. The first way, usually at the beginning of words, you produce it rather like a fricative by curling the tip of the tongue up and back. The second way, usually after a vowel or at the end of a word, you produce it as a glide that sounds like a vowel. Both ways are considered to produce a glide because the articulators are in motion.

□ Production — Method 1 □

1. Open your mouth slightly. Protrude your lips just a bit.
2. Raise the tip of your tongue to a point slightly behind the gum ridge, but don't make contact. At the same time, spread the sides of your tongue so that they touch the upper side teeth. You don't want air to escape from the sides of your mouth.
3. Produce voice.

□ Production — Method 2 □

1. This time keep the tongue tip down and slightly in back of the lower front teeth while you raise the center portion. This position is not used as much as Position 1.

Problems

[r] is one of the most troublesome sounds in our language and for a variety of reasons. Normally, it's one of the last sounds children master, and many

191

DICTION: THE CONSONANTS

times certain nonstandard productions, such as substituting [w] for [r], as in *wed* for *red,* can be continued into adult speech patterns. Many nonnative speakers have difficulty producing [r] due to the fact that it may not exist in their language at all or is very similar to another sound. The use of [r] varies from region to region, so it's confusing even to native speakers. We'll cover the problems in production first and then go over regional usage.

Problem 1. Trilled [r]

The sound of a trilled [r] is almost that of a [t] or [d]. It's produced by tapping the tongue very lightly and quickly against the gum ridge. Try this: say the word *car.* If you've trilled the [r], you'll feel the tongue tip touch.

□ *Production Drill* □

Say the word *are* very slowly, almost separating it into vowel–consonant. Say it a few times. Monitor your production carefully. Try to keep the tip of your tongue from touching anything. Now try the following drill: say the word *are,* stop completely, but don't move your tongue at all. Then add the [r] word that follows. As you read across, make your pause shorter and, finally, drop the *are.*

are . . . red	are . . red	are . red	are red	red
are . . . ripe	are . . ripe	are . ripe	are ripe	ripe
are . . . rode	are . . rode	are . rode	are rode	rode

Here's another way. Say the vowel [ɝ] as in the word *early.* Hold it for a moderately long time, then add the [r] word that follows. Read across.

er . . . red	er . . red	er . red	er red	red
er . . . rose	er . . rose	er . rose	er rose	rose
er . . . rye	er . . rye	er . rye	er rye	rye
er . . . rain	er . . rain	er . rain	er rain	rain
er . . . raw	er . . raw	er . raw	er raw	raw

Problem 2. Overlabialization and [w] for [r]

One of the most common problems is an [r] that sounds rather like a [w]. This happens if you purse your lips too much or if your tongue is inactive while the [r] is produced. Try the following:

□ *Contrast Drill for* [w] *and* [r] □

Say the following words aloud. Use a mirror and note the position of your lips. Try to minimize lip movement for the [r] words. First read the list of [w] words, then the list of [r] words. Then read across, contrasting the pairs of words. Repeat the words and watch your lips in the mirror.

[w]	[r]	[w]	[r]
weep	reap	wage	rage
weed	reed	wise	rise
wed	red	twice	trice
wing	ring	twain	train
wipe	ripe	twist	tryst
west	rest	twill	trill
wait	wait	tweeze	trees
won	run	tweet	treat
woe	row		

Problem 3. Substitution of [l] for [r]

If English is your second language, your [r] may sound like an [l], so that *red* becomes *led*. This is especially true of people whose first language was an Oriental one. Native speakers of Oriental languages tend to produce the [r] with the tongue tip touching the gum ridge.

□ *Contrast Drill for* [r] *and* [l] □

Say the words in the following list aloud. First, read the list of [l] words. Notice the contact between your tongue and the gum ridge. Then read the list of [r] words. Try to keep your tongue tip from touching anything as you produce the [r]. Purse your lips slightly. Finally read across, contrasting the pairs of words.

[l]	[r]	[l]	[r]
leaf	reef	blew	brew
leap	reap	blight	bright
lid	rid	bland	brand
lip	rip	bled	bread
late	rate	class	crass

(Lists continue on p. 194)

(Lists continue on p. 194)

(Lists continue on p. 194)

193

DICTION: THE CONSONANTS

[l]	[r]	[l]	[r]
lend	rend	clew	crew
lag	rag	cloud	crowd
law	raw	glass	grass
lot	rot	flesh	fresh
lug	rug	flank	frank
light	right	flay	fray
play	pray	fly	fry

Problem 4. Intrusive [r]

When a word that ends with a vowel is followed by a word that begins with a vowel, some people will bridge the gap between the words with an [r]. We call this type of [r] *intrusive*.

□ *Practice Drill* □

Say the following phrases carefully making sure you don't add an [r].

law and order	Alaska and Alabama
saw a man	go to Africa on vacation
vanilla ice cream	Havana is the capital of Cuba.
drama and speech	Your idea is okay.

Special Problems

It's possible that you still are having difficulty in producing an acceptable [r] sound even after trying all the drills. If so, talk to your instructor about this. Perhaps you should read Appendix B (Special Speech Problems) or check with a local speech and hearing center to see if you can get (or need) additional help.

Level 1 Drills for [r]

How (r) is pronounced varies with the regions of the country. Pronunciation of [r] preceding a consonant in medial position (as in *tired*) and in final position (as in *care*) can be considered optional. Ask your instructor and listen to the way educated people in your area talk before you decide on the correct pronunciation.

□ *Practice Words for* [r] □

Say the words in the following lists slowly and clearly. Listen carefully and correct your production until you are satisfied you have produced the desired sound. Start with the Beginning words. The Middle words all contain an [r] that should be pronounced. And even though the final [r] may be optional, say the final [r] in the End words so that you can get an auditory and tactile feeling for it. Just don't overdo it by curling your tongue too far back. The final [r] is just a small amount of [r] added on to a vowel or diphthong.

Beginning	*Middle*	*End*
reap	marry	peer
reed	merit	dear
rim	hurry	mere
rig	around	car
ray	array	fare
rake	berry	near
red	arrow	fire
ran	carrot	hair
rock	sorry	pair
roam	sherry	cure
room	orange	air
root	pirate	chair
rye	terrific	chore
rise	story	floor

□ *Practice Phrases for* [r] □

red rocks	orange carrot	carfare
ran into the red	terrific story	mere chore
reap the rye	hurry around	near the chair

□ *Practice Sentences for* [r] □

1. I *roamed* the *room* looking for the *rake*.
2. I put the *rocks near* the *rim*.
3. The *rays* of the sun helped the *rye* to *rise* in the fields.
4. I had to *hurry around* to find the *carfare*.
5. The *pirates* told a *terrific story*.
6. Put the *berries around* the *carrots*.

7. The *chair* was *near* the *fire.*
8. The *reeds* had *roots* that *ran* deep.
9. I was *married* in *Orange* County, *Florida.*
10. I'm *sorry* about the *arrow* in your *rig.*

Level 2 Drills for [r]

The [r] words at this level are more difficult to produce because of the presence of other sounds such as [l]. In addition, the Middle words contain [r] preceding a consonant, so you may have doubts as to local pronunciation. We suggest that you pronounce the [r] (even if others in your area don't) simply to get experience. Take your time with these words. Say them slowly and clearly. If you have doubts as to the accuracy of your production, ask your instructor or another member of the class.

□ *Practice Words for [r]* □

Beginning	*Middle*	*End*	*Combination*
real	barrel	leer	rather
rile	florist	velour	burger
roll	warm	clear	farther
rail	alarm	implore	armory
royal	spiral	millionaire	roar
rasp	Lawrence	lair	rare
Ralph	fork	pearl	rural
rules	storm	father	barrier
ruffle	burn	mother	carrier
raffle	birthday	sister	purser
rubble	girl	bother	farmer
			dormitory

□ *Practice Sentences for [r]* □

1. It's rare to find a real pearl.
2. The carrier was on a rural route.
3. Ralph has the list of rules for the raffle.
4. I burned the burgers on the barbecue fork.
5. My mother said I'd be a millionaire.
6. It was clear after the storm.
7. The florist climbed the spiral staircase.

8. I implore you not to bother my sister.
9. The purser threw the roll over the rail.
10. The bear chased my father with a roar.

Level 3 Drills for [r]

This level has some difficult blends you might want to practice.

☐ *Practice Words for* [pr] ☐

If you purse your lips too much, the [pr] blend may sound like [pw]. Use a mirror and try these words:

preach	priest	pretty
prince	price	prank
prime	prize	pray
April	appropriate	apricot

☐ *Practice Words for* [br] ☐

This blend can be misarticulated the same way as [pr].

breed	bred	broad
bring	brown	break
breeze	broom	bride
abrupt	abrasive	upbringing
abridge	abroad	Hebrew

☐ *Practice Words for* [kr] *and* [gr] ☐

Make sure to produce these as true blends. Don't let a vowel creep in between the two consonants.

[gr]	[kr]	[gr]	[kr]
greet	creek	grave	crave
gram	cram	aground	accrue
grow	crow	aggravate	acrid
grate	crate	angry	across
grime	crime	ingrained	script

□ *Practice Words for* [fr] □

Don't let a consonant separation occur here, either.

friend	fried	French
freedom	fragile	freeze
front	frown	frame
affront	African	afraid
defraud	belfry	

□ *Practice Words for* [tr] □

If you press your tongue too firmly against the gum ridge when you make the [t] and then slide your tongue back, the sound produced is somewhat like [tʃr]. To avoid this, press the tongue lightly against the palate and make a clean break on the way back to making the [r].

[tr]		
trim	tree	troop
true	trash	train
tribe	trend	track
trunk	trigger	try
attractive	entreat	oaktree
entrance		

□ *Practice Words for* [dr] □

Produce these the same way as [tr]. Just add voice early enough.

[dr]		
dream	drink	drew
drip	drape	drive
drum	dragon	drain
address	Andrew	undress

□ *Practice Sentences for* [r] □

1. The prime rate rose three points this year.
2. April gives us freedom from the trials of winter.

3. I put the French vanilla ice cream in the freezer.
4. I'll have a burger, rare, and an order of fries.
5. When you're angry, a frown spreads across your face.
6. He broke the bottle of apricot brandy.
7. She prided herself on her freeze-frame photography.
8. That's where the schooner ran aground.
9. I purchased an unabridged dictionary.
10. It was a plot to defraud the African prince.
11. He was a firm believer in law and order.
12. The bumpy drive aggravated my injuries.
13. The fragile crystal broke in the crate.
14. I brought red roses home for our anniversary.
15. She won the blue ribbon for her brown bread.

---

[j]
yes

Sample: YES. IN MY OPINION THAT VIEW IS FAMILIAR.

Spellings: *y* as in *yes*
io as in *opinion*
ie as in *view*
u as in *use*
e as in *few*
ia as in *familiar*

Description

[j] is a voiced glide. You produce it by raising the tongue toward the palate and gliding it toward the position of the next sound. [j] is voiced.

☐ *Production:* [j] ☐

1. Open your mouth slightly.
2. Place the tip of your tongue behind your lower front teeth.

3. Raise the front of your tongue toward the hard palate. Keep the tip in place behind your lower front teeth, and pull your lips slightly back.
4. Produce voice and let your tongue and lips glide to the position of the next sound. Don't let any air out your nose.

Problems

Because of its vowel-like qualities, most people don't have much trouble producing [j] accurately. Most of the problems involve regional usage or result from learning English as a second language, but are not misarticulations.

Problem 1. Substitution of [dʒ] for [j]

If your native language doesn't have this sound, you will probably substitute the sound associated with the letter *j*. In other words, *yet* would become *jet*. Use the Contrast Drill below to reinforce the difference between the two sounds.

☐ *Contrast Drill for* [j] *and* [dʒ] ☐

Say the words in the following lists aloud. Read the list of [dʒ] words first. Feel the way the tongue tip touches the gum ridge. Then read the list of [j] words. As you say the first sound of each word, be sure to keep your tongue tip down behind the front teeth. Finally, read across, contrasting the pairs of words.

[dʒ]	[j]	[dʒ]	[j]
jet	yet	Jack	yak
jam	yam	jeer	year
Jews	use	jail	Yale
Jell-o	yellow	jowl	yowl
Jess	yes	jarred	yard
joke	yoke	jot	yacht

Problem 2. Omission of [j]

Even native English speakers become confused as to whether to pronounce [j] when it's represented by a letter other than *y*. The general rule is that you use [j] after consonants such as *k, b, f, v, h,* and *p,* with such spellings as *ue, uc, eu, ew.* Pronounce the [j] when *u* is followed by *n.* It almost doesn't make sense to state rules such as these when they have a great many exceptions. Perhaps the best way is to simply observe usage.

Level 1 Drills for [j]

Since there are few production problems with [j], the drills are all Level 1. The pronunciation of [j] is optional in those words that are starred. Note: there are no words ending with the [j] sound.

□ *Practice Words for* [j] □

([j] is optional in starred words.)

Beginning	Middle
year	onion
yes	senior
use	communicate
you	beyond
Yankee	usual
yawn	cue
yard	Tuesday*
youth	reduce*
unit	institute*
Europe	cute
yellow	duke*

□ *Practice Sentences for* [j] □

1. *Yes, you* can have the *yacht* tonight.
2. The *Institute* sent Jeff to *Europe* last *year.*
3. They sold *millions* of lemon *yellow units.*
4. Bakers *use* egg *yolks* by the *yard.*
5. I tried to *communicate* with that *cute senior.*

	LATERAL	
	VS	V
Bilabial (both lips)		
Labio–dental (lip–teeth)		
Lingua–dental (tongue–teeth)		
Lingua–alveolar (tongue-gum ridge)	[l]	page 202
Lingua–palatal (tongue–palate)		
Lingua–velar (tongue–soft palate)		
Glottal (vocal folds)		

[l]
left

Sample: LAURA LEFT THE YELLOW PILLOW IN THE HALL.

Spellings: *l* as in *left*
ll as in pi*ll*ow

Description

[l] is a voiced lateral continuant. You produce it by dropping the sides of the tongue and allowing air to escape around the sides.

□ *Production:* [l] □

1. Place the tip of your tongue against your upper gum ridge.
2. Open your mouth wide enough to slip the tip of your finger between your teeth.
3. Keep the sides of the tongue down.
4. Produce voice. Don't let any air through your nose.

Problems

Problem 1. Distinguishing between "dark" [l] and "clear" [l]

The [l] we described above is called the "clear" [l]. It's the [l] that occurs in the beginning of a word or immediately after a beginning consonant. Try the word *let*. You should feel as though you're making the sound entirely with the front of your tongue. The tongue tip remains touching the gum ridge throughout the [l] and the back stays down.

The "dark" [l] is called dark because it is produced, to a certain extent, by the back of the tongue and is slightly muffled. Say the word *ball*. You should feel your tongue tip still touching the gum ridge, but the back of your tongue lifts slightly.

The "dark" [l] exists in all dialects of English, usually at the ends of words and sometimes in the middle. Some people, though, use the "dark" [l] in beginning positions. Others may even drop the tongue tip from the gum ridge and produce the [l] entirely with the back portion near the palate. Try the Contrast Drill below to see how you produce the [l].

□ *Contrast Drill for "clear"* [l] *and "dark"* [l] □

Read the following pairs of words aloud. Make sure your tongue tip is touching the gum ridge each time you produce the sound [l]. Use the "clear" [l] in the first word of each pair and the "dark" [l] in the second.

"clear" [l]	"dark" [l]
let	tell
lap	pal
lip	pill
lean	kneel
lead	deal

(*Lists continue on p. 204*)

lick	kill
late	tail
led	dell
load	dole
Luke	cool
lost	stall
light	tile

If you are having difficulty producing the "clear" [l], we suggest that you refer to Appendix B, Special Speech Problems.

Problem 2. Substituting [r] for [l]

If your first language was one of the Oriental languages, you may have difficulty with the [l]. Chances are you produce this sound with your tongue tip *behind* the gum ridge. The result is a sound similar to the [r]. Try the following Contrast Drill.

□ *Contrast Drill for* [r] *and* [l] □

Read the words in the following lists aloud. Read them across, in pairs. The first word of each pair will start with [r], the second with [l]. Notice how the tongue is back farther in the mouth for [r], and it's more in the front for [l]. Make sure the part of the gum ridge you're touching for [l] is just behind the upper teeth.

[r]	[l]	[r]	[l]
red	led	brew	blue
reed	lead	pray	play
right	light	frame	flame
rode	load	fry	fly
rate	late	grow	glow
rush	lush	graze	glaze
rise	lies		

Practice these words a few times, concentrating on the differences between [l] and [r]. Ask your instructor or a classmate to listen to you. When you're satisfied with your production, try the Level 1 Practice Words.

Problem 3. Omission of [l]

This happens usually when [l] either precedes or follows another consonant such as in the word *already*. When you're trying the practice words, make sure you pronounce the [l] in each word.

Problem 4. Substitution of [w] for [l]

You are making this substitution if you pronounce the word *late* so that it sounds like *wait*. Read Appendix B and do the drills for [l] there before you start on the Level 1 drills in this chapter.

Level 1 Drills for [l]

☐ *Practice Words for* [l] ☐

Say the words in the following lists slowly and clearly. Make sure the tip of your tongue touches the gum ridge behind your upper front teeth: not on the teeth, and not behind the gum ridge, but squarely on the gum. Listen carefully and monitor your production until you're sure that you are producing the "clear" and "dark" [l] accurately and that you're using the "dark" [l] only where it's appropriate. Start with the Beginning words.

Beginning	Middle	End
lean	allow	kneel
lid	alike	deal
late	daylight	bail
let	pillow	fell
led	yellow	mill
laugh	eleven	bell
lot	always	tall
lawn	follow	ball
long	dolly	style
like	telling	pile
look	along	motel
lunch	believe	pool
loud	balloon	cruel

late lunch	look alike	laugh a lot
always believing	follow a balloon	daylight yellow
motel pool	tall pile	fell in the pool

□ *Practice Sentences for* [l] □

1. I *let lunch* go on too *long.*
2. *Eleven always follows* ten.
3. That *motel pool* has *style.*
4. I don't *believe* how *loud* that *laugh* was.
5. I was *kneeling* on the bridge when I *fell* in the *mill* pond.
6. She was *telling* me about the *"look alike"* contest.
7. Take the *yellow pillow along.*
8. They're *always* too *late* to make a *deal.*

Level 2 Drills for [l]

The words on this level are generally more difficult to produce because the sounds in them may require a wider range of movement by the articulators and because of the [pl], [bl], and [lp] blends. If you say each word carefully and make sure that your tongue tip touches your gum ridge, you should be ready to try these blends.

One additional difficulty results with production of the syllabic [l]. You produce the syllabic [l] when it is in an unstressed syllable following [t], [d], or [n], as in the words *petal, pedal,* and *channel.* To produce the syllabic [l], you leave your tongue touching the gum ridge; you don't remove it after producing the sound before the [l]. The [l] is made by simply dropping the tip of the tongue. Here are some words to try:

□ *Production Drill* □

Read down each column. Don't remove your tongue from the gum ridge before making the [l].

[tl]	[dl]	[nl)
petal	pedal	channel
bottle	paddle	panel

(*Lists continue on p. 207*)

[tl]	[dl]	[nl]
little	muddle	funnel
settle	middle	kennel
rattle	candle	arsenal

Listen carefully and try the words again. If you are producing the syllabic [l] correctly, you won't hear a vowel between the [l] and the sounds that go before.

☐ Practice Words for [l] ☐

Read the words in the following lists slowly and carefully. Take special time with the words that contain [pl], [bl], [lp], [fl], and syllabic [l]. Don't let a vowel creep in between the two consonants of the blend.

Beginning	Middle	End
lure	plank	apple
leaves	blue	bobble
lapse	raffle	quarrel
leases	glide	schedule
lustrous	railing	quail
lair	help	pearl
link	twelve	curl
liar	garlic	eagle
leer	belt	triple
laws	glue	shrill

☐ Practice Sentences for [l] ☐

1. I love the smell of garlic.
2. I heard the shrill call of the eagle.
3. A liar is a person with a lot of memory lapses.
4. You don't find cultured pearls in clams.
5. He had a triple black belt.

Level 3 Drills for [l]

The following drills are more difficult than the ones you've done so far. The words combine the blends you practiced in Level 2, and we've added others, such as [lz], along with words containing more than one [l]. Remember, if a word starts and ends with [l], the first [l] will be "clear," sometimes the second will be "dark."

□ *Practice Words for* [l] □

lonely	fields	lull
lilt	bells	lulls
lately	jails	literally
liability	faultless	boils
welds	lollipop	collegial
helpless	scheduled	swelter
likely	lethal	logical

□ *Practice Sentences for* [l] □

1. She's not likely to be lonely.
2. The sweltering heat leaves me feeling helpless.
3. I'm planning for limited liability.
4. I was sweltering in the glow of collegial smiles.
5. The lock was literally welded closed.

	NASALS		
	vs	v	
Bilabial (both lips)		[m]	page 209
Labio–dental (lip–teeth)			
Lingua–dental (tongue–teeth)			
Lingua–alveolar (tongue-gum ridge)		[n]	page 211
Lingua–palatal (tongue–palate)			
Lingua–velar (tongue–soft palate)		[ŋ]	page 213
Glottal (vocal folds)			

[m]
man

Sample: THE MAN WAS CALM AFTER HE HIT HIS
THUMB WITH THE HAMMER.

Spellings: *m* as in *man*
mm as in *hammer*
mb as in *thumb*
lm as in *calm*
mn as in *column*
gm as in *diaphragm*

Description

[m] is a voiced nasal continuant. It is a vowel-like consonant for which you
emit the breathstream through your nose.

☐ *Production:* [m] ☐

1. Close your lips but keep your teeth very slightly apart.
2. Lower your soft palate, and rest your tongue on the floor of the mouth.
3. Produce voice.

Problems

There are very few problems with the production of [m]. This is one of the
first and easiest sounds that children learn. When problems do exist, they are
usually errors of omission or of assimilating [m] into the next sound. All the
drills for [m] are in Level 1.

Level 1 Drills for [m]

☐ *Practice Words for* [m] ☐

Say the words in the following lists slowly and clearly. Make sure your lips are
closed, and seal off the mouth entirely. Pronounce each [m] distinctly. Don't

allow it to become part of the next consonant. Start with the Beginning words.

Beginning	Middle	End
me	hammer	thumb
mitt	coming	team
mate	gleaming	tempt
metal	demand	fame
mask	clamp	time
moving	tomcat	name
mister	summer	bomb
middle	semester	broom
mistake	camera	column
milk	woman	term
mammoth	family	groom
mime	omen	salmon
mimic	remember	autumn
mouse	fireman	synonym
month	somewhere	crumb

□ Practice Phrases for [m] □

room full	come true	time out
I'm going	remember me	time bomb
some fun	summer time	fame game
tempt me	term paper	team name

□ Practice Sentences for [m] □

1. I'm going to school for one summer semester.
2. It was a mistake to wear the metal mask.
3. It's time to make an effort to complete my term paper.
4. He's the only man I know who isn't coming with the team.
5. Don't tempt me with a room full of cameras.
6. The fireman clamped his thumb on the gleaming bomb.
7. You can call me mister, if you can't remember my name.
8. The Romans certainly made mammoth columns.

[n]
no

Sample: DUE TO P̲NEUMONIA HE COULD N̲OT PICK UP
P̲EN̲N̲IES WITH A K̲NIFE.

Spellings: n   as in *no*
            nn as in *penny*
            kn as in *knife*
            gn as in *gnat*
            pn as in *pneumonia*
            mn as in *mnemonic*

Description

[n] is a voiced nasal continuant. It's a vowel-like consonant you produce by blocking the airstream at the gum ridge with your tongue and emitting it nasally.

□ *Production:* [n] □

1. Open your mouth slightly. Place the tip of your tongue on the upper gum ridge. At the same time, place the sides of your tongue along the upper inside surface of the molars.
2. Lower the soft palate so that air can leave via your nostrils.
3. Produce voice.

Problems

There are very few problems with [n]. We learn this sound very early in life, so misarticulations are seldom serious. The most common problems are omission of [n] and assimilating it into the sounds surrounding it. [n] is most often assimilated when it is followed by another consonant. It then takes on the characteristics of that consonant. For example, in the phrase *in cold water,* [ɪn kold wɔtɚ], the [n] changes to [ŋ] and the word becomes *ink.* Here are some phrases and words in which this happens. Try them slowly, making sure to produce the [n].

income tax	in cold water	concrete
in capitals	in front	unpopular
infrequent	unbiased	in back
in fact	tin whistle	incomplete

Level 1 Drills for [n]

Since [n] is a relatively easy sound to produce, all the drills are at Level 1.

□ *Practice Words for* [n] □

Say the following words slowly and clearly. Listen to your production, and feel it as well. Make sure you use only the tip of your tongue for the [n]. Don't omit it, and don't assimilate it.

Beginning	*Middle*	*End*
knee	penny	keen
knit	peanut	tin
name	cannot	mane
nap	many	pan
north	honey	mine
nose	finish	began
next	cleaner	token
nation	lightning	satin
nail	flint	alone
needle	opener	spoon
knowledge	bench	mitten
gnarled	tunnel	brown
pneumatic	blend	burn
number	blond	drawn
Nancy	concern	scorn
nearing	incomplete	mention
nil	inquire	barn

□ *Practice Sentences for* [n] □

1. She began knitting the cap in November.
2. The flint knife was found in the abandoned tin mine.

3. I inquired about the tenpenny nails.
4. He used satin-finish varnish on the table.
5. The price of peanuts is nearing a penny a pound.
6. The old brown barn burned last night.
7. Nancy didn't have any subway tokens.
8. With all our knowledge, thunder and lightning still frighten many of us.
9. Some students get incomplete grades because they procrastinate.
10. He put his sore hand in cold water for an hour.

[ŋ]
sing

Sample: I THINK THAT SINGING IS GOOD EXERCISE FOR YOUR TONGUE.

Spellings: ng   as in *sing*
nk   as in *think*
nc   as in *anchor*
n   as in *anxious*
ngue as in *tongue*

Description

[ŋ] is a voiced nasal continuant. It is a vowel-like consonant you produce by blocking off the breathstream with the tongue and soft palate and letting the air out through the nostrils.

□ **Production:** [ŋ] □

1. Open your mouth fairly wide.
2. Place the back of your tongue against your soft palate, as though you were going to say the first sound of the word *go*.
3. Lower your soft palate, produce voice, and let the air and sound leave through your nose.

Problems

Problem 1. Deciding whether to use [ŋ] or [n]

This is a sound we learn very early as children, and it's easy to produce. Almost no one has problems with accurate production, as long as they produce it. But a good many people have difficulty deciding *when* to use [ŋ], and many inadvertently substitute [n] for [ŋ].

Here's a Production Drill for [ŋ], and a Contrast Drill to help you distinguish between [n] and [ŋ].

□ Production Drill □

Let's borrow a word from baseball—*inning*. This word contains the sound [n] in the middle, and the sound [ŋ] in the end. Say the word slowly, and feel the way the tongue moves. Maintain the same pause in the middle as you read across the page.

in . . . ning   in . . . ning   in . . . ning   in . . . ning   in . . . ning

Repeat this line another five or six times. Make sure you feel the back of your tongue touching the soft palate in the second syllable.

Now say the following, slowly and distinctly, reading across. Again, make sure to make contact between your tongue and soft palate.

sing . . . sing . . . sing . . . sing . . . sing . . . sing . . . sing . . . sing
sing . . . ing   sing . . . ing   sing . . . ing   sing . . . ing
singing . . . singing . . . singing . . . singing . . . singing . . . singing
kink . . . kink . . . kink . . . kink . . . kink . . . kink . . . kink . . . kink
kink . . . ing   kink . . . ing   kink . . . ing   kink . . . ing
kinking . . . kinking . . . kinking . . . kinking . . . kinking . . . kinking

Now try the following words. Say them slowly.

sing	king	ring
sting	wing	bring
long	strong	wrong
hang	gang	rang

If you're satisfied with your production of [ŋ], you can go on to the Contrast Drill below.

Read across the page, contrasting the pairs of words. Notice the difference between [n] in the first word and [ŋ] in the second. You should be able to feel and hear the difference. Read slowly and distinctly. If you're not sure of your production, ask your instructor or a member of the class to help.

[n]	[ŋ]	[n]	[ŋ]
thin	thing	lawn	long
sin	sing	ton	tongue
win	wing	stun	stung
ban	bang	run	rung
fan	fang	gone	gong
pan	pang	sun	sung

Problem 2. [ŋ] spelling confusion

A great many people, especially nonnative speakers, become confused by English spelling and don't know when to use [ŋ] alone and when to follow it with [g]. For example, *finger* is pronounced [fɪŋgɚ], with [g] following the [ŋ]. But the word *singer* has no [g]. It's pronounced [sɪŋɚ]. Here are some simple rules that should clear up some of the confusion:

• Use [ŋ] when the word ends in *ng.*
Example: *sing* [sɪŋ]

• Use [ŋ] when *ng* or another suffix is added to a root word ending in *ng.*
Example: *singing* [sɪŋɪŋ]

• Use [ŋ] + [g] when the *ng* is in the middle of the original word.
Example: *finger* [fɪŋgɚ]

• Exceptions: Use [ŋ] + [g] in the superlative and comparative forms of certain words such as *long, longer, longest; strong, stronger, strongest; young, younger, youngest.*

Here are more examples:

[ŋ] + [g]

longer	stronger	linger
finger	hunger	language

[ŋ] alone

singing	ringing	banging
hanging	prolonging	bringing
hangar	belonging	flinging
singer	swinger	ringer

Note: *nge* is *not* pronounced [ŋ], but [ndʒ] as in *lunge*. For example, *stranger, arrange, hinge, orange, sponge,* and *change* do not contain the sound [ŋ].

Problem 3. Uncontrolled addition of [k] and [g]

Even if you do know the rules, you may be adding these sounds and not be aware of it. For example, adding [k] to *thing* turns it into *think*. If this is a problem for you, try this:

☐ *Contrast Drill for* [ŋ] *and* [ŋk] ☐

Say the following pairs of words. The first word in each pair ends in [ŋ]; the second ends in [ŋk].

[ŋ]	[ŋk]
thing	think
sing	sink
ring	rink
wing	wink
sting	stink
clang	clank

☐ *Production Drill* ☐

Now say the words in the following lists very slowly. Don't remove your tongue from your soft palate until you have completed the [ŋ]. Listen for any telltale "clicking" sound.

sing . . . . sing . . . . sing . . . . sing . . . . sing . . . . sing
sing . . . ing   sing . . . ing   sing . . . ing   sing . . . ing   sing . . . ing

Now try the same thing with the words in the Contrast Drill above.

Level 1 Drills for [ŋ]

☐ *Practice Words for* [ŋ] ☐

At this level, you won't have to worry about the rules of usage. All the words in the Level 1 drills have [ŋ] alone, not followed by [g].

Say the words in the following lists slowly and clearly. Make sure you feel contact between the back of your tongue and your soft palate. Monitor your production carefully. If you have doubts, ask your instructor or a member of the class to help. There are no words in English that begin with the [ŋ] sound.

Middle	End	Middle	End
bangs	herring	hangman	amazing
ringer	icing	wings	among
singer	king	tongs	jogging
length	tongue	youngster	racing
strength	gang	stingers	nursing
gangster	strong	things	dancing
thronged	asking	gongs	staying
ringed	wrong		

□ *Practice Phrases for* [ŋ] □

staying among	amazing throng	doing wrong
racing and jogging	strong hanger	amazing wings
gongs and things	asking the singer	buying rings

□ *Practice Sentences for* [ŋ] □

1. I'm always *asking* the *wrong* questions.
2. Those are *amazing racing* shoes.
3. *Nursing* is one of the *helping* professions.
4. The *king* was *staying* in the middle of *things*.
5. We stopped *jogging* and started *dancing*.

Level 2 Drills for [ŋ]

□ *Practice Words for* [ŋ] □

The words at this level have been divided into two lists: words containing [ŋk] and words with [ŋg]. Read them slowly and carefully. Be sure you have them right before you go on to the sentences.

[ŋk]	[ŋg]	[ŋk]	[ŋg]
bank	finger	junk	England
anchor	longer	donkey	angle

(*Lists continue on p. 218*)

[ŋk]	[ŋg]	[ŋk]	[ŋg]
drinker	stronger	larynx	penguin
thinker	hunger	thanks	younger
jinx	hungry	planks	tangle
ink	angry	bankrupt	mingle

□ *Practice Sentences for* [ŋ] □

These sentences contain the [ŋk] and [ŋg] blends as well as words from Level 1.

1. Thanks for taking my change to the bank.
2. I'm still hungry after I eat junk food.
3. The tongue is located above the larynx.
4. I don't have the strength for jogging.
5. English vowels are longer than Spanish vowels.
6. Two triangles make one rectangle, I think.
7. The song they were singing so strongly was annoying.
8. She's staying later for the dancing.
9. Donkeys have an amazing amount of strength.
10. Thanks to you I didn't get a single one wrong.

	AFFRICATES		
	vs	v	
Bilabial (both lips)			
Labio–dental (lip–teeth)			
Lingua–dental (tongue–teeth)			
Lingua–alveolar (tongue–gum ridge)	[tʃ]	[dʒ]	page 219
Lingua–palatal (tongue–palate)			
Lingua–velar (tongue–soft palate)			
Glottal (vocal folds)			

[tʃ]   [dʒ]

chair   judge

Sample: [tʃ] THE KITCHEN CHAIR HAD A NATURAL WOOD COLOR.
[dʒ] THE JUDGE SAT ON THE EDGE OF HIS SEAT AS HE HEARD THE SOLDIER ACCUSE THE GYPSY.

Spellings:
ch	as in *chair*	*j*	as in *judge*
tch	as in *kitchen*	*g*	as in *gypsy*
tu	as in *natural*	*dg*	as in *edge*
ti	as in *question*	*dj*	as in *adjective*
c	as in *cello*	*d*	as in *soldier*

Description

[tʃ] and [dʒ] are cognate sounds. [tʃ] is voiceless, and [dʒ] is voiced. They are affricate sounds, which you produce by blocking off the breathstream between the tongue and gum ridge, partially for a plosive and partially for a fricative. The [tʃ] is a blend combined of [t] and [ʃ]. The [dʒ] is a blend of [d] and [ʒ].

□ *Production:* [tʃ] □

1. Open your mouth slightly.
2. Place the tip of your tongue against the gum ridge, and lift the sides to touch the teeth, as though you were going to make the sound [t].
3. Build up air pressure.
4. Release the air pressure very suddenly, but only allow a very small portion of your tongue tip to leave the gum ridge. Although you started with [t], you'll finish with [ʃ].

□ *Production:* [dʒ] □

1. Follow the same steps used for [tʃ]. The only difference is voice. Produce voice as soon as you feel your tongue touch the gum ridge.

Problems

If you have difficulty producing any of the sounds that make up [tʃ] and [dʒ], read the sections of this chapter that apply to those sounds. Once you or your instructor are satisfied with your production of the component sounds, you can go ahead and work on [dʒ] and [tʃ].

Problem 1. Failure to voice [dʒ]

If you don't produce enough voice, you make the sound [tʃ] instead of [dʒ]. This turns the word *joke* into *choke*. To avoid this, you must start voicing at the very beginning of the [dʒ] and hold it all the way through the [dʒ]. Try the following Contrast Drill:

☐ *Contrast Drill for* [tʃ] *and* [dʒ] ☐

Read the words in the following lists aloud, slowly and carefully. First read down the column of [tʃ] words. Notice how your voicing begins in the middle of the words after the [ʃ] is complete. Then read down the list of [dʒ] words. You should feel voicing right at the start. Then read across the page, contrasting pairs of words, listening and feeling for the differences between the voiceless and voiced sounds. Read the lists a few times until you're sure you can distinguish the two sounds.

[tʃ]	[dʒ]	[tʃ]	[dʒ]
choke	joke	lunch	lunge
cheer	jeer	etch	edge
chain	Jane	britches	bridges
cheap	Jeep	searches	surges
chew	Jew	riches	ridges
chin	gin	batches	badges
chip	gyp	cinches	singes
chump	jump		

Problem 2. Substitution of [ʃ] for [tʃ]

Nonnative speakers often make this substitution. Here are some Contrast Drills that may help.

Say the following words aloud. First read down the list of [ʃ] words. Then read the list of [tʃ] words, making sure you say the portion of the blend. Finally read across, contrasting pairs of words. Feel for the hard contact between the tongue and alveolar ridge for [tʃ]. Notice how there isn't any hard contact for [ʃ].

[ʃ]	[tʃ]	[ʃ]	[tʃ]
sheet	cheat	wash	watch
ship	chip	dish	ditch
share	chair	marsh	march
shanty	chanty	lashing	latch
shop	chop	washed	watched
shore	chore	mashing	matching
shoe	chew	wishing	witching
cash	catch		

Problem 3. Substitution of [j] for [dʒ]

This substitution usually results from confusion between the letter *j* and the sound [j]. This is due to the fact that the letter *j* is pronounced as [j], as in *yes,* in some other languages, and this problem is usually experienced only by nonnative speakers. To correct this problem, you must replace one association pattern with another. Here's a Contrast Drill that will help.

□ *Contrast Drill for* [j] *and* [dʒ] □

Read the following words aloud. Read across the page, contrasting the pairs of words. The first word contains the sound [j], and so shouldn't have the tongue tip touching at all. Feel for tongue–gum ridge contact in the second word. Read the lists a few times until you're satisfied that you're pronouncing the words correctly. Then go on to Level 1 words.

[j]	[dʒ]
yoke	joke
use	juice

(*Lists continue on p. 222*)

[j]	[dʒ]
yule	jewel
yellow	Jell-o
yet	jet
yam	jam

Level 1 Drills for [tʃ]

□ *Practice Words for* [tʃ] □

Say the words in the following lists slowly and clearly. Listen carefully and correct your production until you are sure it is accurate. Make sure to produce the full blend, and not just a [ʃ]. Start with the Beginning words.

Beginning	Middle	End
chief	kitchen	beach
chin	hatchet	finch
chain	hitchhike	catch
chest	patching	coach
champion	punctuate	ouch
chat	question	peach
chalk	hatching	much
choice	coaching	pitch
chance	bunches	hitch
check	munches	inch
chowder	watches	touch
choose	teaches	itch

□ *Practice Phrases for* [tʃ] □

cheap chowder	chitchat	chief choice
kitchen matches	munches lunches	teaches coaches
touch and itch	catch much	inch of beach

□ *Practice Sentences for* [tʃ] □

1. My *chief* complaint is about the *chowder*.
2. He *chose* to *question* the *teacher*.
3. He was the *champion catcher* and *pitcher*.
4. *Peach* fuzz will make you *itch* if you *touch* it.
5. The *coaches* ate *lunch* in the *kitchen*.

Level 2 Drills for [tʃ]

□ *Practice Words for* [tʃ] □

Say the words in the following lists slowly and carefully. Make sure you produce the full [tʃ] blend, even though it appears with other sounds that may be difficult to make.

Beginning	Middle	End
chair	achieved	bleach
cheer	fracture	reach
chill	ritual	rich
charm	ratchet	scorch
sketch	researching	mulch
chicken	bachelor	porch
church	preaches	leach
Charley	watched	clutch
chunky	lunched	breech
children	actual	crouch
cello	marching	grouch
chirp	marched	birch

□ *Practice Sentences for* [tʃ] □

1. I gave a bowl of chili to each of the children.
2. Charley actually led the marching.
3. The mulch pile reached up almost to the porch.
4. We bleached the stain out of the birch chair.
5. I drew a sketch of the preacher at the church.

Level 1 Drills for [dʒ]

□ *Practice Words for* [dʒ] □

Say the words in the following lists slowly and carefully. Listen closely. Make sure you are voicing the entire consonant blend. Start with the Beginning words.

Beginning	Middle	End
jeep	imagine	age
jeans	enjoy	bandage

(Lists continue on p. 224)

Beginning	Middle	End
gyp	agent	cabbage
jab	gadget	damage
jump	wages	vintage
jaw	digit	strange
John	object	teenage
junk	lodging	adjust
jug	pigeon	fudge
joy	magic	wedge
gender	edgy	hedge

□ *Practice Phrases for* [dʒ] □

jump for joy	jab at the jaw	gypped John
magic object	imagine the wages	edgy pigeon
vintage cabbage	adjust for damage	strange wedge

□ *Practice Sentences for* [dʒ] □

1. *John* ripped his *jeans.*
2. I *enjoyed* the *magician's* act.
3. Don't *damage* the *hedge.*
4. I *jumped* for *joy* at the sight of the new *jeep.*
5. He was pouring *vintage* wine from the *strange jug.*

Level 2 Drills for [dʒ]

□ *Practice Words for* [dʒ] □

These words combine sounds with more difficult articulatory movements. Say the words slowly and clearly. Make sure to voice the [dʒ]. Start with the Beginning words.

Beginning	Middle	End
George	agile	pledge
geranium	bulges	college
ginger	fragile	foliage
jelly	registrar	wreckage
judge	suggest	grudge

(*Lists continue on p. 225*)

Beginning	Middle	End
jealous	exaggerate	garbage
genial	dodged	privilege
gentle	wedged	sausage
jarred	psychology	dosage
gerbil	rigidly	bridge

☐ *Practice Sentences for* [dʒ] ☐

1. Attending college is a privilege.
2. The judge was gentle as well as genial.
3. Sausage and ginger don't mix.
4. I was jarred by the wreckage of the garage.
5. George was jealous of my beautiful geraniums.
6. The registrar let me take psychology at another college.
7. The garbage can was wedged rigidly against the wall.

☐ *Level 2 Sentences for* [dʒ] *and* [tʃ] ☐

1. He majored in lunch at college.
2. That was a strange choice to make.
3. I almost choked when I saw the damage to my jeans.
4. I suggested that the children chew more quietly.
5. Charley was known to exaggerate about his courage.
6. He actually worked his way through college selling gadgets.
7. Jeff caught a big striped bass in the channel near the beach.
8. He was teaching seamanship as we watched.
9. Jane lost her gold chains and engagement ring.
10. She wrote about range wars and prairie justice.

Diction:
The Vowels
and Diphthongs

On the following pages you'll find drills for working on vowels and diphthongs. Please note that we are presenting words that are pronounced in different ways in different regions of the country. Therefore, word examples we may list for pronunciation of a particular vowel may be pronounced differently in your area of the country. If that's the case, ignore the examples that don't match pronunciation in your region.

Don't, however, assume that a different pronunciation is always regional; it could be nonstandard for your area. Check with your instructor or someone else who is knowledgeable about pronunciation in your region. We do not advocate any particular regional dialect as being preferable over another. We do, however, advocate "standard for your area" as being preferable over nonstandard.

We've arranged the vowels in the following order:

FRONT VOWELS

---

[i]
see

Sample: SHE COULD SEE THE REAPING MACHINES IN THE FIELD.

Spellings:
- *e* as in *he*
- *ea* as in *eat*
- *eo* as in *people*
- *ey* as in *key*
- *ee* as in *see*
- *ie* as in *field*
- *ei* as in *receipt*
- *is* as in *debris*

Description

[i] is a high, front, tense vowel.

1. Open your mouth very slightly. Spread your lips just a little and pull the corners back slightly, as though you were going to smile. Your teeth should be almost touching.
2. Touch the back molars with the sides of the back of the tongue.
3. Put the tip of the tongue behind the lower teeth and arch the tongue up and forward. Continue to touch the rear upper teeth. Keep the soft palate tensed so that there's no nasal emission of air.
4. Produce voice.

Problems

[i] is not a difficult sound to produce. Probably the most frequently occurring problem is the addition of the schwa ([ə]) after [i] when it is followed by [l]. Try the following:

□ *Production Drill* □

If you add [ə] to [i], you should feel your jaw drop slightly as you say it. If there is no extra sound, your jaw will remain steady. Say the words in the following list slowly and carefully, reading across the page. First you'll break a word into two parts. Then you'll join the parts together. As you say the words, place the back of your hand so that it is touching the underside of your jaw to feel if your jaw drops. You can also use a mirror for this.

fee . . . l	fee . . l	fee . l	feel
mee . . . l	mee . . l	mee . l	meal
dee . . . l	dee . . l	dee . l	deal
whee . . . l	whee . . l	whee . l	wheel
ree . . . l	ree . . l	ree . l	reel
hee . . . l	hee . . l	hee . l	heel
stee . . . l	stee . . l	stee . l	steel

Level 1 Drills for [i]

□ *Practice Words for* [i] □

Say the words in the following lists slowly and clearly. Alter your production until you are sure you are saying the sound acceptably. If you're not sure of the standard sound, ask your instructor to identify a word that you *do* say correctly. Use that word as your comparison word when you're in doubt.

Beginning	Middle	End
east	seed	see
eat	peep	key
even	teach	fee
easy	keep	tea
each	speed	she
eager	heat	me

□ **Practice Phrases for [i]** □

to each his own	*East of Eden*	easy pieces
keep up speed	eat the seed	see the key
pay the fee	the tea to me	even heat

□ **Practice Sentences for [i]** □

1. That's *easy* for *me* to say.
2. I paid the *fee* for the new *key*.
3. *Teach me* how to *heat* the *seeds*.
4. *She even* made the *tea*.
5. *Keep* heading toward the *east*.

Level 2 Drills for [i]

The following drills contain [i] in more difficult contexts, including words in which [l] follows [i].

□ **Practice Words for [i]** □

Say the words in the following lists slowly and carefully. Monitor your production until you're sure you're saying the sound in the desired way.

Beginning	Middle	End
ear	steel	agree
eel	heel	glee

(*Lists continue on p. 231*)

Beginning	Middle	End
eagle	please	plea
evil	fleas	flea
either	cheese	three
eerie	greet	free

□ *Practice Sentences for* [i] □

1. At that price, the cheese was a steal.
2. My dog really has fleas.
3. Please don't step on my heels.
4. I've got the feeling that you agree with me.
5. It's either the eagle or me.
6. I got three greeting cards free.

[I]
sit

Sample: THE RICH SYRUP SPILLED ON THE ENGLISH
BOOK.

Spellings: *i* as in *it*   *y* as in *syrup*   *o* as in *women*
           e as in *English*   *u* as in *busy*
           ui as in *build*   *ee* as in *been*

Note: [I] does not normally occur at the ends of words, except when the letter *y* occurs in unstressed position, as in the
word *pretty*. Speakers in the South and New England will
frequently use [I] instead of [i] at the ends of such words.

Description

[I] is a high, front, lax vowel. It is very much like [i], being made in almost the
same place and the same way. The difference is that [I] is lax, and [i] is tense,
so [I] is a shorter, slightly lower pitched sound.

1. Open your mouth very slightly. Your upper and lower teeth should be close together, but not quite as close as for [i]. Spread your lips slightly, but don't smile for this vowel.
2. Touch the back sides of your tongue to the upper molars. Place the tip behind the lower front teeth. The back of the tongue will be slightly lower than it was for [i].
3. Produce voice.

Problems

[ɪ] is actually not a difficult vowel to produce for native English speakers. Some people who have learned English as a second language, however, may have difficulty if the sound [ɪ] does not appear in their native language. Such languages are the Romance languages—Spanish, French, Italian, and other languages developed from Latin. If you have difficulty distinguishing between [ɪ] and [i], try the following Contrast Drill.

□ *Contrast Drill for* [ɪ] *and* [i] □

Read the words in the following lists aloud slowly and carefully. First read down the columns, then read across. When you read across, contrast the pairs of words, listening for the differences between the [i] in the first word, and the [ɪ] in the second.

[i]	[ɪ]	[i]	[ɪ]
eat	it	jeep	gyp
seat	sit	bean	been
heat	hit	peak	pick
meat	mitt	cheek	chick
cheap	chip	bead	bid
Jean	gin	deep	dip
reach	rich	beat	bit
peel	pill	steal	still

Problem 2. Elongation of [ɪ]

If you hold on to [ɪ] too long, you may add an extra sound, the schwa ([ə]), to it. For example, the word *pill* becomes [pɪəl] instead of [pɪl]. [ɪ] is a shorter sound than [i]. Read the words presented in the Contrast Drill above to feel the difference in length. When you read the words in the drills that follow, make sure to cut the [ɪ] off without adding [ə].

Level 1 Drills for [ɪ]

☐ *Practice Words for* [ɪ] ☐

Read the words in the following lists slowly and carefully. Monitor your production until you're sure it's correct. Ask your instructor to identify a word that you say correctly. Use that word for comparison. Start with the Beginning words.

Beginning	*Middle*	*End* (*y*)
it	bit	city
itch	bin	pretty
in	sit	heavy
ink	pitch	kitty
is	wink	funny
if	king	busy
isn't	wind	any

☐ *Practice Sentences for* [ɪ] ☐

1. The *dinner* was *fit* for a *king.*
2. *It* was too *windy* in the *city.*
3. *Isn't* the *ink pretty?*
4. I'm *itching* from *sitting* in poison *ivy.*
5. *Is* he too *busy* to *pitch?*

Level 2 Drills for [ɪ]

☐ *Practice Words for* [ɪ] ☐

In the lists below, we've included some words that have the letter *i* in an unstressed position, such as in the word *Africa.* The alternate standard pronunciation of these words is with a schwa [ə], instead of [ɪ]: [æfrəkə]

Make sure that you are cutting off the [ɪ] and not adding a schwa to it.

Beginning	*Middle*
ill	sill
irritate	wilt
igloo	flinch
English	slit
Illinois	strip
	still
	pill
	script
	trip
	written

☐ *Practice Sentences for* [ɪ] ☐

1. I had to take a bitter pill when I was sick.
2. Chicago is a big city in Illinois.
3. Read it as it's written in the script.
4. The flower will wilt on the window sill.
5. My English teacher irritates me.

---

[e]
ate

Sample: THE LADY SAID THE TRAIN WAS DELAYED EIGHT HOURS.

Spellings:
a as in *ate*	*ei* as in *eight*
ea as in *break*	*ay* as in *delay*
ai as in *train*	*ee* as in *matinee*

Description

[e] is a mid, front, tense vowel. In stressed syllables, especially those in final position, we tend to use the diphthong, [eɪ], which is longer than [e] and drops in pitch.

□ *Production:* [e] □

1. Lower your tongue to a point just a bit lower than the position for [ɪ]. Open your mouth slightly. Just the rear of your tongue should touch the upper back teeth, and the tip should be behind the lower front teeth.
2. Produce voice. As you do, pull the corners of your lips back very slightly.

Problems

Problem 1. Addition of [ə]

When [e] is followed by [l], we sometimes add the schwa between the [e] and the [l]. If you do this, try the following:

□ *Production Drill* □

Say the following words, reading across the page. The words will be broken at first, but you'll join the parts together as you go across. Make sure to stop producing voice entirely during the breaks, which will become shorter and shorter.

may . . . l	may . . l	may . l	mail
say . . . l	say . . l	say . l	sail
pay . . . l	pay . . l	pay . l	pail
ray . . . l	ray . . l	ray . l	rail
fay . . . l	fay . . l	fay . l	fail
tray . . . l	tray . . l	tray . l	trail

Problem 2. Clipped [e]

Some nonnative speakers tend to shorten the [e] too much. This tends to give their speech a characteristically clipped sound. Do you do this? Compare the following pairs of words. The first word in each pair should have a shorter [e] than the second. The second word should have a noticeably longer [e].

| rate – raid | face – faze |
| mate – maid | race – raze |

If both words in the pairs have vowels the same length, try giving them longer duration when you do the following drills. Since [e] is a sound of relatively few problems, all the drills are Level 1.

Level 1 Drills for [e]

☐ *Practice Words for* [e] ☐

Say the words in the following lists slowly. Listen carefully as you say them, and try to make the vowel [e] the correct length. Avoid adding the schwa before [l].

Beginning	*Middle*	*End*
able	break	delay
eight	train	matinee
age	label	away
ace	great	gray
ache	place	repay
April	flake	payday
angel	scrape	replay
aim	slate	relay
ape	relation	weigh

☐ *Practice Phrases for* [e] ☐

great place	break the label	eight hundred and eight
matinee day	able to repay	relay race

☐ *Practice Sentences for* [e] ☐

1. It would be great to take the day off.
2. I'll pay you back on Thursday.
3. We'll be able to meet you at the train by eight.
4. Show the instant replay of the relay race.
5. Wednesday and Saturday are matinee days.
6. Scrape the snowflakes off the slate.
7. This backache won't go away today.
8. They won't take it if you break the label.

$$[\varepsilon]$$
bet

Sample: I DIDN'T USE MY HEAD WHEN I MADE A BET
WITH MY FRIEND.

Spellings: *e* as in *bet*   *ea* as in *head*   *ai* as in *again*
          a as in *any*   *ie* as in *friend*

Description

[ɛ] is a mid, front, lax vowel. It is shorter than [e] and lower pitched.

☐ *Production:* [ɛ] ☐

1. Open your mouth slightly wider than for [e].
2. The very back of the tongue is touching the upper molars, and the tip is
behind the lower front teeth.
3. Produce voice.

☐ *Contrast Drill for* [ɛ] *and* [e] ☐

Contrast the following pairs of words:

[e]	[ɛ]
late	let
bait	bet
fade	fed
pain	pen
paste	pest

Problems

This sound is one of the most often used in the English language. There are
few real difficulties in producing the sound. There are some substitutions of

other sounds for [ɛ], however. A common substitution is [ɪ] for [ɛ] as in *pin* for *pen*. Try the following Contrast Drill:

☐ *Contrast Drill for* [ɛ] *and* [ɪ] ☐

Say the words in the following lists slowly, reading across the page. The first word of each pair contains the sound [ɪ] and the second contains the sound [ɛ]. Ask your instructor or a fellow student to listen to you and to correct your pronunciation.

[ɪ]		[ɛ]	[ɪ]		[ɛ]
pin	—	pen	sit	—	set
bit	—	bet	tin	—	ten
wrist	—	rest	lid	—	led
him	—	hem	lint	—	lent
been	—	Ben	mint	—	meant
hid	—	head	rid	—	red
since	—	cents	sinned	—	send

Level 1 Drills for [ɛ]

[ɛ] is a relatively easy sound to produce accurately, so we've provided only Level 1 Drills. Just make sure you're producing [ɛ] and not another vowel in these drills.

☐ *Practice Words for* [ɛ] ☐

Say the words in the following lists slowly. Monitor your production to make sure you are producing the desired sound. Ask your instructor or a classmate to listen to you if you're not sure of your pronunciation. Start with the Beginning words. Note: [ɛ] does not occur in end position in English.

Beginning	*Middle*	*Beginning*	*Middle*
end	pen	any	rent
edge	pledge	echo	center
eggs	again	elderly	pledge
extra	gentle	engineer	forget
every	tent	exit	energy
enter	sent	elbow	said
ever	heaven	educate	mess

heaven sent	gentlemen's pledge	any exit
sent the rent	bent elbow	a mess again
every edge	extra echo	center entrance

□ *Practice Sentences for* [ɛ] □

1. Eggs again?
2. I sent the rent on Wednesday.
3. I pledged my help to the Center for the Elderly.
4. The squeak of Fred's pen set my teeth on edge.
5. I need every bit of extra energy I can get.
6. I missed the exit because of the mess.
7. The sunset tinted the tent a pale yellow.
8. The engineers couldn't get rid of the extra echoes.
9. Don't forget to give me the fifty cents.
10. He got his education sitting in front of thc TV set.

[æ]
pat

Sample: **A FLAT TIRE IS NO LAUGHING MATTER.**

Spellings: *a* as in *pat*   *au* as in *laugh*
ai as in *plaid*

Description

[æ] is a low, front, slightly tense vowel. It is a longer sound than [ɛ] and lower pitched.

□ *Production:* [æ] □

1. Drop your lower jaw noticeably from the position for [ɛ].
2. Place your tongue tip behind the lower front teeth. Flatten the entire tongue slightly, and raise the middle and back slightly.

2. Produce voice. Make sure to keep the soft palate energized to prevent nasal emission of air.

Problems

Problem 1. Distinguishing between [ɛ] and [æ]

If you raise the back and sides of the tongue just a little too much, you change an [æ] word to an [ɛ] word. For example, *bat* becomes *bet*. There are some regional differences, too. Say the words, *merry, marry, Mary.* If you live in the Northeast, you probably say each word with a different vowel. In other parts of the country, you may be saying them the same, with the vowel [ɛ]. For words in which there's an [r], then, we would consider the use of [ɛ] to be regional. Substituting [ɛ] for [æ], as in *bet* and *bat*, is generally considered nonstandard regardless of region. Try the following Contrast Drill:

□ *Contrast Drill for* [ɛ] *and* [æ] □

Say the words in the following list slowly, reading across the page, contrasting the pairs of words. The first word of each pair will contain the vowel [ɛ], the second word will contain [æ]. Listen carefully to hear the difference between the two. Ask your instructor to check your pronunciation.

[ɛ]	[æ]	[ɛ]	[æ]
bet	— bat	fed	— fad
ten	— tan	led	— lad
end	— and	head	— had
Ed	— add	set	— sat
Ken	— can	lend	— land
send	— sand	bed	— bad
said	— sad	pest	— past
left	— laughed	leg	— lag

Problem 2. Distinguishing between [ɒ] and [æ]

Sometimes people have difficulty distinguishing [ɒ] as in *hot* from [æ] as in *hat.* Try the following:

Say the words in the following list slowly, reading across the page. Contrast the pairs of words. Ask your instructor to check your pronunciation if you're not sure. The first word of each pair will have the sound [æ], the second word will have [ɒ].

[æ]	[ɒ]	[æ]	[ɒ]
hat	hot	cat	cot
map	mop	shack	shock
pat	pot	cap	cop
jab	job	tap	top
sack	sock	Dan	Don

Problem 3. Diphthongization

You may be in the habit of producing [æ] with your jaw too high, near the position for [ɛ]. This will result in a diphthong [ɛæ], instead of the pure vowel [æ]. This most often happens before voiced consonants, especially the nasals. To prevent this, you must move the articulators quickly. The following Transfer Exercises* will help.

□ *Transfer Exercises* □

The beginning word of each line below is one in which [æ] is not as likely to change to a diphthong as in some of the words following on that line. Avoiding diphthongization is likely to be more difficult in later words on the same line. Listen carefully to your production of [æ] in the first word of a line. Then, in producing every other word in the line, try to copy the same pure [æ] vowel you produced in the first word. Circle the words you find most difficult and practice them repeatedly, transferring the vowel sound from a "safe" word in that line to your troublesome word.

1. at add ant aunt act actor actual
2. bat bad bath bass bash batch balance back bag bang bank
3. fat fad fan fast fact fang fashion
4. sat sad sand sash sack sang sank
5. hat had half hand hash hatch hack hang hank
6. pat pad pan path pass patch pack pang

---

* Hilda B. Fisher, *Improving Voice and Articulation, Second Edition.* Houghton Mifflin, Boston, 1975.

7. cat cad can cash catch can't
8. mat mad matter mass man mash match mangle
9. lad laugh lass lash latch lap lab lamb lamp lank
10. dad Dan dash dab dam damp dank
11. tat tan tap tab tam tack tag tang tank
12. rat radish rather raft wrap rash ran ram rang
13. gap gaff gander gallon gash gag gang
14. gnat nab nap nasty gnash knack nag
15. chat chatter chap chastise champion chant
16. plait plaid plan plant plaque
17. blab bland blast black blank
18. glad glass gland glance
19. grad grab grand grass gramp
20. trap tramp trash track
21. stab stamp stand staff stash stack stank
22. slap slab slash slant slam slack slang
23. snap snack snatch snag
24. flat flap flab flash flask flack flag flank
25. exact example examine examination

Note: There is an allophone of [æ] that is used mostly in New England. This can be considered a low front vowel, [a] as in the words *ask, half, park.* That vowel is produced in a position somewhere in between the [æ] as in *hat* and the [ɑ] as in *father.*

Level 1 Drills for [æ]

□ *Practice Words for* [æ] □

Say the words in the following lists slowly. Listen carefully as you say them. If you're not sure of your production, ask your instructor or a classmate to listen to you and identify a word you say correctly to use for comparison. Start with the Beginning words. Do not go on to the phrases or sentences until you have had enough practice on single words. There are no English words ending with the [æ] sound.

Beginning	Middle	Beginning	Middle
at	bat	add	pat
actor	fast	and	can
after	habit	attic	sack
apple	Jack	as	fact
act	wax	happy	packed

□ *Practice Phrases for* [æ] □

after the actors   up in the attic
packed his sack   wash or wax
at bat   fast answer

□ *Practice Sentences for* [æ] □

1. *Anthony packed* his *sack.*
2. *Can* I *have* my car *waxed?*
3. The *ants* were in the *last sack.*
4. I'll *have* a *stab at* it *after* the *exam.*
5. He *acted as* though we were *answering back.*

Level 2 Drills for [æ]

□ *Practice Words for* [æ] □

Say the words in the following lists slowly and carefully. Make sure you don't nasalize the vowel when there's a nasal consonant in the word. Also, many of the words at this level are easily diphthongized. Listen carefully. If you're not sure of your production, ask your instructor or a classmate to listen to you.

Beginning	*Middle*	*Middle*	*Middle*
angle	can't	class	plant
amplify	ham	grant	grand
ankle	bland	band	plan
angry	sandwich	handy	pants
adding	fans	grass	brand
asking	lands	stranded	standing

□ *Practice Sentences for* [æ] □

1. I can't stand it!
2. The fans were standing while the band played the National Anthem.
3. He gets angry with me for asking too many questions in class.
4. They were stranded on the grass strip after the crash.
5. The ham sandwiches in the snack bar are pretty bland.

DICTION: THE VOWELS AND DIPHTHONGS

[ɑ]
calm

Sample: IT DIDN'T BOTHER HIM AS HE CALMLY LOCKED
THE CAR.

Spellings: *a* as in *calm*   *o* as in *lock*
ea as in *heart*

Description

[ɑ] is a low, back, lax vowel. It's the widest open of all the vowels. The tongue has only the very back part slightly raised, the rest of it is relaxed.

□ *Production:* [ɑ] □

1. Open wide and say *ahhh*.

Problems

Very few. There are a couple of substitutions, but they are regional or sub-cultural. For example, New Englanders might say *park* with the vowel [a], and certain New Yorkers or West Indians might say the word *hot* with the vowel [ɒ]. It probably doesn't matter which you say as long as you are consistent.

Level 1 Drills for [ɑ]

□ *Practice Words for* [ɑ] □

Say the words in the following lists slowly. Listen carefully to your production as you say each word. All the drills for [ɑ] are Level 1. There are no English words (except slang words) that end in [ɑ].

Beginning	Middle	Beginning	Middle
arms	calm	on	top
are	frog	ah	father
honest	bomb	alarm	stars
obvious	locker	occupy	guard
art	spot	onset	response
argue	palms	arson	stopping
arch	smart	army	follow

☐ *Practice Phrases for* [ɑ] ☐

obvious response	calm frog
argue about art	smart bomb
on top of	spot the guard

☐ *Practice Sentences for* [ɑ] ☐

1. They had an honest argument with their father.
2. Stopping is the obvious response when the guard is armed.
3. The fog crept in the harbor on little frog's feet.
4. Sighing "ahh" can be calming.
5. Watch them stop the cars at the top of the yard.

[ɔ]
awful

Sample: I THOUGHT THE LAUNDRY DID AN AWFUL JOB
IN A SHORT TIME.

Spellings: *aw* as in *awful*   *au* as in *laundry*   *oo* as in *door*
o as in *wrong*   *ough* as in *thought*   *augh* as in *taught*

Description

[ɔ] is a mid, back, lax vowel. The lips are usually rounded.

□ *Production:* [ɔ] □

1. Close the mouth very slightly from the position of [ɑ], and slightly round your lips. Elevate the back of your tongue a bit, but don't touch your upper teeth.
2. Produce voice. Make sure there's no nasal emission.

Problems

Use of [ɔ] varies almost from word to word, region to region. Words that are pronounced with [ɔ] in one region may be pronounced with [ɔ] or [ɒ] in others. For example, the word *water* may be pronounced with [ɒ] in upstate New York and with [ɔ] in downstate New York. Floridians usually say *Florida* with [ɔ], but northerners say it with [ɑ]. How do *you* say such words as *wash, caught, coffee,* and *auto?*

In the drills that follow, we've used words that are pronounced with [ɔ] in at least one regional dialect. You'll have to determine the usage in your area by consulting with your instructor or someone else who is knowledgeable on the subject.

Problem 1. Nonstandard [ɔ]

Although use of [ɔ] varies greatly around the country, there is a nonstandard production. It occurs when you round your lips too much and close your mouth slightly. It frequently is associated with the dental and gum ridge consonants because they require a slight closing of the mouth. Look at your mouth in a mirror as you say *awful.* Do your lips suddenly round before you make the sound? Is your mouth almost closed? If so, you are probably producing the nonstandard sound. Here's another test: put the back of your hand lightly against the underside of your chin and say "all." Did your jaw drop? It should.

The nonstandard sound that results is a diphthong close to [ɔə]. Actually, there are two changes in the sound: the [ɔ] is said with too much lip-rounding, and the [ə] results because the jaw is moving before you stop the [ɔ]. If you're producing the sound this way, try the following exercise.

□ *Production Drill* □

Say the following pairs of words, reading across. The first word of each pair contains the sound [ɑ]. The second has the sound [ɔ]. Hold your chin and look in a mirror while you say the words. Don't let your jaw rise or your lips round. In other words, go from the position for [ɑ] to the position for [ɔ] without moving anything except your tongue. You should be able to produce the correct sound. Ask your instructor to listen.

[ɑ]	[ɔ]	[ɑ]	[ɔ]	[ɑ]	[ɔ]
cot	– caught	hot	– haught	la	– law
on	– awning	hock	– hawk	tot	– taught
lot	– lawn				

Level 1 Drills for [ɔ]

☐ *Practice Words for* [ɔ] ☐

Say the words in the following lists slowly and carefully. Listen carefully. If a particular word sounds strange because it's not pronounced with [ɔ] in your area, eliminate it. (Check with your instructor first.) Find a word you consistently pronounce correctly, and use that word as your standard for comparison.

Beginning	Middle	End
awful	tall	law
often	stall	straw
August	always	draw
auction	thought	jaw
also	wrong	saw

☐ *Practice Phrases for* [ɔ] ☐

awfully tall	always thought	August auction
wrong side of the law	took a draw	stop stalling

☐ *Practice Sentences for* [ɔ] ☐

1. I *always thought* he'd break the *law*.
2. *August* can be *awfully* hot.
3. We drew *straws also*.
4. Have you been *wrong often*?
5. We *saw* her at the *auction*.

Level 2 Drills for [ɔ]

☐ *Practice Words for* [ɔ] ☐

Many [ɔ] words couple [ɔ] and [r]. You should make an extra effort to stop your jaw from rising and your lips from overly rounding. Say each word slowly, comparing it with a word you know you say correctly. If you're not sure, ask your instructor or a classmate to listen.

Beginning	*Middle*	*Middle*	*Middle*
oar	born	morning	sports
crawl	store	drawn	broad
orchid	four	order	north
all	small	storm	sore
audio	cough	cloth	corn

☐ *Practice Sentences for* [ɔ] ☐

1. I ordered it all at the store.
2. I bought a small audio amplifier.
3. The storm washed an oar up on the shore.
4. He steered a broad course by the North Star.
5. I had an awful cough all morning.

---

[o]

so

Sample: S͟O, I ASKED HIM TO R͟O͟W THE B͟O͟A͟T HOME.

Spellings: *o*   as in *so*   *oa* as in *boat*
                ow   as in *row*   *oe* as in *toe*
                ough as in *dough*   *ew* as in *sew*

Description

[o] is a mid, back, tense vowel. The jaw is up slightly higher than for [ɔ], and your lips are rounded.

□ *Production:* [o] □

1. Open your mouth about halfway. Round your lips and slightly purse them. Touch the tip of your tongue to the back of your lower teeth, but do it lightly.
2. Raise the back of your tongue as you purse the lips. Produce voice. Make sure there's no nasal emission.

Problems

[o] is fairly easy to produce accurately. Actually, most native speakers produce the diphthong [ou] more than the pure vowel [o], especially in stressed syllables and before voiced consonants. Sometimes, nonnative speakers who have only the pure vowel [o] in their native languages shorten their vowels consistently in English. It doesn't really matter which you use for meaning. See if you can hear a difference in length in the following pairs of words:

rope – robe   coat – code   post – posed

The second word of each pair contains the diphthong [ou]. You can practice lengthening your vowel on the Level 1 drills that follow.

Level 1 Drills for [o]

□ *Practice Words for* [o] □

Say the words in the following lists slowly. Listen for length: do you use the vowel [o] or the diphthong [ou]?

Beginning	Middle	End
open	road	flow
over	boat	toe
oh	bowl	dough
oak	sewing	throw
oats	pole	show
ocean	coal	mow
own	grown	grow
omit	stone	follow
odor	whole	glow

1. He *owned* an *ocean-going boat*.
2. Put the *oatmeal* in the *bowl* next to the *stove*.
3. We *opened* the *coal stove* and began to *choke* on the *smoke*.
4. She was *sewing closed* a *hole* in the *toe*.
5. It's hard to *follow* such a *glowing show*.

[U]
book

Sample: **I WISH YOU WOULD PUT THE BOOK IN THE WOODEN BOX.**

Spellings: *oo* as in *book*   *ou* as in *would*
          u as in *put*

Description

[U] is a high, back, lax vowel. Your lips are slightly rounded.

□ *Production:* [U] □

1. Open your mouth to a position slightly higher than for [o]. Round and slightly protrude your lips.
2. Touch your lower front teeth with the tip of your tongue.
3. Produce voice. Make sure there's no nasal emission.

Problems

[U] is a fairly easy vowel to produce. Most of the problems occur when a speaker isn't sure of how to pronounce a word and substitutes [u] for [U]. For example, *should* becomes *shooed*. (See the drills on [u] for this.)

The drills for [U] are all level 1. Just be sure you're using [U] and not [u].

Level 1 Drills for [ʊ]

☐ *Practice Words for* [ʊ] ☐

Say the words in the following lists slowly and carefully. Listen closely, and be sure you are not saying [u] instead of [ʊ]. [ʊ] does not occur in end or beginning positions.

Middle

wood	book	could	put
stood	should	sugar	pull
look	cook	bushel	bully
hook	hood	wooden	couldn't
brook	butcher	wool	bush
wouldn't	cookie	took	good

☐ *Practice Sentences for* [ʊ] ☐

1. I couldn't push the wood through the bush.
2. I would do it by hook or by crook.
3. He took the meat off the butcher block.
4. The bully stood still against the pull.
5. The sugar cookies were too good to crumble.

---

[u]
too

Sample: HE WAS TOO LATE TO GO ON THE CRUISE AS A CREW MEMBER.

Spellings: *o* as in *to*   *oo* as in *too*
            ew as in *crew*   *ui* as in *cruise*
            ou as in *you*   *u* as in *tuba*

Description

[u] is a high, back, tense vowel. It's the highest back vowel, and we make it with our lips considerably rounded.

□ *Production:* [u] □

1. Put your jaw in the same place as for [ʊ]. Round your lips so as to leave only a small opening, as for [w].
2. Raise the back of your tongue so that it almost touches your soft palate. The tip should be just touching the gum behind the lower front teeth.
3. Produce voice. Make sure there's no nasal emission.

Problems

[u] is not often misarticulated. It's fairly easy to produce, so only Level 1 Drills are given. Sometimes, though, nonnative speakers may be confused as to which sound to use—[u] or [ʊ]. And there are some regional variations in the pronunciation of words such as *roof* and *root*. Here's a Contrast Drill to help reinforce the differences between [u] and [ʊ].

□ *Contrast Drill for* [u] *and* [ʊ] □

Say the words in the following lists slowly, reading across the page. Contrast the pairs of words. The first word of each pair uses a [ʊ] and the second a [u].

[ʊ]	[u]	[ʊ]	[u]
soot	– suit	pull	– pool
look	– Luke	full	– fool
would	– wooed	could	– cooed
stood	– stewed	cookie	– kooky

Level Drills for [u]

□ *Practice Words for* [u] □

Say the words in the following lists slowly. Make sure you're not saying [ʊ] for [u]. Ask your instructor or a classmate to listen to you if you're not sure. There are only a few words beginning with [u].

Beginning	Middle	Middle	End	End
oodles	pool	stool	crew	two
ooze	fool	coupon	true	through
oolong	dues	moon	stew	blue
	dunes	whose	shoe	grew
	tube	soup	flew	glue
	food	stoop	knew	who

1. He jumped in the pool like a fool.
2. Food tubes are the stews of tomorrow.
3. We found a coupon for a soup spoon.
4. Is it true he flew the coop?
5. I carried my shoes while we walked through the dunes.

MID VOWELS

[ʌ]

up

Sample: HE WAS LUCKY TO DOUBLE HIS MONEY IN UNDER A MONTH.

Spellings: *u* as in *up*   *o* as in *month*
ou as in *double*

Description

[ʌ] is a mid, central vowel that occurs in stressed syllables and words.

□ *Production:* [ʌ] □

1. Open your mouth about as wide as for [ɔ] and slightly higher than for [ɑ]. Don't round your lips.
2. Raise the center of your tongue very slightly. Produce voice. Make sure there's no nasal emission.

Problems

[ʌ] is one of the least complicated vowels to produce. But because it doesn't exist in many other languages, nonnative speakers will frequently substitute another sound for [ʌ]. Most often, [ɑ] is substituted, so here's a Contrast Drill to help you distinguish between [ɑ] and [ʌ].

□ Contrast Drill for [ɑ] and [ʌ] □

Read the words in the following lists aloud. First read down the list of [ɑ] words. Then read down the list of [ʌ] words. Finally read across the page, contrasting the pairs of words. The first word of each pair will contain [ɑ], and the second [ʌ].

[ɑ]	[ʌ]	[ɑ]	[ʌ]
hot	hut	rob	rub
cop	cup	lock	luck
not	nut	rot	rut
calm	come	mock	muck
cot	cut	dock	duck
gone	gun		

Note: [ʌ] occurs *only* in stressed words and syllables. It does not occur at the ends of words. Because it is easy to produce accurately, all the drills for [ʌ] are Level 1.

Level 1 Drills for [ʌ]

□ Practice Words for [ʌ] □

Say the words in the following lists slowly. Monitor your production to make sure you are producing the sound correctly and not substituting [ɑ] for [ʌ]. If you aren't sure of your production, ask your instructor or a classmate to listen to you. Start with the Beginning words.

Beginning	*Middle*	*Beginning*	*Middle*
up	double	under	month
uncle	nothing	other	mother
oven	brother	us	discuss
onion	instructor	ugly	tough
usher	enough	ultimate	bubble

nothing under   tough and ugly   the other onion
enough ushers   double up   under discussion

□ *Practice Sentences for* [ʌ] □

1. There's nothing cooking in the oven.
2. We have enough ushers this month.
3. My uncle and my brother have the matter under discussion.
4. My mother doesn't cry when she peels onions.
5. The other instructor is a tougher grader.
6. I blew the ultimate bubble with that ugly looking gum.
7. What's coming up for us next?

[ə]

banana

Sample: THE PRICE OF BANANAS WENT DOWN AGAIN.

Spellings: a, e, i, o, u, plus combinations, in unstressed syllables.

Description

[ə] is a low, mid vowel. It does not occur in any stressed syllables or in stressed single-syllable words.

□ *Production:* [ə] □

1. [ə] is produced in the same way as [ʌ]. The only difference is in stress (loudness). Open your mouth to a position about the same as for [ɔ]. Rest your tongue in the bottom of your mouth.
2. Produce voice, but not as loud as for [ʌ] or as long.
   Notes: [ə] is the vowel we use more than any other in our language. That's because the *other vowels tend to change from their original form to* [ə] *when*

they are unstressed. This vowel actually can't be pronounced alone, since it only occurs in unstressed positions, so you may be confused as to what its sound is. For now, let's say that *it sounds just like* [ʌ], *but weaker*. As a matter of fact, the name of this vowel, *schwa*, is from the German word for "weak."

Here are some words that may help explain this. Say the word *above*. It has the stress on the second syllable, so the vowels are [ə] and [ʌ]: [əbʌv]. Say the word a few times to get the feeling of the first sound. Make sure to say the word normally, with the first sound so weak that it's almost not there. Now say *above* with equal stress on both syllables, as you would in a word such as *Ping-Pong*. Sounds strange, doesn't it. When you said *above* that way, you used the vowel [ʌ] twice. Here's another example: the word *the* can be said in two ways. Try these phrases: *the beginning, the end*. Say them a couple of times. You should hear a difference: in phrases in which *the* comes before a consonant sound, we say [ə]; in phrases in which *the* comes before a vowel sound, we say [i]. You have to listen to the stress to decide which vowel was used.

In summary, [ə] is produced in the same way and sounds just like [ʌ], only it is weaker. You use [ə] when other vowels change because they are unstressed.

Problems

The difficulties with [ə] are really not production difficulties. They are basically difficulties caused by confusing [ʌ] and [ə], omission of [ə], and addition of [ə], such as in the word *athlete*. Here's a Contrast Drill to help you distinguish between [ə] and [ʌ].

☐ *Contrast Drill for* [ə] *and* [ʌ] ☐

Say the following words and phrases slowly. Each word or phrase contains both the [ə] (marked ‿) and the [ʌ] (marked ‾).

a͜bōve	co͜me ūp	sun ūp	a͜brūpt
cūt u͜p	cu͜t ūp	fūnda͜mental	bū͜ttercu͜p
seve͜n ūp			

Level 1 Drills for [ə]

☐ *Practice Words for* [ə] ☐

The words in the following lists all contain the vowel [ə]. Because you can spell [ə] so many ways, and the same letter can be pronounced differently in the same word, we've underlined the letters that are to be pronounced [ə]. Say the words slowly and carefully, but make sure to use the conventional stress pattern. Check with your instructor or a classmate if you're not sure.

Beginning	*Middle*	*End*
about	lion	soda
around	banana	Canada
another	connect	sofa
again	official	tuba
agree	police	vanilla
away	elephant	Carolina

Level 2 Drills for [ə]

□ *Practice Words for* [ə] □

Here are more words containing [ə]. This time, though, there's no underlining. Check with your instructor if you're not sure of pronunciation.

Beginning	*Middle*	*End*
afraid	dictionary	Roberta
amend	university	area
aloud	parade	camera
asleep	possible	arena
across	zoology	visa
appreciate	professor	panda

□ *Practice Sentences for* [ə] □

Since you can spell [ə] with any vowel, you may have to double-check the pronunciation of some of the new words in these sentences.

1. Look it up in the dictionary.
2. Did you bring your camera to the parade?
3. Roberta was afraid she would fall asleep in class.
4. I was in that professor's class last semester.
5. I understand that rain is possible later in the day.
6. He walked across the restricted area.
7. I learned about the giant panda in Zoology.
8. The elephant charged around the arena.
9. He was an undercover agent.
10. They couldn't agree on an official solution.

257

DICTION: THE VOWELS AND DIPHTHONGS

Sample: THE <u>EAR</u>LY T<u>UR</u>TLE IS THE F<u>IR</u>ST ONE IN THE H<u>ER</u>D.

Spellings: er as in *herd*   ur as in *turtle*
                   ear as in *early*   ir as in *first*

Description

[ɝ] is a high, mid, tense vowel that occurs only in stressed words and syllables. It has an [r] sound to it, but it is different from the consonant in that it is longer and can form a syllable on its own.

The amount of [r] varies in different areas of the country. Less [r] is used in large areas of the South, East, and Northeast. That pronunciation can be transcribed with another symbol, [ɜ]. We won't use that symbol because we don't think it's important to distinguish between [ɝ] and [ɜ].

☐ *Production:* [ɝ] ☐

1. Open your mouth to the position to say [ɔ], about halfway. Don't round your lips.
2. Raise the middle section of the tongue slightly, and *curl the tip back* until it's pointing to the palate just behind the upper gum ridge. Produce voice. Make sure there's no nasality.

Problems

Problem 1. Overpronunciation

Some people tend to curl their tongues too far back and "work" too hard at the [r] quality. Ask your instructor to listen to your pronunciation of some [ɝ] words if you think you may be overpronouncing.

Problem 2. Substitution of [ɜɪ] for [ɝ]

There is a nonstandard pronunciation that occurs mostly in the East when [ɜɪ] is substituted for [ɝ]. In this substitution, the word *bird* would become something like *boid* because of the addition of the [ɪ] after the [ɜ]. This substitution is used by only a small number of speakers, so we suggest you check with your instructor or see Appendix B for more help.

Only Level 1 Drills are given for [ɝ]. Try not to overpronounce.

Level 1 Drills for [ɝ]

☐ *Practice Words for* [ɝ] ☐

Say the words in the following lists slowly and carefully, but don't overdo it. Determine the amount of [r] used in your area by checking with your instructor or some other person knowledgeable about your regional dialect.

Beginning	Middle	Beginning	Middle
early	first	earnest	turtle
earn	nervous	urn	word
irk	attorney	urban	burn
earth	learn	urgent	girl
urge	curve	herb	whirl

☐ *Practice Sentences for* [ɝ] ☐

1. He burned the first dollar he ever earned.
2. She was learning about the curvature of the Earth.
3. The attorney received an urgent message.
4. Where on Earth did you get that turtle?
5. It was too early for the girl to get a sunburn.
6. He nervously urged me to slow down on the curves.

[ɚ]
father

Sample: HER FAT<u>HER</u>'S LETT<u>ER</u> GAVE THE GOVERN<u>OR</u> PLEA<u>SURE</u>.

Spellings: Any vowel and [r] combination.

Description

[ɚ] is a mid, back, tense vowel with an [r] quality. In large areas of the South, East, and Northeast, the pronunciation is optional, with the [ə] being used instead. [ɚ] *is used only in unstressed syllables and words.* It is a shorter, unstressed version of [ɝ].

□ *Production:* [ɚ] □

1. [ɚ] is produced in the same way as [ɝ]. The only difference is in stress (loudness). Open your mouth to the position to say [ɔ], about halfway. Don't round your lips.
2. Curl the tongue tip back until it points just behind the upper gum ridge and raise the center. Produce voice, but not as loud or as long as for [ɝ].

Problems

[ɚ] is a relatively simple sound to produce. One problem may be that of the "optional" pronunciation. That could occur should you relocate to an area of the country where [ə] isn't optional from an area where it is. In that case you may want to consider pronouncing the [ɚ]. There are some omissions that are nonstandard, though. The [ɚ] should be pronounced when it is followed by a vowel, as in *difference, burying,* and *furry.*
    Only Level 1 Drills are given for [ɚ].

Level 1 Drills for [ɚ]

□ *Practice Words for* [ɚ] □

Say the words in the following lists slowly. Although all the drills for [ɚ] are on Level 1, you may have some difficulty deciding when to use [ɚ] and [ɝ]. When both sounds occur in a word or a sentence, we've marked [ɚ] with _. Ask your instructor about the optional pronunciation of [ə] in your area. Remember, [ɚ] is unstressed.

Middle	*End*	*Middle*	*End*
eastern	father	western	dollar
perhaps	wonder	furry	after

(Lists continue on p. 261)

Middle	End	Middle	End
barn	bother	American	caller
paper	actor	answered	sailor
percent	matter	modern	tire
personality	buyer	sister	tar
cart	burger	anchorman	turner
beer	earner	surrender	runner

□ *Practice Sentences for* [ɚ] □

1. A burger and fries cost a dollar.
2. I'd rather surrender first.
3. Are those American sailors over there?
4. That actor sure has personality.
5. The cart goes on the eastern end of the street.
6. Answer the other caller first.
7. My sister ordered a western omelet.
8. Something's bothering my father.
9. Perhaps you'd like more modern furniture?

DIPHTHONGS

[aɪ]
ice

Sample: I WOULD LIKE TO BUY SOME ICE SKATES
SOMETIME.

Spellings: *i* as in *ice*   *y* as in *cry*
ie as in *lie*   *uy* as in *buy*
igh as in *light*   *eigh* as in *height*

Description

[aɪ] is a diphthong beginning with a low back vowel and gliding toward a high front vowel.

□ *Production:* [aɪ] □

1. Open your mouth to the position for [a]. Your tongue should be flat in the bottom of your mouth, relaxed. Your lips should not be rounded.
2. Produce voice. As you do, close the mouth slightly, and lift your tongue slightly. Move toward the position of [ɪ].

Problems

Problem 1. Substitution of [a] for [aɪ]

In many areas the [aɪ] is "broadened"; in other words, the first part of the diphthong has its normal value, but the second part is greatly diminished. This happens particularly in the South and Southeast. There is a nonstandard pronunciation, however, in which the second part of the diphthong is entirely missing. The word *time* [taɪm] would become [tam] *tahm*. Check with your instructor to see if you make this substitution. If you do, try the following Production Drill.

□ *Production Drill* □

Read across the page, saying the "broken" words slowly. Bring the parts together as you read across. Say the first part with the vowel [a] as in *calm*, and say the second part with the vowel [ɪ] as in *sit*.

ta . . . it	ta . . it	ta . it	ta it	tight
la . . . it	la . . it	la . it	la it	light
na . . . it	na . . it	na . it	na it	night
ba . . . it	ba . . it	ba . it	ba it	bite
ka . . . it	ka . . it	ka . it	ka it	kite
ra . . . it	ra . . it	ra . it	ra it	right
sa . . . it	sa . . it	sa . it	sa it	sight

Problem 2. Substitution of [əɪ] for [aɪ]

If you raise your jaw a little too much, you'll produce a diphthong, [əɪ], instead of [aɪ], the same sound you'd get if you substituted *loin* for *line*. The problem seems to occur most often in words in which [aɪ] is followed by a voiced consonant. Do you hear a difference between *right* and *ride?* Between *sight* and *side?* If you make this substitution, try the Problem 1 drill presented above. Then try the following Contrast Drill:

☐ *Contrast Drill for* [aɪ] *and* [əɪ] ☐

Read the words in the following lists slowly. First read down the *vs* column, next down the *v* column, and then across the page. When you contrast the pairs of words, try to hold your jaw position constant: don't let it move up.

vs	v	vs	v
right	ride	ice	eyes
sight	side	slights	slides
height	hide	strife	strive
lice	lies	ricing	rising
rice	rise	slighting	sliding
light	lied	sighting	siding
a bite	abide	righting	riding
tight	tide	device	devise

If you seem to have difficulty, try using a mirror to look for lip-rounding, which would be associated with lifting your jaw.

Level 1 Drills for [aɪ]

☐ *Practice Words for* [aɪ] ☐

Say the words in the following lists slowly and carefully. You may want to use a mirror and feel your lower jaw to see if you're closing too much. Start with the Beginning words. [aɪ] doesn't occur in unstressed syllables.

Beginning	Middle	End
ice	sight	tie
item	kite	sigh

(*Lists continue on p. 264*)

Beginning	Middle	End
eye	rice	shy
ice cream	bite	hi
isotope	fright	thigh

☐ *Practice Phrases for* [aɪ] ☐

an eye for an eye	out of sight
sky high	frightening sight

☐ *Practice Sentences for* [aɪ] ☐

1. *I* read an *item* in the text about *isotopes.*
2. The *kite* was so *high* it was out of *sight.*
3. *I* was too *shy* to say *hi.*
4. She spilled *rice* pudding all over *my tie.*
5. He *sighed* when he put the *ice pack* on his mosquito *bites.*

Level 2 Drills for [aɪ]

☐ *Practice Words for* [aɪ] ☐

These words contain [aɪ] in more difficult sound contexts. Say the words slowly and listen carefully. If you're not sure of your production, ask your instructor or a classmate to listen to you.

Beginning	Middle	End
idea	rise	lie
iron	dime	cry
island	alive	buy
I've	dried	dry
I'm	tried	try
idle	crime	rely
I'll	climb	deny
aisle	pliers	fry
ideal	hide	guy

    1. He said he didn't find the pliers at the scene of the crime.
    2. I tried to buy some dry clothes.
    3. I'm sure I dropped the dime in the aisle.
    4. He climbed the cliffs on the north side of the island.
    5. I try not to rely on ideal solutions.
    6. We could see the steam rising from the iron.

[aʊ]
how

    Sample: THE CROWD SHOUTED AND HOWLED WHEN THE BALL WENT FOUL.

    Spellings: *ou* as in *shout*   *ow* as in *crowd*

Description

[aʊ] is a diphthong beginning with a low, back vowel, and gliding to a high, back vowel.

□ *Production:* [aʊ] □

1. Open your mouth for the position of [ɑ]. Your tongue should be relaxed and flat in the mouth. Your lips should not be rounded.
2. Produce voice. As you do, close your mouth slightly, and round your lips. Your tongue should elevate. Move toward the position for [ʊ].

Problems

Problem 1. Substitution of [ɛaʊ] for [aʊ]

This substitution happens if you don't open your mouth enough and if you draw back the corners of your mouth. If you smile when you say this diph-

thong, it will be distorted. This substitution is a frequent nonstandard production. Check with your instructor to see if you produce [aʊ] in this way. If
you do, try the following Production Drill.

☐ *Production Drill* ☐

Say the following "broken" words, reading across the page. The first part of
each word has the sound [ɑ] as in *calm*. The second has the sound [ʊ] as in
push. Gradually join the parts together as you read across. It may be very
helpful to use a mirror to see your lips.

ba . . . u	ba . . u	ba . u	ba u	bow
ka . . . u	ka . . u	ka . u	ka u	cow
na . . . u	na . . u	na . u	na u	now
ha . . . u	ha . . u	ha . u	ha u	how
va . . . u	va . . u	va . u	va u	vow
ta . . . un	ta . . un	ta . un	ta un	town
da . . . un	da . . un	da . un	da un	down

Level 1 Drills for [aʊ]

☐ *Practice Words for* [aʊ] ☐

All the practice exercises for [aʊ] are on Level 1. Say the following words
slowly and carefully. You may want to use a mirror to see lip-rounding and to
help prevent the smile. Having someone else watch and listen to you can also
help.

Beginning	*Middle*	*End*
out	town	cow
ouch	couch	allow
hour	cloud	plow
ours	towel	how
ounce	powder	now
outside	allowance	eyebrow
oust	growl	downtown
outlaw	about	chow

☐ *Practice Phrases for* [aʊ] ☐

our couch	allow an hour	allowance now
how to plow	brown towel	how about

1. It took an hour to get downtown.
2. They didn't raise an eyebrow about the cow.
3. Where's the brown towel you took outside?
4. An ounce of prevention is worth a pound of cure.
5. The outlaws only stole about an ounce of gold.
6. Some flowers don't open on cloudy days.
7. I said more than ouch when I dropped the couch.
8. Coffee grounds were floating around in my cup.
9. The county raised our mileage allowance.
10. My stomach gave a loud growl in the crowded elevator.

[ɔɪ]
coin

Sample: ROY TOOK GREAT JOY IN COIN COLLECTING.

Spellings: *oy* as in *joy*   *oi* as in *coin*

Description

[ɔɪ] is a diphthong beginning with a mid, back vowel and gliding to a high, front vowel. Your lips should be slightly rounded.

□ *Production:* [ɔɪ] □

1. Open your mouth to the position for [ɔ]. Raise the back of your tongue slightly and round your lips.
2. Produce voice. As you do, let your tongue lift toward the position for [ɪ], relax your lip rounding, and draw the corners of your mouth back. Make sure there's no nasal emission.

Problems

The problems with [ɔɪ] are generally caused by too much lip rounding and not opening the mouth enough. The drills for the vowel [ɔ] will help you here.

Problem 1. Substitution of [ɝ] for [ɔɪ]

If you make this substitution, you would say, for example, *curl* for *coil*. This substitution happens occasionally in the New York area and in some areas of the South. Although it does happen rather infrequently, it's very noticeable to those who don't make the substitution. The substitution also happens the other way around: *verse* could become *voice*. If you make this substitution, try the following Contrast Drill.

□ *Contrast Drill for* [ɔɪ] *and* [ɝ] □

Say the following word pairs slowly and carefully. Read across the page, contrasting [ɔɪ] in the first word with [ɝ] in the second.

[ɔɪ]	[ɝ]		[ɔɪ]	[ɝ]
coil	– curl		loin	– learn
poise	– purrs		foist	– first
poison	– person		oil	– Earl
boys	– burrs		voice	– verse

Level 1 Drills for [ɔɪ]

□ *Practice Words for* [ɔɪ] □

The drills for [ɔɪ] are all on Level 1. Say the following words slowly and carefully. Listen to your production and make sure you're not substituting [ɝ] or closing your mouth too much.

Beginning	*Middle*	*End*
oil	boil	Roy
oyster	join	employ
ointment	appointment	noise
oilcan	soy sauce	boy
	toys	enjoy
	boycott	annoy

□ *Practice Sentences for* [ɔɪ] □

1. They served oysters cooked in soy sauce.
2. Please oil that noisy hinge.
3. I have an appointment for an employment physical.
4. The little boys really enjoyed the toys.
5. I need some ointment for that annoying boil.

appendix A

Ear Training

Speech pathologists tell the apocryphal story of the mother who was trying to correct her child's pronunciation of the word *soap*. It seems that the child was saying, *thoap*. The mother said to the child, "The word is *soap*, not *thoap*. Now say, *sssss*." And the child did. "Say it again," said the mother, "say *sssss* – *sssss* – *sssss*." Of course the child said it, perfectly. "Now say, *soap*." And the child said, *"thoap."*

Like that child, you and I have an auditory image of how each word we say should sound. And when you customarily say a word and misarticulate a sound or sounds in that word, you hear your own pronunciation as being correct. The way you pronounce your words and articulate your sounds becomes the comfortable, familiar, and "right" way. You may not notice that your production of a sound is different from the way others pronounce that sound.

When you change the way you articulate a sound from an incorrect to a correct production, it is important to monitor the way you make that sound until you are able to make it correctly without consciously trying. It is therefore important that you learn to discriminate, auditorially, between your accurate and inaccurate productions of that sound. We call the process of learning to discriminate accurately *speech discrimination* or *ear training*.

Here are a few simple rules to follow that will make the process of ear training as effective and worthwhile as possible:

1. **Work with someone**, possibly a partner from your speech class, who pronounces your sounds correctly.

2. Your partner should use normal voice, but also **your partner should always keep his or her mouth covered in some way.** That's so you won't be getting visual cues.

3. **Always go from an easier performance task to a more difficult task.** Ear training performance tasks range from easy to difficult in the following categories:

Recognition

1. Train your ear to recognize whether the target sound occurs in a word spoken by the partner.

2. Train your ear to recognize *where* the target sound is in a word (beginning, middle, end) when spoken by the partner.

Discrimination

1. Train your ear to distinguish between both correct and incorrect productions of the target sound as produced by your partner in random order, and being able to point out and distinguish the correct from the incorrect version.

2. Train your ear to distinguish between correct and incorrect productions, but with the target sound at the beginning, then the end, then the middle of nonsense syllables.

3. Train your ear to distinguish between correct and incorrect productions, but with the target sound occurring at the beginning, end, and then middle of actual words.

Example A: Your partner says, "I'm going to say a word two times. Tell me whether I say it the same way or differently: *soap – thoap.*" **Answer:** "Differently."

Example B: Your partner says, "I'm going to say the same word twice, but the [s] sound will be correct in one and incorrect in the other. Tell me which is correct, the first word or the second word: *soap – thoap.*" **Answer:** "The first word."

4. Train your ear to distinguish between correct and incorrect productions, but with the target sound in words, phrases, then sentences.

Perform tasks 1 through 4 using a tape recorder to record your sound production. Then listen to the tape with your partner and identify your own correct and incorrect productions of the target sound. Then repeat tasks 1 through 4 without the tape recorder.

When you practice ear training, you'll do better if you make sure you're performing each task at a satisfactory level before you advance to the next. If you follow this procedure, by the time you've repeated the tasks, you probably will be able to accurately monitor your own productions of the target sound. Then you should repeat the tasks each time you practice your target sound or sounds.

appendix  B

Special Speech Problems

Now that you've studied all the sounds of the language, you probably realize that some of the phonemes are harder to accurately produce than others. Because they are difficult, it's fairly common to find some phonemes misarticulated by children, and it's not unusual to hear the same misarticulations by teenagers and adults. Possibly your speech instructor, or someone else, has told you that you misarticulate one or more of these phonemes. We assume that's why you're reading these pages now; you want to correct your misarticulation.

THE CORRECTION OF DIFFICULT SOUNDS

The phonemes we are talking about include [s] and [z], [ʃ] and [ʒ], [l], [r], and for some people [θ] and [ð]. It is important for you to determine which sounds you misarticulate to get as much information about your productions as possible.

Kinds of Misarticulations

There are three kinds of misarticulations: *omissions, substitutions,* and *distortions.* When you *omit* a phoneme, you're not producing the sound at all where it belongs. For example, a child may say "poon" [pun] instead of "spoon" [spun]. When you *substitute,* you are producing one phoneme in the place of the desired one. Have you ever heard someone utter "thpoon" [θpun] instead of "spoon" [spun] or "mouf" [maʊf] instead of "mouth" [maʊθ]? These are both forms of substitutions. The third kind of misarticulation, *distortion,* is a bit harder to define, and also to identify. A distorted production of a phoneme is one that resembles the correct production closely enough to be identified as part of the same phoneme but different enough that it sounds incorrect. Perhaps you have heard someone whose [s] sounds were accompanied by a whistle or sounded "mushy" instead of sharp and clear. You knew it was an [s], but it didn't sound right to you.

After you have determined the type of misarticulation you are producing, you should determine the severity and frequency with which it occurs. Is the misarticulation present when you produce the phoneme at the beginning of words? The middle? The ends of words? Does it occur when you say the sound by itself, in a single word, or in a phrase or sentence? Is your misarticulation obvious enough to be noticed by most people? Only a few people? Only by a trained speech person?

In addition to determining the severity and frequency of the misarticulation, you should establish a baseline of production. Use a tape recorder, if possible, and read a list of words containing the target sound. Play it back and, perhaps with the help of another person, determine the percentage of words in which that sound is misarticulated. You can use this baseline figure later to measure your progress as you work on the sound.

At this point, if there is a speech clinic or speech and hearing center at your school, or conveniently located in your community, your instructor may wish to refer you there for an evaluation of your articulation. A hearing test may also be indicated because many misarticulations can be related to a mild-to-moderate loss of hearing, particularly in the high frequency range. Possibly the speech clinic may want to work with you to help eliminate the misarticulations.

If there is no such service available, the following steps may help you to work on correcting the sound or sounds either with the assistance of your instructor or under your own direction.

Steps in Correction

Step 1

Read Appendix A and follow the ear training procedures explained there. Use the sound or sounds you misarticulate until you are able consistently to recognize your own errors.

Step 2

If possible, ask your instructor to teach you how to make the sound correctly by itself. You might make a tape recording of your instructor producing the sound in a variety of contexts, perhaps using the drill exercises included in this text. Listen to the tape often enough that you get a clear impression of the sound the way that is considered standard. If your instructor can't make the tape for you, ask a member of your speech class who produces the sound correctly.

Step 3

Begin working on your own correct productions of the sound using the drill exercises you'll find later in this section. Begin by making the sound by itself, then combine it with vowel sounds so that the sound is at the beginning, end, and middle of sound groups. Then put the sound into words in all three positions. Start with beginning, go on to end position, and finally to the middle of words. During the beginning stages, try to have someone listen to you who can tell you whether you are making the sound correctly or not. After a while your ear will be sufficiently trained so that you can make that judgment your-self.

Step 4

Go on to phrases, sentences, and connected speech. Still use the drill exercises in the text and any other materials you can find using your target sound. For variety, get a partner and make up some games to play using words that contain your target sound; for example, "Scrabble," with every word containing your sound.

Remember, you've probably been misarticulating your target sounds for sixteen or seventeen or more years. You're not going to change the way you produce them overnight. Only after frequent, regular, and conscientious work on your part will you begin to see changes. Short, regular practice sessions will work better than long, infrequent ones. Work on your speech every day and those changes will start to happen.

Frontal and Lateral Distortion of [s] *and* [z]

If your [s] and [z] sound like your [θ] and [ð], you are probably producing them with the tip of your tongue either against or between your teeth. This is called a *lingual protrusion or frontal lisp.* Here are some drills you can use to correct this misarticulation.

Step 1

Practice making a groove down the center of the tongue, from front to back. You may find it useful to use a thin plastic mixing stick or applicator stick for this. Place the stick along the center of your tongue and wrap the sides of your tongue around the stick. Remove the stick slowly, but keep the sides of your tongue up. Once you are able to do this consistently, you are ready for the next step.

Step 2

Place your tongue against the alveolar ridge in the position to make the [t] sound. Start to make the [t] sound, but instead of pulling your tongue sharply away, let the tip drop very slightly downward slowly, while keeping the sides up. Keep the teeth almost closed, with a very narrow opening between them. Force air between your teeth, aiming it with your tongue right down the center. You should now be producing a sharp, clear [s].

Step 3

Place your tongue in position for the [t] sound, but drop the tip slightly before you begin to breathe out. Make sure you maintain the groove down the center of your tongue. You should still be able to produce a sharp, clear sound.

Step 4

Once you are able to initiate a good, clear [s] sound, practice the following comparisons:

[s] – [θ] – [s] – [θ] – [s] – [θ]
sɑ – θɑ – sɑ – θɑ – sɑ – θɑ
si – θi – si – θi – si – θi
so – θo – so – θo – so – θo

Then

θɑ – sɑ – θɑ – sɑ – θɑ – sɑ
θi – si – θi – si – θi – si
θo – so – θo – so – θo – so

Next

sɪn – θɪn – sɪn – θɪn – sɪn – θɪn
sʌm – θʌm – sʌm – θʌm – sʌm – θʌm
sim – θim – sim – θim – sim – θim

Note: make sure there is a sharp distinction between the [θ] and [s] sounds in each pair of sounds, syllables, and words.

You should now be ready to follow the general procedures explained under the heading, "The Correction of Difficult Sounds."

Distortion of [l] *as in* [lɛt]

Sometimes this sound is distorted so that it resembles [w] as in "wet." This happens if you lower the tip of the tongue and purse the lips and produce a bilabial glide instead of the lateral continuant. Another misarticulation that is less frequent is caused by lowering the tongue tip and raising the *back* of the tongue against, or near, the soft palate. This type of sound resembles the French uvular trilled [r].

To produce [l] correctly, raise the tip of the tongue to your alveolar ridge with your mouth open fairly wide. Make sure to keep the back and sides of your tongue low. Now, keeping the tip of the tongue at the alveolar ridge and the back and sides low, begin to phonate. The sound you are producing should be a fairly accurate [l]. Ask your instructor or a classmate to check your production of the sound. When you are able to produce the sound consistently with your mouth wide open, practice the sound while maintaining a space of one finger between your upper and lower teeth.

You are probably now ready to produce the [l] sound followed by some of the vowels:

la – la – la
li – li – li
lo – lo – lo
lu – lu – lu

Next produce the vowel before the [l].

il – il – il
ɛl – ɛl – ɛl
ol – ol – ol

Now make the vowel sound before and after the [l].
ala – ala – ala
ili – ili – ili
olo – olo – olo

If you're satisfied with your production so far, try the following comparisons. Make sure there is a marked difference between the consonant sounds.

la – wa – la – wa – la – wa – la
li – wi – li – we – li – we – li
lo – wo – lo – wo – lo – wo – lo
la – ga – la – ga – la – ga – la
li – gi – li – gi – li – gi – li
lo – go – lo – go – lo – go – lo

Now go back to the previously outlined procedures for "The Correction of Difficult Sounds."

Distortion of [r]

This is one of the most difficult sounds to correct. There are several different misarticulations of this sound. The one that is most troublesome is a substitution of [w] as in "wed" for [r] as in "red." To correct this substitution, try the following procedures.

Step 1

Ask one of the students in your class to read aloud the following sentence: *The rainbow circled around part of the sky after the rain ended.* Now read the sentence aloud yourself. Do you produce the [r] sounds the same way as your classmate? If your production of "rainbow" or "rain" sounds somewhat like "wainbow" or "wain" you are probably making the [r] sound only with your lips rather than with your tongue *and* your lips.

Step 2

Produce the [z] sound. See if you can feel where you're placing the tip of your tongue. Produce the [z] sound again. Without stopping, produce the syllable [zra]. Focus your attention on what happens to the tip of your tongue. You will feel, we hope, the tip of the tongue drop slightly away from the gum ridge while the sides remain raised. Repeat the syllable slowly as many times as are necessary for you to get an accurate perception of the correct tongue position for the [r] sound.

Step 3

Once you have learned the proper tongue position, try making the [r] sound by itself. Ask your speech instructor to check your production of the sound before you proceed. If your instructor is not available, perhaps a classmate with a good ear for sounds can check you out.

Step 4

Once you are fairly certain that you are producing the sound accurately, follow the procedures outlined in Appendix A for ear training and the procedures at the beginning of this Appendix.

Since this is a difficult sound to correct, your instructor may wish to refer you to the college's or university's speech clinic or a community clinic for additional help.

appendix C

Pronunciation List

The words in the following lists are, for a number of reasons, frequently mis-pronounced. They're all fairly common words, and with a little practice you should be able to pronounce them correctly. We've grouped them according to the type of mispronunciation, so we suggest you work within one type before moving on to the next. Have someone listen to you, or tape your practice session for review later.

A word about the "correct" way to pronounce words; our language is always changing, and a pronunciation that was preferred at one time may not be so widely used today. We used the 1980 *Random House Dictionary* for our guide to preferred pronunciations; you may find that your dictionary shows another. If so, consult your instructor to determine which pronunciation is preferred in your area.

REVERSALS

The words in this section are often mispronounced because of the reversal of two sounds. For example, the word "ask," standardly pronounced [æsk], becomes "ax" when the two consonant sounds are reversed.

Standard Pronunciation

Word	(Dictionary)	(IPA)	Nonstandard
1. ask	ask	[æsk]	[æks]
2. asked	askt	[æskt]	[ækst]
3. asterisk	as′ tə risk	[æstərɪsk]	[æstərɪks]
4. children	c͟hil′ drən	[tʃɪldrən]	[tʃɪldɚn]
5. hundred	hun′ drid	[hʌndrɪd]	[hʌnɚd]
6. introduction	in′ trəduk′ shən	[ɪntrədʌkʃən]	[ɪntɚdʌkʃən]
7. larynx	lar′ ingks	[lærɪŋks]	[lærnɪks]
8. lisp	lisp	[lɪsp]	[lɪps]
9. perform	pər fôrm′	[pɚfɔɚm]	[prəfɔɚm]
10. perspiration	pûr′ spə ra′ shən	[pɚspəreʃən]	[prəspəreʃən]
11. pharynx	far′ingks	[færɪŋks]	[færnɪks]
12. prescription	pri skrip′shən	[prɪskrɪpʃən]	[pɚskrɪpʃən]
13. professor	prə fes′ər	[prəfɛsɚ]	[pɚfɛsɚ]
14. southern	sut͟h′ ərn	[sʌðɚn]	[sʌðrən]

OMISSIONS

The following words are often mispronounced when people omit one or more of the sounds which should be present. Say these words carefully. Make sure each sound is there that should be there.

Standard Pronunciation

Word	(Dictionary)	(IPA)	Nonstandard
1. accelerate	ak sel′ə rat′	[æksɛləræt]	[æsɛləret]
2. accessory	ak ses′ ə rē	[æksɛsəri]	[æsɛsəri]
3. and	and	[ænd]	[æn]
4. antidote	an′ti dōt′	[æntədot]	[ænədot]
5. arctic	ärk′tik	[ɑɚktɪk]	[ɑɚtɪk]
6. basketball	bas′kit bôl′	[bæskətbɔl]	[bæskəbɔl]
7. candidate	kan′di dāt′	[kændədet]	[kænədet]
8. contact	kon′takt	[kɑntækt]	[kɑntæk]
9. correct	kə rekt′	[kərɛkt]	[kərɛk]
10. couldn't	kood′ənt	[kʊdnt]	[kʊdn]
11. entertain	en′tər tān′	[ɛntɚten]	[ɛnɚten]
12. environment	en vī′rənmənt	[ɛnvaɪrənmənt]	[ɛnvaɪrəmənt]
13. February	feb′rōo er′ē	[fɛbrueri]	[fɛbjueri]
14. friendly	frend′lē	[frɛndli]	[frɛnli]
15. frustrate	frus′trāt	[frʌstret]	[fʌstret]
16. hundred	hun′drid	[hʌndrɪd]	[hʌnɚd]
17. library	lī′brer′ē	[laɪbrɛɚɪ]	[laɪbɛɚi]
18. museum	myōo zē′əɪɪɪ	[mjuziəm]	[mjuzim]
19. orange	or′inj	[ɑɚəndʒ]	[ɑɚndʒ]
20. perhaps	pər haps′	[pɚhæps]	[præps]
21. picture	pik′chər	[pɪktʃɚ]	[pɪtʃɚ]
22. poem	pō′əm	[poəm]	[pom]
23. probably	prob′ə blē	[prɑbəbli]	[prɑli]
24. quiet	kwī′it	[kwaɪɪt]	[kwaɪt]
25. recognize	rek′əg nīz′	[rɛkəgnaɪz]	[rɛkənaɪz]
26. regular	reg′yə lər	[rɛgjəlɚ]	[rɛgəlɚ]
27. robbery	rob′ə rē	[rɑbəri]	[rɑbri]
28. scrupulous	skrōo′pyə ləs	[skrupjələs]	[skrupələs]
29. skeptical	skep′ti kəl	[skɛptɪkəl]	[skɛpəkəl]
30. slept	slept	[slɛpt]	[slɛp]
31. specific	spi sif′ik	[spəsɪfɪk]	[pəsɪfɪk]
32. substitute	sub′sti tōot′	[sʌbst tut]	[sʌbsətut]
33. temperature	tem′pər ə chər	[tɛmpərətʃɚ]	[tɛmpətʃɚ]
34. throw	thrō	[θroʊ]	[θoʊ]
35. twenty	twen′tē	[twɛnti]	[twɛni]
36. veteran	vet′ər ən	[vɛtərən]	[vɛtrən]
37. wonderful	wun′dər fəl	[wʌndɚful]	[wʌnɚful]
38. wouldn't	wōod′ənt	[wʊdnt]	[wʊnt]

SUBSTITUTIONS

These words are mispronounced by substituting one sound for another.

Word	Standard Pronunciation (Dictionary)	(IPA)	Nonstandard
1. architect	är′ki tekt′	[ɑɚkətɛkt]	[ɑɚtʃətɛkt]
2. asphalt	as′fôlt	[æsfɔlt]	[æʃfɔlt]
3. attaché	at′ə shā′	[ætəʃe]	[ætətʃe]
4. banquet	bang′kwit	[bæŋkwɪt]	[bænkwɪt]
5. Beethoven	bā′tō vən	[betovən]	[beθovən]
6. beige	bāzh	[beɪʒ]	[beɪdʒ]
7. brochure	brō shoor′	[broʃuɚ]	[brotʃuɚ]
8. charisma	kə riz′mə	[kərɪzmə]	[tʃərɪzmə]
9. charlatan	shär′lə tən	[ʃɑrlətən]	[tʃɑrlətən]
10. chasm	kaz′əm	[kæzəm]	[tʃæzəm]
11. chef	shef	[ʃɛf]	[tʃɛf]
12. chic	shēk	[ʃik]	[tʃɪk]
13. chiropractor	kī′rə prak′tər	[kaɪrəpræktɚ]	[tʃaɪrəpræktɚ]
14. Chopin	shō′pan	[ʃopæn]	[tʃopæn]
15. clique	klik	[klɪk]	[klikeɪ]
16. connoisseur	kon′ə sûr′	[kanəsuɚ]	[canəʃuɚ]
17. crux	kruks	[krʌks]	[krʊks]
18. cuisine	kwi zēn′	[kwɪzin]	[kjuzin]
19. data	dā′ tə	[detə]	[dætə]
20. deluge	del′yōōj	[dɛljudʒ]	[dɛljuʒ]
21. diphthong	dif′thông	[dɪfθaŋ]	[dɪpθaŋ]
22. diphtheria	dif thēr′ēə	[dɪfθiriə]	[dɪpθiriə]
23. et cetera	et set′ərə	[ɛt sɛtərə]	[ɛksɛtərə]
24. faux pas	fō pä′	[fo pa]	[fɔks pæs]
25. filet	fi lā′	[fɪleɪ]	[fɪlɪt]
26. futile	fyoot′ᵊl	[fjutəl]	[fjutaɪl]
27. gesture	jes′chər	[dʒɛstʃɚ]	[gɛstʃɚ]
28. gist	jist	[dʒɪst]	[gɪst]
29. harbinger	här′bin jər	[hɑɚbɪndʒɚ]	[hɑɚbɪŋɚ]
30. hearth	härth	[hɑɚθ]	[hɚθ]
31. height	hīt	[haɪt]	[haɪθ]
32. heinous	hā′nəs	[heɪnəs]	[haɪnəs]
33. heir	âr	[ɛɚ]	[hɛɚ]
34. herald	her′əld	[hɛrəld]	[hærəld]
35. houses	hou′ziz	[haʊzɪz]	[haʊsɪz]
36. indict	in dīt′	[ɪndaɪt]	[ɪndɪkt]
37. indigent	in′di jənt	[ɪndɪdʒənt]	[ɪndɪgənt]

Word	(Dictionary)	(IPA)	Nonstandard
38. Italian	i tal′yən	[ɪtæljən]	[aɪtæljən]
39. length	leñgkth	[leɪŋkθ]	[lɛnθ]
40. lingerie	län′zhə rā′	[lanʒəre]	[lɪŋgəre]
41. longevity	lon jev′i tē	[lɔndʒɛvɪti]	[lɔŋgevɪti]
42. longitude	lon′ji tōōd′	[lɔndʒɪtud]	[lɔŋgɪtud]
43. malingerer	mə liñg′ gərər	[məlɪŋgərɚ]	[məlɪndʒərɚ]
44. masochistic	mas′əkis′tik	[mæsəkɪstɪk]	[mæsətʃɪstɪk]
45. mocha	mō′kə	[mokə]	[motʃə]
46. oil	oil	[ɔɪl]	[ɝl]
47. onus	ō′nəs	[oʊnəs]	[ɑnəs]
48. orgy	ôr′jē	[ɔɚdʒi]	[ɔɚgi]
49. pathos	pā′thos	[peθos]	[pæθos]
50. pique	pēk	[pik]	[pike]
51. placard	plak′ärd	[plækɚd]	[plekɚd]
52. poignant	poin′yənt	[pɔɪnjənt]	[pɔɪgnənt]
53. police	pə lēs′	[pəlis]	[polis]
54. posthumous	pos′chə məs	[pastʃəməs]	[pasθjməs]
55. prestige	pre stēzh′	[prɛstiʒ]	[prɛstidʒ]
56. regime	rə zhem′	[rəʒim]	[rədʒim]
57. salient	sā′lēənt	[seɪliənt]	[sæliənt]
58. strength	streñgkth	[strɛɪŋkθ]	[strɛnθ]
59. suave	swäv	[swɑv]	[sweɪv]
60. suite	swet	[swit]	[sut]
61. taciturn	tas′i tûrn′	[tæsɪtɚn]	[tækɪtɚn]
62. taupe	tōp	[top]	[tɔp]
63. thyme	tīm	[taɪm]	[θaɪm]
64. tremendous	tri men′dəs	[trɪmɛndəs]	[trɪmɛndjuəs]
65. virile	vir′əl	[vɪɚəl]	[vaɪɚəl]
66. Worcester	woŏs′tər	[wʊstɚ]	[wɝcɛstɚ]
67. worsted	woŏs′tid	[wʊstɪd	[wɝstɪd]
68. zealot	zel′ət	[zɛlət]	[zilət]
69. zoology	zō ol′ ə jē	[zoɑlədʒi]	[zuɑlədʒi]

The words in this list are mispronounced by adding sounds that don't belong there.

Standard Pronunciation

Word	(Dictionary)	(IPA)	Nonstandard
1. across	əkrôs′	[əkrɔs]	[əkrɔst]
2. almond	ä′mənd	[amənd]	[almənd]
3. athlete	ath′lēt	[æθlit]	[æθəlit]
4. balk	bôk	[bɔk]	[bɔlk]
5. balmy	bä′mē	[bami]	[balmi]
6. burglar	bûr′glər	[bɝglɚ]	[bɝgjələ]
7. business	biz′nis	[bɪznɪs]	[bɪzinɪs]
8. calm	käm	[kam]	[kalm]
9. chimney	chim′nē	[tʃɪmni]	[tʃɪmbli]
10. column	kol′əm	[kalʌm]	[kalʌmn]
11. condominium	kon′də min′ē əm	[kandəmɪniəm]	[kamndəmɪniəm]
12. consonant	kon′sə nənt	[kansənənt]	[kanstənɛnt]
13. corps	kôr	[kɔɚ]	[kɔɚps]
14. drowned	dround	[draʊnd]	[draʊndəd]
15. electoral	i lek′tər əl	[ɪlɛktərəl]	[ɪlɛktɔriəl]
16. escalator	es′kə lā′tər	[ɛskəletɚ]	[ɛskjəletɚ]
17. escape	e skāp′	[ɛskep]	[ɛkskep]
18. evening	ēv′ning	[ivnɪŋ]	[ivənɪŋ]
19. facetious	[fəsē′shəs]	[fəsiʃəs]	[fəsiʃiəs]
20. film	film	[fɪlm]	[fɪləm]
21. grievous	[grē′vəs]	[grivəs]	[griviəs]
22. momentous	mō men′təs	[momɛntəs]	[momɛntʃuəs]
23. monstrous	mon′strəs	[manstrəs]	[manstərəs]
24. nuclear	noo′klē ər	[nukliɚ]	[nukjələ]
25. often	ô′fən	[ɔfən]	[ɔftən]
26. once	wuns	[wʌns]	[wʌnst]
27. psalm	säm	[sam]	[salm]
28. righteous	rī′chəs	[raɪtʃəs]	[raɪtʃuəs]
29. schism	siz′əm	[sɪzəm]	[skɪzəm]
29. soften	sô′fən	[sɔfən]	[sɔftən]
30. sophomore	sof′môr	[safmɔɚ]	[safəmɔɚ]
31. statistics	stə tis′tiks	[stətɪstɪks]	[stəstɪstɪks]
32. subtle	sut′əl	[sʌtəl]	[sʌbtəl]
33. sword	sōrd	[sɔɚd]	[swɔɚd]
34. tremendous	tri men′dəs	[trɪmɛndəs]	[trɪmɛndjuəs]

The following words are all frequently mispronounced due to misplaced syllable stress; that is, emphasizing the wrong syllable.

Standard Pronunciation

Word	(Dictionary)	(IPA)	Nonstandard
1. abdomen	ab'də mən	[æb'dəmən]	[æbdo'mən]
2. absurd	ab sûrd'	[æbsɚd']	[æb'sɚd]
3. admirable	ad'mər ə bəl	[æd'mərəbəl]	[ædmaɪr'əbəl]
4. applicable	aplə kə bəl	[æp'ləkəbəl]	[əplɪk'əbəl]
5. bravado	brə vä'dō	[brəva'do]	[bra'vədo]
6. Caribbean	kar'ə bē'ən	[kær'əbi'ən]	[kɚɪb'iən]
7. cement	si ment'	[simɛnt']	[si'mɛnt]
8. chagrin	shə grin'	[ʃəgrɪn']	[ʃʌ'grɪn]
9. conduit	kon'dōō it	[kan'duɪt]	[kəndu'ɪt)
10. delight	di līt'	[dilaɪt']	[di'laɪt]
11. deluge	del'yōōj	[dɛl'judʒ]	[dɛljudʒ']
12. finance	fi'nans'	[fɪnæns']	[faɪ'næns]
13. guitar	gi tär'	[gɪtaɚ']	[gɪ'taɚ]
14. impotent	im'pə tənt	[ɪm'pətənt]	[ɪmpo'tɛnt]
15. incomparable	in kom'pər ə bəl	[ɪnkam'pɚəbəl]	[ɪnkampɛɚ'əbəl]
16. incongruous	in kong'grōō ə s	[ɪnkaŋ'gruəs]	[ɪnkangru'əs]
17. infamous	in'fə məs	[ɪn'fə məs]	[ɪnfɛm'əs]
18. inquiry	inkwiər'ē	[inkwaɪ'ɚi]	[ɪn'kwɚi]
19. irreparable	i rep'ər ə bəl	[ɪrɛp'ərəbəl]	[ɪrɛpɛɚ'əbɔl]
20. maintenance	mān'tənəns	[meɪn'tənəns]	[meɪnteɪn'əns]
21. mischievous	mis'chə vəs	[mɪs'tʃəvəs]	[mɪstʃi'vəs]
22. omnipotent	om nip'ə tənt	[amnɪp'ətənt]	[amnɪpo'tənt]
23. police	pə lēs	[pəlis']	[po'lis]
24. preclude	pri klōōd'	[priklud']	[pri'klud]
25. preferable	pref'ərə bəl	[prɛf'ərəbəl]	[prəfɚ'əbəl]
26. preference	pref'ər əns	[prɛfərəns]	[prəfɚ'əns]
27. respite	res'pit	[rɛs'pɪt]	[rəspaɪt']

appendix D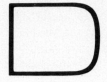

Glossary

This is an informal glossary of words that are used in this book. We have given definitions that could be considered to be "working definitions," and they might not always be the best definitions in other contexts.

abdominal breathing: A pattern of breathing that is typified by controlled movements of the abdominal muscles.

accent: Stress given to a syllable in a word—see stress.

acoustic: Pertaining to sound, or the qualities of a sound.

adaptor: Unintended nonverbal behaviors, such as head scratching, nose rubbing, and foot tapping, that reflect our unconscious needs or drives.

affect display: Nonverbal display, usually by facial expression, of your emotional state.

affricate: A single consonant sound that you produce by following a plosive closely with a fricative. The first sound in the word "shoe" is an affricate.

allophone: A variation of a phoneme.

alveolar ridge: The gum ridge just behind the upper front teeth.

amplify: To increase in loudness.

articulation: Movements of the speech organs to produce speech sounds.

articulators: The organs of speech used to produce speech sounds: tongue, lips, soft palate, hard palate, alveolar ridge, teeth.

assimilation: The process by which speech sounds become part of the sounds around them. For example: "Jeet?" (Did you eat?)

audition: The process of hearing.

bi-labial sounds: Sounds produced using both lips.

blend: A sound which is the result of joining two sounds closely and smoothly together. For example: *gl*ass, *br*ass, *bl*ack.

breathiness: An excessive loss of air while speaking. A breathy voice has a "whispery" quality.

breathstream: Air released from the lungs that is used to start vocal fold vibration.

cluster: A grouping of consonants in the same syllable, with no vowel between them.

cognate sounds: Two consonant sounds that are made in the same place and in the same manner. The only difference is that one is voiced and the other is voiceless.

consonant: A type of speech sound that is produced by completely or partially blocking the breathstream using the articulators. The first and last sounds in the word "kiss" are consonants.

decibel: The measurement unit of sound intensity.

defective speech: Speech that results in a handicap for the speaker. The speaker may need help in producing a standard sound.

denasality: Too little nasal resonance resulting in a voice that sounds as if the speaker has a stuffed nose.

dialect: A form of a language that is spoken in a specific geographical area that differs from the official language of the larger area.

diaphragm: The main muscle of respiration. It is located between the chest and abdominal cavities.

diction: The production of the sounds of a particular language, and the selection of words of the language when speaking.

diphthong: A glide composed of two vowels, blended together, produced in a single syllable.

duration: How long a sound is held when produced.

emblem: A nonverbal action that has a direct verbal translation.

emphasis: Stress given to a word in a phrase.

excessive nasality: A voice quality resulting from too much nasal resonance.

frequency: The number of cycles (vibrations) per second of a sound. The unit of frequency is Hz (Hertz).

fricative: A type of consonant sound produced when the breathstream is forced through a narrow opening between two articulators. The first sound in the word "see" is a fricative.

glide: A consonant sound produced while the articulators are moving. The first sound in "west" is a glide.

glottal fry: A rough, bubbly, cracking voice quality that usually occurs in the lower part of the pitch range.

glottis: The opening between the vocal folds.

habitual pitch: The pitch level at which a person usually begins producing voice.

hard glottal attack: A way of producing vowel sounds. The vocal folds are very tense, and the vowels begin very abruptly. The vowels have a hard, explosive quality.

hard palate: The roof of the mouth, lying between the alveolar (gum) ridge and the soft palate.

harsh voice: A rough-sounding voice that results from irregular vibration of the vocal folds.

hoarse voice: A voice that sounds both harsh and breathy. The vocal folds are not able to close completely.

Hz (Hertz): The unit of measurement of frequency.

illustrator: Nonverbal behaviors that accompany speech used to emphasize, clarify, or illustrate ideas. For example, describe with words *and* actions a figure eight.

inflection: Pitch changes that occur *during* phonation. They may be rising, falling, or circumflex (a combination of both).

innervation: The process of supplying nerve impulses to muscles.

International Phonetic Alphabet (IPA): An alphabet that uses a special set of symbols to represent the sounds of a language.

intonation: The pattern of pitch changes in connected speech.

key: The average pitch level of a segment of connected speech.

kinesics: All the nonverbal behaviors you can observe visually.

labio-dental sounds: Consonant sounds produced by using the lower lip and upper teeth. The first sound in "first" is a labio-dental consonant.

larynx: The structure for producing voice. Composed of cartilage and muscle, it is the uppermost part of the trachea.

lateral consonant: The first sound in the word *leaf*. It is produced with the gum ridge and tongue. Air is emitted at the sides of the mouth (laterally).

lingua-alveolar consonant: Consonant sounds that are produced with the tongue touching or near the gum ridge. The first and last sounds in "sit" are lingua-alveolar consonants.

lingua-dental consonants: Consonant sounds that are produced with the tongue touching the front teeth. The first sound in the word "thumb" is a lingua-dental consonant.

lingua-palatal consonants: Consonant sounds that are produced with the middle and back of the tongue raised toward the hard palate. The first sound in "ship" is a lingua-palatal consonant.

linguistics: The study of language, in general, or the study of the sounds and structure of a particular language.

loudness: The psychological sensation of sound intensity.

metallic voice: A usually high-pitched voice that sounds both strident and harsh.

nasality: The quality of voice that results from the degree of resonance by the nasal cavities.

nonstandard speech: Speech which is significantly different from the speech generally considered to be "standard."

optimum pitch: The pitch level at which a particular person can produce the loudest voice and best vocal quality with the least effort; producing the pitch your body was "designed" to produce.

paralanguage: The range of nonverbal cues that accompany verbal language: how you say something, rather than what you say.

pharynx: The throat.

phonation: The production of vocal sounds using the vocal folds.

phoneme: A "family" of sounds in a language; acoustically very similar. We generally recognize the entire sound family as one sound, different from all the other phonemes of the language.

phrasing: Grouping words for better understanding or meaning. Not to be considered a complete sentence.

pitch: The subjective perception of the highness or lowness of a sound.

plosive: A consonant sound produced by blocking the airstream completely, building up pressure, and suddenly exploding the air. The first and last sounds in "top" are plosives.

proxemics: The study of the use, and perception, of space by humans.

pure-tone: A sound consisting of only one frequency of vibration.

quality: The subjective interpretation of a sound, based on frequency, intensity, phase, etc.

rate: The number of words spoken per minute.

regionalism: That type of speech used and accepted in a particular area; similar to a dialect.

regulator: Nonverbal cues, such as eye contact or head nodding, that regulate the back-and-forth nature of conversation.

resonance: Amplification and modification of sound either by an air-filled chamber or another object that vibrates sympathetically.

soft palate: The soft, muscular, movable, rearmost portion of the roof of the mouth.

spectrum: The graphic display of a sound, showing the component frequencies and their relative intensities.

standard speech: The way the majority of educated speakers in a large area speak. The generally accepted "correct" style of speaking.

stress: Making a syllable or word appear to be "larger" and louder by applying more force.

stridency: A high-pitched, tense, metallic vocal quality.

tenseness: A vocal quality resulting from excess tension in the larynx.

thorax: The chest.

throaty: A vocal quality that seems lacking in resonance and strength; it seems to come from the back of the throat.

trachea: The "windpipe."

velum: The soft palate.

vocal folds: Two small bands of tissue located in the larynx. They can be made to vibrate in the airstream from the lungs, and create voice.

vocal fry: See *glottal fry*.

voiced consonant: A consonant sound produced with voice. The first sound in "back" is voiced; the last is voiceless.

voiceless consonant: A consonant sound produced without voice. The first sound in "kid" is voiceless; the last is voiced.

vowel: Voiced sounds produced without blocking the airstream.

appendix E

Speech Check List

APPENDIX E

SPEECH CHECK LIST

Name _____   Course _____

Rater _____   Date _____

Voice

Pitch:
   Appropriate   Too High   Too Low   Patterned   Monotonous   Other _____

Volume:
   Appropriate   Too Loud   Too Weak   Monotonous   Uncontrolled   Other _____

Rate:
   Appropriate   Too Fast   Too Slow   Hesitant   Monotonous   Other _____

Quality:
   Pleasant   Nasal   Denasal   Breathy   Hoarse   Other _____

Target Areas: _____

Articulation

Consonants		Vowels	Diphthongs
p pat _____	ʃ she _____	i see _____	aɪ ice _____
b boat _____	ʒ beige _____	ɪ sit _____	aʊ how _____
t top _____	h hot _____	e ate _____	ɔɪ coin _____
d dog _____	hw where _____	ɛ bet _____	
k key _____	w wet _____	æ pat _____	
g go _____	r red _____	a ask _____	
f four _____	j yes _____	ɑ calm _____	
v very _____	l left _____	ɔ awful _____	
θ thin _____	m man _____	o so _____	
ð the: _____	n no _____	ʊ book _____	
s snake _____	ŋ sing _____	u too _____	
z zoo _____	tʃ chair _____	ʌ up _____	
	dʒ judge _____	ə banana _____	
		ɜ-ɝ early _____	
		ɚ father _____	

Other Articulatory Features:

Consonant omissions _____	lisp (type)_____
Consonant additions _____	excess sibilance _____
dentalized d, t _____	assimilation _____
intrusive r _____	dialect (type) _____
final unvoicing _____	other _____

Target sounds: _____

APPENDIX E

SPEECH CHECK LIST

Name _____   Course _____

Rater _____   Date _____

Voice

Pitch:
   Appropriate   Too High   Too Low   Patterned   Monotonous   Other ____

Volume:
   Appropriate   Too Loud   Too Weak   Monotonous   Uncontrolled   Other ____

Rate:
   Appropriate   Too Fast   Too Slow   Hesitant   Monotonous   Other ____

Quality:
   Pleasant   Nasal   Denasal   Breathy   Hoarse   Other ____

Target Areas: _____

Articulation

Consonants		Vowels	Diphthongs
p pat _____	ʃ she _____	i see _____	aɪ ice _____
b boat _____	ʒ beige _____	ɪ sit _____	aʊ how _____
t top _____	h hot _____	e ate _____	ɔɪ coin _____
d dog _____	hw where _____	ɛ bet _____	
k key _____	w wet _____	æ pat _____	
g go _____	r red _____	a ask _____	
f four _____	j yes _____	ɑ calm _____	
v very _____	l left _____	ɔ awful _____	
θ thin _____	m man _____	o so _____	
ð the: _____	n no _____	ʊ book _____	
s snake _____	ŋ sing _____	u too _____	
z zoo _____	tʃ chair _____	ʌ up _____	
	dʒ judge _____	ə banana _____	
		ɜ-ɚ early _____	
		ɚ father _____	

Other Articulatory Features:

Consonant omissions _____	lisp (type) _____
Consonant additions _____	excess sibilance _____
dentalized d, t _____	assimilation _____
intrusive r _____	dialect (type) _____
final unvoicing _____	other _____

Target sounds: _____

APPENDIX E

SPEECH CHECK LIST

Name _____   Course _____

Rater _____   Date _____

Voice

Pitch:
   Appropriate Too High Too Low Patterned Monotonous Other ____

Volume:
   Appropriate Too Loud Too Weak Monotonous Uncontrolled Other ____

Rate:
   Appropriate Too Fast Too Slow Hesitant Monotonous Other ____

Quality:
   Pleasant Nasal Denasal Breathy Hoarse Other ____

Target Areas: _____

Articulation

Consonants		Vowels		Diphthongs	
p	pat _____	i	see _____	aɪ	ice _____
b	boat _____	ɪ	sit _____	aʊ	how _____
t	top _____	e	ate _____	ɔɪ	coin _____
d	dog _____	ɛ	bet _____		
k	key _____	æ	pat _____		
g	go _____	a	ask _____		
f	four _____	ɑ	calm _____		
v	very _____	ɔ	awful _____		
θ	thin _____	o	so _____		
ð	the: _____	ʊ	book _____		
s	snake _____	u	too _____		
z	zoo _____	ʌ	up _____		

Consonants (cont.)	
ʃ	she _____
ʒ	beige _____
h	hot _____
hw	where _____
w	wet _____
r	red _____
j	yes _____
l	left _____
m	man _____
n	no _____
ŋ	sing _____
tʃ	chair _____
dʒ	judge _____

Vowels (cont.)	
ə	banana _____
ɜ-ɝ	early _____
ɚ	father _____

Other Articulatory Features:
Consonant omissions _____   lisp (type)_____
Consonant additions _____   excess sibilance _____
dentalized d, t _____   assimilation _____
intrusive r _____   dialect (type) _____
final unvoicing _____   other _____

Target sounds: _____

APPENDIX E

Reading: _____

SPEECH CHECK LIST

Name _____   Course _____

Rater _____   Date _____

Voice

Pitch:
  Appropriate   Too High   Too Low   Patterned   Monotonous   Other ____
Volume:
  Appropriate   Too Loud   Too Weak   Monotonous   Uncontrolled   Other ____
Rate:
  Appropriate   Too Fast   Too Slow   Hesitant   Monotonous   Other ____
Quality:
  Pleasant   Nasal   Denasal   Breathy   Hoarse   Other ____

Target Areas: _____

Articulation

Consonants		Vowels	Diphthongs
p pat _____	ʃ she _____	i see _____	aɪ ice _____
b boat _____	ʒ beige _____	ɪ sit _____	aʊ how _____
t top _____	h hot _____	e ate _____	ɔɪ coin _____
d dog _____	hw where _____	ɛ bet _____	
k key _____	w wet _____	æ pat _____	
g go _____	r red _____	a ask _____	
f four _____	j yes _____	ɑ calm _____	
v very _____	l left _____	ɔ awful _____	
θ thin _____	m man _____	o so _____	
ð the: _____	n no _____	ʊ book _____	
s snake _____	ŋ sing _____	u too _____	
z zoo _____	tʃ chair _____	ʌ up _____	
	dʒ judge _____	ə banana _____	
		ɝ-ɝ early _____	
		ɚ father _____	

Other Articulatory Features:

Consonant omissions _____	lisp (type) _____
Consonant additions _____	excess sibilance _____
dentalized d, t _____	assimilation _____
intrusive r _____	dialect (type) _____
final unvoicing _____	other _____

Target sounds: _____

APPENDIX E

SPEECH CHECK LIST

Name _____   Course _____

Rater _____   Date _____

Voice

Pitch:
   Appropriate   Too High   Too Low   Patterned   Monotonous   Other ____

Volume:
   Appropriate   Too Loud   Too Weak   Monotonous   Uncontrolled   Other ____

Rate:
   Appropriate   Too Fast   Too Slow   Hesitant   Monotonous   Other ____

Quality:
   Pleasant   Nasal   Denasal   Breathy   Hoarse   Other ____

Target Areas: _____

Articulation

Consonants		Vowels	Diphthongs
p pat ____	ʃ she ____	i see ____	aɪ ice ____
b boat ____	ʒ beige ____	ɪ sit ____	aʊ how ____
t top ____	h hot ____	e ate ____	ɔɪ coin ____
d dog ____	hw where ____	ɛ bet ____	
k key ____	w wet ____	æ pat ____	
g go ____	r red ____	a ask ____	
f four ____	j yes ____	ɑ calm ____	
v very ____	l left ____	ɔ awful ____	
θ thin ____	m man ____	o so ____	
ð the: ____	n no ____	ʊ book ____	
s snake ____	ŋ sing ____	u too ____	
z zoo ____	tʃ chair ____	ʌ up ____	
	dʒ judge ____	ə banana ____	
		ɝ-ɜ early ____	
		ɚ father ____	

Other Articulatory Features:

Consonant omissions _____	lisp (type)_____
Consonant additions _____	excess sibilance _____
dentalized d, t _____	assimilation _____
intrusive r _____	dialect (type) _____
final unvoicing _____	other _____

Target sounds: _____

APPENDIX E

SPEECH CHECK LIST

Name _____   Course _____

Rater _____   Date _____

Voice

Pitch:

   Appropriate   Too High   Too Low   Patterned   Monotonous   Other _____

Volume:

   Appropriate   Too Loud   Too Weak   Monotonous   Uncontrolled   Other _____

Rate:

   Appropriate   Too Fast   Too Slow   Hesitant   Monotonous   Other _____

Quality:

   Pleasant   Nasal   Denasal   Breathy   Hoarse   Other _____

Target Areas: _____

Articulation

Consonants		Vowels	Diphthongs
p pat _____	ʃ she _____	i see _____	aɪ ice _____
b boat _____	ʒ beige _____	ɪ sit _____	aʊ how _____
t top _____	h hot _____	e ate _____	ɔɪ coin _____
d dog _____	hw where _____	ɛ bet _____	
k key _____	w wet _____	æ pat _____	
g go _____	r red _____	a ask _____	
f four _____	j yes _____	ɑ calm _____	
v very _____	l left _____	ɔ awful _____	
θ thin _____	m man _____	o so _____	
ð the: _____	n no _____	ʊ book _____	
s snake _____	ŋ sing _____	u too _____	
z zoo _____	tʃ chair _____	ʌ up _____	
	dʒ judge _____	ə banana _____	
		ɜ-ɝ early _____	
		ɚ father _____	

Other Articulatory Features:
Consonant omissions _____   lisp (type) _____
Consonant additions _____   excess sibilance _____
dentalized d, t _____   assimilation _____
intrusive r _____   dialect (type) _____
final unvoicing _____   other _____

Target sounds: _____

APPENDIX E

SPEECH CHECK LIST

Name _____   Course _____

Rater _____   Date _____

Voice

_____

Pitch:

   Appropriate   Too High   Too Low   Patterned   Monotonous   Other _____

Volume:

   Appropriate   Too Loud   Too Weak   Monotonous   Uncontrolled   Other _____

Rate:

   Appropriate   Too Fast   Too Slow   Hesitant   Monotonous   Other _____

Quality:

   Pleasant   Nasal   Denasal   Breathy   Hoarse   Other _____

Target Areas: _____

Articulation

_____

Consonants		Vowels	Diphthongs
p pat _____	ʃ she _____	i see _____	aɪ ice _____
b boat _____	ʒ beige _____	ɪ sit _____	aʊ how _____
t top _____	h hot _____	e ate _____	ɔɪ coin _____
d dog _____	hw where _____	ɛ bet _____	
k key _____	w wet _____	æ pat _____	
g go _____	r red _____	a ask _____	
f four _____	j yes _____	ɑ calm _____	
v very _____	l left _____	ɔ awful _____	
θ thin _____	m man _____	o so _____	
ð the: _____	n no _____	ʊ book _____	
s snake _____	ŋ sing _____	u too _____	
z zoo _____	tʃ chair _____	ʌ up _____	
	dʒ judge _____	ə banana _____	
		ɝ-ɚ early _____	
		ɚ father _____	

Other Articulatory Features:

Consonant omissions _____   lisp (type)_____

Consonant additions _____   excess sibilance _____

dentalized d, t _____   assimilation _____

intrusive r _____   dialect (type) _____

final unvoicing _____   other _____

Target sounds: _____

APPENDIX E

SPEECH CHECK LIST

Name _____   Course _____

Rater _____   Date _____

Voice

Pitch:

   Appropriate   Too High   Too Low   Patterned   Monotonous   Other _____

Volume:

   Appropriate   Too Loud   Too Weak   Monotonous   Uncontrolled   Other _____

Rate:

   Appropriate   Too Fast   Too Slow   Hesitant   Monotonous   Other _____

Quality:

   Pleasant   Nasal   Denasal   Breathy   Hoarse   Other _____

Target Areas: _____

Articulation

Consonants		Vowels	Diphthongs
p pat _____	ʃ she _____	i sec _____	aɪ ice _____
b boat _____	ʒ beige _____	ɪ sit _____	aʊ how _____
t top _____	h hot _____	e ate _____	ɔɪ coin _____
d dog _____	hw where _____	ɛ bet _____	
k key _____	w wet _____	æ pat _____	
g go _____	r red _____	a ask _____	
f four _____	j yes _____	ɑ calm _____	
v very _____	l left _____	ɔ awful _____	
θ thin _____	m man _____	o so _____	
ð the: _____	n no _____	ʊ book _____	
s snake _____	ŋ sing _____	u too _____	
z zoo _____	tʃ chair _____	ʌ up _____	
	dʒ judge _____	ə banana _____	
		ɝ-ɚ early _____	
		ɚ father _____	

Other Articulatory Features:

Consonant omissions _____	lisp (type) _____
Consonant additions _____	excess sibilance _____
dentalized d, t _____	assimilation _____
intrusive r _____	dialect (type) _____
final unvoicing _____	other _____

Target sounds: _____

Index

Note: I.P.A. symbols are listed in the order in which they appear in this book.